Isadora Duncan
THE RUSSIAN YEARS

Isadora Duncan
THE RUSSIAN YEARS

ILYA ILYICH SCHNEIDER

Translated by David Magarshack

MACDONALD : LONDON

792·8/

/338,815

SBN 356 02436 2
FIRST PUBLISHED IN GREAT BRITAIN IN 1968 BY
MACDONALD & CO. (PUBLISHERS) LTD.,
49 POLAND STREET, LONDON W.I.
MADE AND PRINTED IN GREAT BRITAIN BY
PURNELL & SONS LTD., PAULTON (SOMERSET) AND LONDON

List of Plates

INTRODUCTION

Many years separate me from the events and encounters described in this book, but I retain a very clear memory of everything connected with them.

Isadora Duncan, of Irish origin but born in America, became famous throughout the world at the beginning of the twentieth century. Her appearance in the world of art produced the effect of an exploding bomb not only because she had given up ballet costume and danced barefoot in a light tunic, but also because she dared to perform her dances to the music of great composers. Isadora Duncan called for a closer link between art and life and for the infusion of beauty into life—slogans considered revolutionary at the time. She tried to find some organic connection between music and dance and a natural expressiveness of movement.

An advocate of "the grand idea of a closer tie between a child's life and happiness and beauty", she demanded a reform of everyday life, of school, and of clothes. Her dearest wish was the creation of a school in which the dance would be the means of artistic and physical training of children—the men and women of a new world, harmoniously developed physically and spiritually.

Isadora Duncan toured Russia several times before the revolution. In the summer of 1921 she arrived in Russia at the invitation of the Soviet Government. Anatoly Vasilyvich Lunacharsky, People's Commissar of Education, delegated me to work with her.

Isadora Duncan and I lived under one roof in Moscow for several years. I accompanied her on her tours to Petrograd, the Ukraine, the Crimea, the Northern Caucasus and Transcaucasia. I worked with her as an organizer of her school, was responsible for all her public performances, created the librettos for her new productions, and was in charge of the lighting effects which she insisted on as an

7

important element of her performances. I had literally hundreds of conversations with her, remember distinctly her ideas and the manner in which she expressed them, and was familiar with her creative plans and aspirations. Finally, I was the witness of her great love affair with Sergei Esenin, one of the outstanding Soviet poets. During the last years of her life she wrote to me constantly from Paris. For more than two decades after her death in 1927 I was in charge, first of her school, later of her studio and, finally, of the studio-theatre bearing her name.

The reader will perhaps reproach me for indulging in some prosaic details. For me Isadora Duncan was a great woman as well as a great artist. Once, talking to a biographer, Isadora said: "You cannot write only half the truth about a great man. A good biography must tell of all the sides of his character, the bad and the good. That is absolutely necessary if we are to achieve a complete picture of the man. Even his thoughts and emotions, provided you can vouch for them, must be described with absolute clarity. I hope that everything written about me will be true, regardless of any feelings for me..."

In 1929 Mary Desti, a close friend of Isadora's, published a book in New York, which, according to her, aimed at completing the work Isadora had left unfinished during the last years of her life. In discussing Isadora's life in Moscow, Desti perpetrated a number of monstrous distortions of fact, partly through ignorance and partly through a desire to dramatize her story. She states, for instance, that for a whole week the Moscow school was closed for lack of fuel. After desperate appeals, Isadora, according to her, was only sent one log, which "she held groaning in her hand in frantic desperation". She further alleges that the children of the school had no proper beds and that Duncan had "to make bunks for them by tearing out planks which were nailed to the wall" and that she was only given "one blanket with which to cover the children who slept three in a bed". She describes the children as "little mites holding out their hands with fingers like straws . . ."

This was written five years after the foundation of the school; and three years earlier I had published an article about the school in the Berlin journal *Die Woche,* with illustrations showing the children at their dancing lessons, at dinner, and during their hours of rest lying on well-made beds in large and airy bedrooms.

The Duncan school in Moscow certainly went through a difficult period at first. I shall discuss it at length later. But if Isadora could read what Desti had written she would have been utterly disgusted. Desti strings together a number of what she described as "Moscow episodes" which are entirely of her own invention. In her book, for instance, we find quite untrue versions of the first and last meetings between Isadora Duncan and Sergei Esenin, together with fantastic accounts of the poet's childhood and youth. A novel, serialized by the Yugoslav paper *Borba* in 1958 under the title of *Duncan and Esenin,* is quite obviously based on the "facts" in Desti's book, and in the same year the scenario of an Italian film called *Isadora Duncan* clearly drew on material from Desti's book.

Isadora Duncan's decision to go to Russia gave rise to a great number of contradictory rumours and completely fictitious stories: to counter them, I have only to remind the reader of what Isadora herself wrote in her book *My Life*:

"On the way to Russia, I had the detached feeling of a soul after death making its way to another sphere. I thought I had left all the forms of European life behind me for ever. I actually believed that the ideal State, such as Plato, Karl Marx and Lenin had dreamed it, had now by some miracle been created on earth. With all the energy of my being, disappointed in the attempts to realise any of my art visions in Europe, I was ready to enter the ideal domain of Communism."

In answer to all sorts of absurd statements to the effect that "Isadora Duncan sold herself to the Bolsheviks," the Soviet writer Nikolai Nikitin wrote in his reminiscences of Esenin:

"To arrive in Soviet Russia without any thought of personal gain at a time when the country had barely recovered from its historic conflagrations, deprivations and famine; to arrive in Bolshevik Moscow with the completely unselfish intention of devoting her talent to our country, is quite a different thing from the modern tours of foreign artists. Only an outstanding personality could have believed in the Russia of those years. To discount riches, and world fame—albeit past its peak—is not so easy ... she could have lived peacefully and in complete comfort. But she used to say at that time that she could not live like that, that

9

Russia alone was a country where art could not be bought for gold."

As for her last and greatest love, it was not only emotion, but also the character and similarity of their ideas that formed the bond between Isadora Duncan and Sergei Esenin.

"However fantastic the conjectures hazarded by sensational purveyors of fiction," writes Korney Zelinsky, the well-known Soviet man of letters, "there is no doubt that the value of their relationship lay in all that they had in common: their artistic nature, the tremendous range of their talent, their fearlessness, their generosity of heart..."

Both of them were keenly alive to the close links between art and life, and thought of art as one of life's implements. In her book Isadora Duncan wrote that she sought for and did at last find "the primary principle of every movement" and that she strove to understand "the sole rhythm of movement in nature." According to Zelinsky, "Esenin's imagery reflects the movements and transformations that take place in life; it is based on the feeling of man's unity with nature."

Do not these quotations emphasize the unity of the creative principles of Duncan and Esenin?

It was my love for the great dancer, my admiration for her remarkable art, her enthusiasm, her unselfishness, her great human feelings and, last but not least, my desire to make the real truth known, that impelled me, one of the few surviving people who knew Isadora Duncan intimately, to write this book.

I

After the revolution I worked in the Press Department of the People's Commissariat for Foreign Affairs, wrote reviews of ballets, and lectured on the history and the aesthetics of the dance at the School of Ballet.

When the "Free Theatre," which brought about the amalgamation of the dramatic and ballet companies, was formed in 1919 in Moscow, I was invited to be the director and producer of the ballet company.

Trying to breathe some life into the archaic forms of the ballet, the Free Theatre announced an open competition for a libretto for a one-act ballet. I decided to take part in it. But when I learned what its theme was to be, "Labour and Capital," I became discouraged. I was sure that it would be much easier to dramatize a telephone directory.... Then, quite suddenly one night, I saw the whole performance in my mind. Indeed, what I saw was a completed choreographic picture and not merely a libretto. I called it *The Golden King*.

I could no longer sleep, and I finished *The Golden King* that very night. Next morning I sent in my libretto to the competition committee, which, quite unexpectedly, awarded it first prize.

But it was never performed. A bomb, thrown by the left wing Social Revolutionaries and Anarchists, destroyed the premises of the Committee of the Moscow Communist Party, which was forced to move into the building set aside for the Free Theatre on Bolshaya Dmitrovka Street.

The Free Theatre was homeless. A suitable building had to be found without delay. That was not so simple. At last, we were successful in getting possession of the Colosseum, a cinema, and work was soon in full swing. But no one thought of producing *The Golden King,* least of all myself, for quite unexpectedly I became "an eminent public figure."

In those years there were only about eighteen Moscow actors and artists who were members of the Communist Party. The rest, all three thousand of them, were neither interested nor involved in politics. It is true, one professional organization was already in existence. For the small trade unions of "orchestral musicians," of "dancers in private ballet companies," and others, had joined the United Trade Union of Workers in the Arts, but the majority were not even members of the union. The first elections of deputies to the Moscow Soviet of Workers, Peasants, and Soldiers were about to take place. Meanwhile the Moscow "Workers in the Arts" organized their own "faction of non-party men" and elected me as its secretary. This "faction" had no political aims, and indeed we, the leaders of a nearly three-thousand-strong unorganized group, had only a vague idea of the particular aims, tasks, and range of our activities. The "faction" held its meetings at "The Bat" Theatre, at which the speakers, conscious of their newly acquired freedoms of public assembly and speech, addressed the members. They revelled in their eloquence—I had to spend whole nights in writing the minutes.

The "Workers in the Arts" put up five candidates for election to the Moscow Soviet, one per five hundred electors. The first name on the list was that of Lunacharsky. I was the fifth.

It was very cold at the Bolshoi Theatre, where the elections were being held. People were wearing fur coats.

The votes were cast for the whole list, but as there were only five hundred electors present, Lunacharsky was the only one to be elected.

At the meeting, which he chaired while I acted as secretary, we sat next to each other and I gave him the rolled-up libretto of *The Golden King.*

"What's this," he asked. "Something for the meeting?"

"No. Something quite different. If you can spare the time, read it at home."

He nodded and slipped the manuscript into the deep pocket of his fur coat. Two weeks later a journalist I knew burst into my room.

"What are you sitting at home for?" he cried. "And so calmly, too!"

"Why? Has anything happened?" I asked in alarm.

"Happened? The Minister of Fine Arts writes an article about him and he sits at home!" the journalist cried, beside himself with excitement.

"What 'Minister'? What article? Written about whom?" I, too, cried, beside myself with excitement.

"Lunacharsky! Minister of Fine Arts and People's Commissar for Education. The same thing. He wrote about you. An article about *The Golden King.* . . . Here it is!" he choked, giving me with shaking hands the folded number of the *Theatrical Herald,* the official journal of the People's Commissariat of Education.

I opened the journal. There was indeed an article by Lunacharsky, in which he discussed *The Golden King.*

Lunacharsky wrote: "I do not know whether Comrade Schneider is right in thinking that his libretto would go well with Scriabin's *Poem of Ecstasy,* but it is quite excellent by itself. His theme is simplicity itself: it is the struggle of the labouring masses against the golden idol and their victory over it. It is worked out very brilliantly, picturesquely, in the best sense of the word, as a fairy-tale ballet. . . . A performance produced with real artistic talent would make this ballet one of the most popular shows for our proletariat, who, both in Moscow and in Petrograd, react very strongly to the fascination of the ballet, with its undeniable skill, its appealing gracefulness, and its exquisite beauty."

I knew that my libretto was pure symbolism, but at the time I did not regard that as a fault, for I failed to realize the sketchy fashion in which I depicted the revolution, and, to be quite honest, I was surprised at the impression it had made on so great a political figure, so eminent a publisher and so talented a dramatist.

Lunacharsky advised me to find a new musical score for *The Golden King.* During a meeting at the Bolshoi Theatre, he introduced me to Vladimir Ivanovich Nemirovich-Danchenko, who had just been appointed director of all academic theatres.

"This is the young author of the ballet I spoke to you about," said Lunacharsky. "I don't think," he added, "he would have any objections if Glazunov were asked to set it to music."

Some time later I was given Lunacharsky's letter to Glazunov. I was about to leave for Petrograd to meet the composer when suddenly I learned that Glazunov had arrived in Moscow. I went to see him that day. I had never met the composer before, but his face, with its massive features and drooping moustache, was very familiar to me from the large number of his portraits.

Glazunov had composed the haunting music of *Raymond,* which carried us back to the Middle Ages. Glazunov had composed *Autumn*, with its famous *Bacchanalia*.

"I'd be very pleased to set your ballet to music," said Glazunov, "but I'm sorry, I can't do it now. It would be very difficult for me at present. You see, I have to keep the stove going myself and chop wood every day in the open air...."

He fell silent, smoothing Lunacharsky's letter and the pages of my libretto with his podgy fingers.

"Now, in the summer," he said, "I shall gladly sit down to it in my little garden."

The artistic committee of the Bolshoi Theatre had met many times to discuss the production of *The Golden King*. But I had long lost interest in my libretto. I did not like its allegorical character, and, above all, I failed to see how the theme of labour and the dances in the finale could be reconciled with the canons of the classical ballet. The managers of the theatre also found themselves between two fires: the order of the People's Commissar and the new forms which demanded the abolition of the traditions of the classical school. I gave up the idea of ever getting *The Golden King* on the stage and went to see the all-powerful Commissar of the Moscow Academic Theatres, Elena Malinovskaya.[1] I asked her to return the manuscript of my libretto to me. She tossed her greying head and looked at me sharply.

"We have an order from the People's Commissar for the production of this ballet," she said.

"I don't think our present ballet companies will be able to produce my ballet," I said.

Malinovskaya flushed. She bent forward as if she were about to jump at me like a tigress defending her cub. She cared passionately for "her theatres" and did not permit anyone to question their merits.

"How am I to understand that?" she asked slowly.

"I hope I'm making myself clear," I replied. "You, Elena Kon-

[1] Elena Malinovskaya was appointed Commissar of the Moscow academic Theatres immediately after the victory of the October Revolution.

stantinovna, know from my reviews how much I love the art of ballet and how highly I regard the Moscow ballet company. But the forms of the modern ballet will have to undergo many changes before they can tackle new themes and get closer to the new audiences."

"You'll have to sign a form stating that you're taking back your libretto at your own request," she said, in a gentle tone of voice.

I agreed. She rang and asked for my manuscript to be brought in.

To break the awkward silence, I attempted to explain myself a little more precisely.

"My libretto must be produced by quite a different type of ballet company," I said. "Besides, I can't think of any producer who could undertake it. There is, I believe, one person who might find its theme congenial and who would be competent to produce it, but that particular person isn't here."

"Who is he?" Malinovskaya asked.

"It's not a he, it's a she," I replied. "It's Isadora Duncan."

Malinovskaya told Lunacharsky of our conversation. I believe he understood me. Lunacharsky was one of those who had a clear idea of Isadora Duncan's role in modern culture and who took a serious view of her art.

His ringing me up on the day of Isadora Duncan's arrival was not, therefore, an accident.

II

In 1878 a grand-daughter was born into the family of an old Irishman settled in America.

At the beginning of the twentieth century, the English critic Titterton wrote of this girl, who was to become one of the greatest artists of our era: "A new idea comes into the world once in a century and today I was the witness of one re-born." Titterton wrote this after having seen Isadora Duncan dance in London. Duncan's name reached Russia for the first time at the very beginning of the eighteen-nineties.

In her reminiscences of her childhood years, Isadora Duncan wrote: "When I could escape from the prison of school, I was free. I could wander alone by the sea and follow my own fantasies. . . . I believe that whatever one is to do in one's later life is clearly expressed as a baby. I was already a dancer and a revolutionist."

She recalls one episode at school when she was six years old: before Christmas, her teacher, on entering the classroom with a box of sweets in her hand, said: "See, children, what Santa Claus has brought you." Isadora got up and solemnly replied: "I don't believe you. There is no such thing as Santa Claus."

The teacher was considerably ruffled. "Candies are only for little girls who believe in Santa Claus," she said. "Then I don't want your candy," replied little Isadora. As a punishment, the teacher ordered her to come forward and sit on the floor. "I came forward," Isadora recalls, "and, turning to the class, made the first of my famous speeches. 'I don't believe lies,' I shouted. 'My mother told me she is too poor to be Santa Claus; it's only the rich mothers who can pretend to be Santa Claus and give presents.'"

This directness in declaring her convictions and thoughts, irrespective of place or person, Duncan preserved throughout her life, as she did her straightforwardness and her high principles in respect of questions of art.

As a child she refused to go to the dancing schools she was sent to. "I dreamed of a different dance," she writes. "I did not know just what it would be, but I was feeling out towards an invisible world into which I divined I might enter if I found the key." She would go to the seashore by herself and dance to the accompaniment of the sound of the waves and the rustle of the trees, trying to achieve a single rhythm of movement in nature.

Having persuaded her mother, a music teacher, to go to Chicago with her, she went to see the director of a famous touring company and told him, in a long speech, that she had "discovered the art" which had been lost for two thousand years, that she had "discovered the dance."

"I bring you the idea that is going to revolutionize our entire epoch. Where have I discovered it? By the Pacific Ocean, by the waving pine-forests of Sierra Nevada."

Before the director stood a thin, strange little girl, who had the audacity to harangue him in that manner. He did not know what to do with the child and asked her to report for rehearsals in New York on the first of October, and he promised to give her a small part. "If you suit," he added cautiously.

However, in New York she met with a disappointment. She had to play a small part in a pantomime which preserved all the false and vapid forms of that type of art. Trying "to adopt a Stoic philosophy to alleviate the constant misery," Isadora recalled how she used to walk behind the scenes with a volume of Marcus Aurelius.

The Duncan family succeeded in renting a small studio in which they worked during the day and slept at night. Isadora composed dances to the music of the popular American composer Ethelbert Nevin, who burst into her studio one day shouting that he forbade her to dance his music because it was not dance music. Isadora took him by the hand. "Sit there," she said, leading him to a chair, "and I will dance to your music. If you don't like it, I swear I will never dance to it again."

And she danced his *Narcissus* for Nevin. The composer was amazed. "Those very movements," he cried, "I saw when I was composing the music." As a result, Nevin composed for Isadora a dance which he called *Spring*. Nevin gave several concerts with Duncan in the small music room of the famous Carnegie Hall. Isadora scored a big success at the first concert and "caused quite a sensation" in New York, after which she received many invitations to appear in different drawing rooms before "a select society."

Isadora was disappointed. "These people," she wrote, "seemed so enwrapped in snobbishness and the glory of being rich that they had no art sense whatever." She began dreaming of going to London, and before long her dream became a reality.

In London, Isadora Duncan gave a performance in one of the picture galleries, and her dances, performed beside a fountain surrounded by flowers and palm trees, were acclaimed by the spectators and in the press. This helped her to meet some of the outstanding artists in London. She danced for the painter Watts, and went to the performances of Henry Irving and Ellen Terry, whose friend she became for the rest of her life. During one of the rehearsals she was asked to dance for the famous actor Beerbohm Tree, who, as Isadora Duncan recalls, hardly looked at her and "kept gazing in a distracted way up to the flies."

"I told him this story afterwards in Moscow," Isadora Duncan writes, "when he had toasted me at a banquet as 'one of the world's greatest artists.'"

"What," he exclaimed. "I saw your dance, your beauty, your youth, and did not appreciate it? Ah! What a fool I was!"

After London, which did not help to improve the financial position of the Duncan family, they left for Paris, where the same thing was repeated: Isadora's dances became known and received the high acclaim of people belonging to the world of art, but her financial position continued to be lamentable. "Yet, in the midst of this poverty and deprivation," Duncan wrote, "I can remember standing alone in our bleak studio, waiting for the moment of inspiration to come to me to express myself in movement.

"I spent long days and nights in the studio seeking that dance which might be the divine expression of the human spirit through the medium of the body's movement. For hours I would stand quite still, my two hands folded between my breasts, covering the solar plexus. My mother often became alarmed to see me remain for such long intervals quite motionless as if in a trance—but I was seeking and finally discovered the central spring of all movement, the crater

18

of motor power, the unity from which all diversities of movements are born, the mirror of vision for the creation of the dance—it was from this discovery that was born the theory on which I founded my school."

It was in that condition of self-contemplation that "a florid gentleman with an expensive fur collar on his coat, and a diamond ring," found her.

"I am from Berlin," he said. "We have heard of your barefoot act (a description of her dancing that shocked her dreadfully). I have come from the largest music hall to make an engagement with you at once."

Isadora declared that she would never consent to take her art into a music hall. She hated the very word all her life, and during her stay in Moscow she constantly impressed upon her pupils the idea of a solicitous attitude towards their art, a concentration of all their dances "in the same programme as performing dogs in some music hall."

The impresario offered her five hundred marks a night. She rejected his offer. The German was beside himself and, at last, offered her one thousand marks a night for one month, promising to advertise Isadora in Berlin as "the first barefoot dancer in the world." Isadora told him that she would refuse if he offered her ten thousand, one hundred thousand marks a night. The furious German called her "a stupid girl," but Isadora shouted that she "had come to Europe to bring about a great renaissance of religion through the Dance, to bring the knowledge of the Beauty and Holiness of the human body . . . and not to dance for the amusement of overfed bourgeoisie after dinner." She added: "I will come to Berlin one day. I will dance for the countrymen of Goethe and Wagner, but in a theatre that will be worthy of them, and probably for more than a thousand marks."

"My prophecy was fulfilled," she recalls, "for this same impresario had the grace to bring flowers to my loge three years afterwards in the Kroll's Opera House, with the Philharmonic Orchestra of Berlin playing for me, when the house was sold out for more than twenty-five thousand marks. He acknowledged his error with a friendly, 'Sie hatten Recht, gnädiges Fräulein. Küss die Hand.'"

But three more years had to pass before that, while Isadora's fame grew in the meantime, though she was still extremely hard up, and neither the dithyrambs of the composer André Messager nor the recognition of "the great Sardou" could help to improve her financial position.

According to Isadora herself, she had found "in some mysterious manner the key which opened to me the hearts and minds of the intellectual and artistic élite of Paris; Paris, which stands in our world, for our times, for what Athens was in the epoch of the glory of Ancient Greece." She was often in the company of Henri Bataille, and she visited the studio of Eugène Carrière, where she met Ilya Metchnikov, who was then working at the Pasteur Institute. It was at that time, too, that she met Rodin, whom she was to regard afterwards as her teacher and friend.

Real fame came to Isadora Duncan after her tours of Hungary, Austria and Germany. "I took Berlin by storm," she wrote. It was in Hungary, in the town of Siebenirchen, incidentally, that she heard of the execution by hanging of the seven revolutionary generals and created, to the music of Liszt's *Rakoczy March*, her dance which she performed as a revolutionary hymn to the heroes of Hungary. She presented this beautiful and exciting march afterwards in Moscow and danced it with seven of her Soviet pupils, who kept it in their repertoire for a long time. The music, performed in furious tempo, represents the galloping of the Hungarian cavalry at the outbreak of the 1848 insurrection.

Early in 1905 Isadora Duncan paid her first visit to Russia, where she gave performances in several cities. She later recalled her arrival in Petersburg. The express train got there at dawn, having been stopped by snowdrifts. She was driven, covered by a fur rug, through the dark and silent Petersburg streets in a "one-horse cab." Suddenly she saw in the distance a long procession of men, "laden and bent under their loads—coffins." She was filled with horror and asked her coachman what it was.

He explained that the workmen shot down before the Winter Palace on "Bloody Sunday," the fatal January 5, 1905, were being carried to their graves.

"This terrible procession," Isadora Duncan was to repeat many times later, "left its mark on all my life afterwards and set me on the right path."

With this indelible impression, a week later she went to Moscow from St. Petersburg. The owners of the Moscow Candy Factory "Einem" (now "Red October") invited her to inspect their products and sent a troika for her.

Isadora walked in silence through the damp cellars of the factory, in which workers cut the long twists of candy with large knives. When the owners saw her off to her troika, holding big boxes of assorted chocolates, they asked her how she liked their factory. Unable to control her feeling of indignation, she replied, standing beside the troika: "The time will come when these men will leave their cellar and cut your throats with their knives!"

In April, 1913, all the Moscow papers published dispatches about the tragic death in Paris of Isadora Duncan's two little children. People all over the world were shocked by that terrible accident, regardless of whether or not they had heard of Isadora Duncan.

Her children were being driven with their nurse in a limousine along the Seine embankment, which had no parapet at that time. The motor-car fell into the river and the children and their nurse were drowned.

The whole street in which Isadora Duncan lived was filled with flowers, for which there was no room left in the house, and more and more flowers were brought by strangers who had been shocked by this tragedy. Students of the Ecole des Beaux Arts bought up all the white flowers in Paris and, at night, affixed them to the trees and bushes in the garden of Duncan's house. The sculptor Emile Bourdelle spent the night pacing the garden. In the morning he walked into the room where for the last two days Duncan had been sitting motionless like a carved stone image, and knelt at her feet. Claude Debussy came in and stood for a long time in silence. Then he sat down at the piano and began improvising a fantasy that was full of grief. It was his *Danse Macabre*.

The world press reported that after the cremation, Isadora Duncan took the two small urns to the seashore and then, after sailing alone far out to sea, scattered the ashes on the waves. But I learned after her own death that the urn with her ashes had been placed in the Père Lachaise cemetery in the same niche as the ashes of her children and her mother.

I once came across a photograph of Isadora Duncan with her little boy and little girl in a French journal. (The boy was three years old and the girl five.) Isadora Duncan was sitting on a bench, the children clinging to her on either side with their heads on her shoulders. Isadora, clasping her children in her arms, as though with a pair of wings, pressed their bodies to herself. Her beautiful eyes looked sad and were directed straight at the lens of the camera. I looked at the photograph for a long time and never thought that, almost ten years later, I should hear about that tragedy, here in Moscow, from Isadora Duncan herself. . . .

She gave no public performances for a long time after the death of her children. Then "the great American woman," as she was called in her country, resumed her work.

Duncan founded her first school in Germany, where, as she herself wrote, her name became "magical." However, recognizing the practical results of Isadora Duncan's system of artistic and physical training, the Germans wished to see in her undertaking merely a school for the physical training of healthy German mothers capable of bearing healthy German children. Duncan transferred her school to France shortly before the outbreak of the First World War, but the capitalist who financed her school became worried about his financial position, and the school was closed.

"I realized then," Duncan told me, "that it was impossible to make a great idea dependent on private capital." At that time, the Greek Prime Minister, Venizelos, inspired by the beautiful dream of a renaissance of ancient Greek culture, invited Isadora Duncan to be his assistant in this undertaking. Isadora responded immediately and went directly to Athens, but Venizelos, an excellent dreamer but an unsuccessful politician, fell from power, and with his fall Duncan's dreams of creating a school in Greece came to nothing. After the failure both of the dictatorial power of Venizelos and of his campaign to revive "the great past of Greece," Isadora realized that other conditions were necessary for the large social experiment she had in mind.

According to Lunacharsky, Isadora Duncan "always wanted to found a school for the poor on a mass scale and to create two classes of experts of the ethical dance: on the one hand, instructors who were capable of propagating her method and, on the other, great numbers of children, who could take part in public processions and festivals, and who could introduce freedom of movement, gracefulness, and lofty humane sentiments into the very heart of the poor population."

Lunacharsky understood perfectly the dancer's ideas and aspirations. In his memoirs he gives what amounts, in my opinion, to an exhaustive analysis of her creative method.

As early as 1913, Lunacharsky reported from Paris to the

monthly *Theatre and Art*: "I am inclined to agree with those who take into account the influence exerted by Loic Fuller[1] on Isadora Duncan's genius. Isadora Duncan is so great, and even, one might say, such an enigmatic cultural phenomenon, at least at first glance, that she deserves an article to herself. All I can say now is that she has, of course, broken through the limitations of the interesting and charming, but fossilized, academic ballet. It was she who brought back emotional freedom to the dance and made it one of the most direct expressions of man's soul, though of course for the time being only for a few artists. But the great wave which is now sweeping across Europe—as shown by the schools of Isadora Duncan's brothers and sisters, by the eurythmics of Dalcroze, and by Dumesnile's aesthetic gymnastics—has its origin in Isadora." Lunacharsky added this "footnote" to his article before including it in the collected editions of his works, published in 1924: "To this, of course, one must add the influence of Delsarte."

"Duncan had a highly idealized conception of the ancient Greek world. She perceived it through its statues, through descriptions in the Greek plays, through the theories of Greek scholars. Isadora had a peculiar way of combining idealism and materialism. Yes, she was a materialist in many things. So, for instance, placed the cult of the body above everything. If one's attention was concentrated on the body, if one had to cultivate it, if one had to obey the laws of its development without in any way violating its freedom, even, indeed, aiding its freedom, the body became beautiful, and not only because of its structure. Isadora considered grace (agreeing in that respect with Spencer, whom she may not have known) the expression of this freedom. Grace meant the extreme ease and simplicity with which the body achieved any chosen aim. Isadora believed that if the body were to be made light, graceful, and free in movement, it would to a great extent influence people's consciousness and even their social life. She maintained that if, on the one hand, man was taught to be in complete control of his body and if he exercised it in the expression of lofty feelings, if he could be made by the movement of his eyes, head, torso, and feet to express calm, deep thought, love, tenderness, friendship, or a proud gesture of majestic refusal of something despicable, inimical and so on, then this would help to broaden his consciousness, his soul.

[1] One of Isadora Duncan's first influences in the art of the dance.

23

"As I have already explained, Isadora believed that the culture of the body and its movements in a form worthy of man must have an effect, not only on his consciousness, but also on his social life. She used to say that a man who was accustomed to move about nobly, not only learned to feel nobly, but also refused to put up with the ugliness that surrounded him and did his best to make sure that he was dressed in conformity with these movements, that he organized his living quarters in conformity with them. As a result, his attitude towards the people who surrounded him must also change."

Isadora's first steps on stage, painted by Franz Haufstaengl

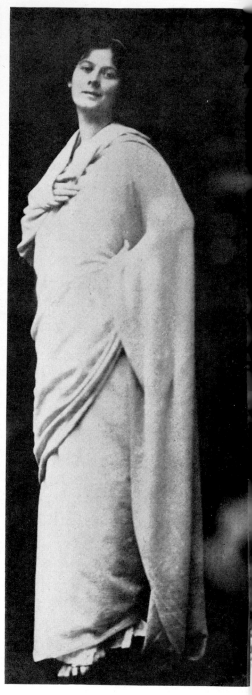

Two studies of Isadora Duncan. The painting is by Franz Hanfstaengl

Four portraits of the young Isadora. In two of them she is wearing
the Grecian-styled tunic in which she preferred to dance

Isadora's first school in
Grünewald, Berlin, 1905, with a
number of her young pupils

Isadora in the Amphitheatre of
Dionysius, Athens, in 1904

Isadora Duncan in Berlin, 1904, with Gordon Craig, the famous
theatrical designer and father of her first child, Deirdre

Isadora's Paris school, 1914

Isadora with Irma Duncan, her constant companion and her most willing and able pupil

A class in Isadora's school in Villegenis, France 1908

A group of pupils at the Villegenis school

Three of the "Duncan Dancers", Liesel, Trina and Margot. Paris 1920

III

Who can foresee the moment when because of some insignificant circumstance one is suddenly faced with a radical change in one's life, the cause of which one really cannot divine and which is usually attributed to fate?

If I had entered my office a minute later, the telephone which had been ringing for some time would have stopped. But it was still ringing, and Flaxerman, Lunacharsky's secretary, told me that the Commissar of Education would like to speak to me.

"We expected Isadora Duncan to arrive in three days' time," Lunacharsky said, "but she arrived unexpectedly yesterday and a room was found for her at the Savoy Hotel, which is far from comfortable and is partly in ruins. Besides, it seems to be infested with rats and bedbugs. Isadora Duncan and her companions left it at night and went walking about the streets sight-seeing till morning. While we are looking for other quarters for her, do you think it would be possible to install her temporarily in the apartment of Yekaterina Vasilyevna Geltser, who is touring the provinces and who, I understand, has asked you to keep an eye on her apartment? I have already sent Flaxerman to the railway station," Lunacharsky continued, "where Isadora Duncan, her pupil Irma, and her dresser are getting out their luggage. I should like you to go to Geltser's apartment, arrange everything for her there, and look after her for the time being."

I rang up Geltser's apartment, told them about the arrival of the unexpected visitors, and asked them if they would get some breakfast ready for them. They could only promise an omelette but, in

25

Isadora in 1912, draped in an embroidered shawl

those days, that, too, was a luxury. I left for the railway station. Flaxerman had gone there in Lunacharsky's car and the only transportation at my disposal was the tram. In those days Moscow had neither taxis nor buses.

I arrived at the Nikolayevsky Station (now Leningrad Station) in Kalanchevsky Square. There was no sign of Lunacharsky's car. I could only assume that Flaxerman had driven away with Isadora Duncan. Suddenly a cart drove out of the gates of the station and my attention was involuntarily drawn to it: it was piled two yards high with trunks, hampers, and suitcases. I realized at once that it was Isadora Duncan's luggage. I left for Rozhdestvensky Boulevard. The visitors were already there.

I had first seen Isadora Duncan, a slim figure in a light tunic, on the stage in 1908 when I was still in my teens. The stage was draped in large, plain curtains, and a plain carpet was on the floor.

To me Isadora Duncan was the personification of extraordinary femininity, grace, poetry, the like of which it was scarcely to be expected that I would ever see. Now I had an unexpected impression: she looked big and monumental, her head set proudly on a regal neck and covered with the reddish copper of smooth, thick, short hair. Before me sat a great artist, the reformer of the art of the dance, the "queen of gesture," as she was called, of whom Auguste Rodin had said that "she took that force from nature which did not go under the name of talent, but of genius." She wore a black satin jacket, which shone like leather, and a white satin waistcoat with a red border. (It is said that after Isadora Duncan had ordered her costume for her journey to Russia, Paul Poiret, the arbiter of fashion in Paris, sold the identical model under the name of *à la Bolshevik*.)

I asked the visitors whether they were satisfied with their apartment and explained that Lunacharsky had asked me to take care of "Miss Duncan and her companions" during the first days of their stay in Moscow.

Duncan frowned. I thought that she must be irritated by my German accent, but a few days later I discovered that the reason for her displeasure was that I called her "Miss Duncan."

Isadora was sickened by all, even the verbal, attributes of the world she had left behind. She was attracted by the new sound resulting from the combination of the name of Duncan with the word *tovarishch* (comrade). I recall another incident connected with the same word. She was not so naïve as to believe that she would drop into socialism the moment she stepped off the train that had brought her to Petrograd. But having believed in the truth of the ridiculous stories about the abolition of the monetary system in Soviet Russia, she had, unfortunately, to pay for her ignorance. She was told in Paris that the word *tovarishch* would be sufficient for any cabman to take her anywhere she liked without any fare, and as she had not brought any money with her (why should she?), she had to do her first sight-seeing on foot. That did not discourage her. She walked along the streets, gazing with interest at the faces of the passers-by. It was July, 1921. The people were badly clothed and they looked worried. It was, therefore, not surprising that Isadora first discovered "the image of the new world" in the expression of the faces and eyes of the Red Army men she happened to meet in the streets of Petrograd.

A very slim girl in a long, silk peignoir entered the room.

"This is Irma, the only one of my pupils who decided to come with me to Russia," said Isadora, introducing me.

She pushed a cigarette box towards me. On it was a picture of a "vamp" smoking a cigarette, and the name of the manufacturer, "Mary Desti," a name that meant nothing to me at the time.

We lit our cigarettes.

"Yes, we were told all sorts of terrible stories," said Isadora with a smile, inhaling rather awkwardly (she did not smoke a great deal). "In Paris I had a visit from the former Russian ambassador Maklakov and a certain Tchaikovsky, a namesake of your famous composer. Who is he?" she asked.

"He was the head of the White Government in Northern Russia, organized by the English after the occupation of Archangel."

"Yes, well, so the two of them—Tchaikovsky even went down on his knees before me—implored me not to go to Russia, for Irma and I would be raped at the frontier, and even if we succeeded in getting as far as Petrograd we would have to drink soup with chopped-off human fingers floating about in it."

A gorgeous, full-breasted young woman suddenly burst into the room and began speaking rapidly in French, opening her eyes wide and gesticulating. It was Jeanne, a French girl without whom Isadora Duncan never travelled and who not only looked after her stage costumes and acted as her dresser, but also managed her daily affairs. It was explained to me that Isadora's luggage had arrived. I went out onto the balcony and caught sight of the tower of trunks, hampers, and suitcases.

The editor of *Izvestia* asked me to write a short article on Isadora Duncan's arrival in Soviet Russia. What I wanted from her was not so much a "statement" as something that was new and fresh, something that explained the social reasons for her desire to live in the Soviet Union. All pre-revolutionary writings about Isadora Duncan as a "light-winged, barefoot dancer, who intended to revive the ancient Greek dance," were quite obviously out of date and would not serve any more. Besides, though Russia had been practically under a blockade for the last seven years, since the war and the revolution, we knew that Isadora Duncan had long ago advanced from "the angel with the violin," which seemed to have been suggested to her by a fourteenth-century Cremona fresco, to the "philosophic treatment" of Tchaikovsky's *Symphonie Pathétique* and *Slavonic March*. Now she was dancing the entire *Fifth Symphony* of Beethoven and the *Unfinished Symphony* of Schubert, and great cycles from the works of Chopin and Liszt.

"I ran away from European art, which is so closely bound up with commerce," said Isadora Duncan. "I prefer the movement of a hunchback inspired by an inner idea to the coquettish, graceful, though effective gesture of a beautiful woman. There is no pose, no movement, no gesture that is beautiful in itself. Every movement is beautiful only when it is expressed truthfully and sincerely. The phrase 'the beauty of line' is—by itself—absurd. A line is beautiful only when it is directed towards a beautiful end."

She spoke excitedly about her plans: to create in Moscow a school in which the dance would be the means of the artistic and physical training of children, new people of a new world, harmoniously developed—physically and spiritually.

The news of her arrival, together with this short statement, was published a few days later in *Izvestia*.

Irma sat down at our table. She was a well-built young woman of medium height, with beautiful chestnut hair, cut *à la* Duncan, and a pair of fine dark eyes, not quite in keeping with her nose, which betrayed her German origin. On the whole, however, she was not only very charming, but quite fascinating. Jeanne, Isadora's dresser, was busy unloading tins of jam and marmalade, chocolate bars, biscuits, and some kind of small packets in greaseproof paper. Tearing them open noisily, Jeanne produced white rolls. I looked into the huge basket from which Jeanne was pulling out all these articles of food.

"Why did you bring so much bread from abroad?" I asked Duncan.

Before she had time to answer, Irma blurted out with a little laugh: "We have two more baskets like this."

Looking a little embarrassed, Isadora said that those were starch-reduced rolls, for she was afraid of putting on weight.... But observing my laughing eyes and the sceptical expression on my face, she laughed and in her peculiar German "dialect," which she sprinkled with French and occasionally English words, she said:

"They all insisted that we should take as much bread as we could with us, because there was no bread in Russia."

From her bag she produced a thick lipstick, applied it, then, running her tongue over her lips, added:

"Anyway, apart from that, it really is dietetic bread."

Irma put on a record and asked me to dance with her. I felt embarrassed and refused her proposal, which seemed a little forward to me, though it was probably quite a commonplace thing to her.

Isadora was covering the lampshades with thin, pinkish-yellow silk shawls.

"I can't bear white light," she explained, putting the shawls carefully over the lampshades so as not to knock over some little porcelain figurine or vase. "I'm afraid I shall never become a collector of these things. The difference between the pretty and the beautiful is too great." Suddenly she stopped before a painting by Tropinin. "Now this is beautiful!" she exclaimed. *"Haben Sie allumettes?"* she asked, again interjecting French words in her German speech as, taking out a cigarette, she offered me the box with the silly top.

"When building a new world and creating new people, one must fight against the false conception of beauty. Every trifle in everyday life, in dress, every label on a box, must train the taste. I believe that here in Russia it will all be so. I came here to carry out important work and I'd like very much to be properly understood here. Think how many years people have been attributing to me a desire to revive the ancient dance! It's so untrue! I studied ancient sculpture, paintings on vases, and the single movements of the ancient dance that became fixed in painting and sculpture, but I regarded

29

them merely as unsurpassed models of man's natural and beautiful movements. My dance is not a dance of the past, it is a dance of the future. For we do not know what the dance of the ancient Greeks was like. It would seem that their music was primitive."

The doorbell rang. Lunacharsky had arrived. Duncan had already met him during the day at the Commissariat of Education. Not wishing to interfere in their conversation, we others went out into the street.

Irma said: "Let's go to a cinema."

It was Monday and all the cinemas were closed. (There were only a few cinemas in Moscow at that time.) Luckily, I remembered that they were showing a few films to the members of the Bolshoi Ballet at the offices of a former private manufacturing firm. We went to Gnezdikovsky Lane. The young ballet dancers and the no less youthful ballet critics were already there. They were all old acquaintances of mine. I told them of Isadora Duncan's arrival and introduced Irma to them.

The "classical" ballet welcomed the representative of the "Duncan school" in a very friendly fashion. But then the young ballet dancers only had a very vague idea of the principles of Isadora Duncan's art.

IV

When we returned to Rozhdestvensky Boulevard, Lunacharsky had left. Isadora Duncan was arguing heatedly about something with Stanislavsky, who, having learned of her arrival, immediately came to see her.

I recalled how, almost thirteen years before, when I was still in my teens, I was standing opposite the stage door in the courtyard of the Moscow Art Theatre, where we lived at the time, and saw a troika driving in through the gates, its harness bells ringing. As though it were happening now, I remember the bright crimson velvet of the seats and back of the sleigh, ornamented with pretzel-shaped silver patterns. The troika stopped outside the stage door. In the sleigh sat a man and a woman and something about her attracted my attention. They were holding hands, looking into one another's eyes, and smiling: he with embarrassment, she excitedly and as though surprised. Her smiling face seemed about to burst into laughter. I knew the man. It was Stanislavsky. The troika was waiting. Its passengers suddenly recollected themselves, rose quickly, and disappeared through the stage door. The door was thrown open again immediately and two actors walked out. One of them, looking round, said: "Isadora Duncan . . ."

I knew the name. There were reports in the papers about the arrival of the famous "barefoot dancer." In the streets large posters announced Isadora Duncan's appearances on the stage.

Now I might perhaps find out from Isadora Duncan herself what they had been talking about in the troika and why Stanislavsky had such an embarrassed smile and why she had seemed so delighted.

A long time later, when she learned that as an adolescent boy I

31

had seen them together in the courtyard of the Moscow Art Theatre, she revealed to me the secret of that love affair that had never happened.

"When, forgetting everything in the world, we were ready to fling ourselves into each other's arms," said Isadora, "he startled me by asking a question with such charming seriousness and such bright, bright eyes: 'And what will happen to our child?'"

That was the end of their "love affair." But the two great artists always remained great friends. Isadora Duncan met Stanislavsky many times afterwards. She was also present at many performances in which Stanislavsky took part.

In his book *My Life in Art,* published after Isadora Duncan's death, Stanislavsky devoted a great part of one chapter to reminiscences of Isadora. He wrote:

"The first appearance of Duncan on the stage did not make a very big impression. Unaccustomed to see an almost naked body on the stage, I could hardly notice and understand the art of the dancer.... But after a few of the succeeding numbers, one of which was especially persuasive, I could no longer remain indifferent to the protests of the general public and began to applaud demonstratively.

"When the intermission came, I, a newly baptized disciple of the great artist, ran to the footlights to applaud.... From that time on I never missed a single one of the Duncan concerts. The necessity to see her often was dictated from within me by an artistic feeling that was closely related to her art. Later ... I came to know that in different corners of the world, due to conditions unknown to us, various people in various spheres sought in art for the same naturally born creative principles. Upon meeting they were amazed at the common character of their ideas. This is exactly what happened at the meeting I am describing. We understood each other almost before we had said a single word."

A former producer of the Imperial Theatres, V. A. Telyakovsky, recorded in his diary in January, 1908:

"Moscow has lately fallen under the spell of the ballet. Everyone is interested in it and talking about it. Not only the balletomanes, but also the young people, even serious people like Stanislavsky, are interested in it.... Last night, Stanislavsky talked to me about the ballet and Isadora Duncan. There can be no doubt that Isadora Duncan has made a great impression on everybody. This year she has been very successful both in Moscow and in Petersburg. Everybody is talking about the classical dances of Greece, Rome, India, China, and other countries. Stanislavsky sees a great future in it and believes in Isadora Duncan's school, which he asked me to support and accept in Petersburg, so that she could transfer her school from Grünewald to Russia. Stanislavsky had seen the children who are trained by Duncan there and was greatly impressed."

A few days later, Telyakovsky again wrote in his diary:

"Isadora Duncan came to see me. In accordance with Stanislavsky's telegram, she came to see me at two o'clock in the afternoon. . . . She began talking to me about the art of the ballet and the art of dancing and asked my permission to visit the ballet school. . . . She spent several hours at the school and was very much interested in the teaching. She asked me for permission to come again. I gave her my permission and asked the producer to tell the members of the ballet company who wished to be present at a demonstration of Isadora Duncan's dances, to assemble in the school, for Duncan has promised to demonstrate her system of dancing."[1]

Stanislavsky advised Isadora not to ask Telyakovsky at first for more than 15,000 roubles a year, "not to abuse the old ballet too much," and to tell him in detail about the principles of her art.

In January, 1908, she wrote to Stanislavsky from Petersburg:

"Last night I danced. I was thinking of you and I danced well. I feel a new, unusual access of energy. Today I worked all morning. I have put a lot of new ideas into my work. Again— rhythms. These ideas you have given to me and I am so happy that I feel like flying up to the stars and dancing round the moon. It will be a new dance, which I am thinking of dedicating to you."[2]

Stanislavsky replied:

"Dear friend, I am so happy! I am so proud! I helped a great artist to find the atmosphere she needed so badly. And all this

[1] The Vakhrushin Central Theatrical Museum: notebook No. 22, pp. 7467–68, 7481–82.
[2] Moscow Art Theatre Museum: K. G. Stanislavsky archives.

happened during a delightful talk, and in a cabaret where vice reigns. How strange life is! How beautiful it is at times! Oh yes, you are good, you are pure, you are noble, and in the great rapturous feeling and artistic admiration for you which I experienced till now, I felt the birth of a deep and true friendship.

"Do you know what you did for me? I haven't yet told you about it.

"In spite of the great success of our theatre and the great number of admirers who surround it, I have always been lonely. (My wife alone supported me in moments of doubt and disappointment.) You were the first who told me in a few simple and convincing words the chief and fundamental thing about the art I wanted to create. That gave me strength at a moment when I was about to give up my artistic career.

"Thank you sincerely, thank you with all my heart.

"Oh, I was waiting impatiently for your letter and danced with joy when I read it. I was afraid that you would put a wrong interpretation on my restraint and mistake my pure feeling for indifference. I was afraid that your feeling of happiness, strength, and energy, with which you had left to create new dances, would desert you before you reached Petersburg.

"Now you are dancing the Moon Dance, while I am dancing my own dance which has as yet no name. I am satisfied. I have been rewarded.

"Let me describe to you in my next letter the impression you made on all your admirers, the enchantment of which has not been dispelled even yet.

"Every free moment, in the midst of our work, we speak of the divine nymph who descended from Olympus to make us happy. We kiss your beautiful hands and we never forget you. I am happy that your new creation has been inspired by my love for you. I would like to see this dance. When shall I see it? Alas, I don't even know your itinerary!!!!"[1]

At the end of January, Stanislavsky wrote to her in Helsingfors, where she was giving performances.

"...Here they are saying that your delightful children will be coming to Petersburg. Does it mean...that your school is about to be founded? My dream is being realized and your great art

[1] Ibid., Vol. 7, p. 378.

will not disappear with you.[1] Do you know that I admire you much more than the beautiful Duse? Your dances have said more to me than the beautiful performance I saw tonight.

"You shattered my principles. After your departure I kept looking in my art for the thing you have created in yours. It is beauty, as simple as nature. Today the beautiful Duse repeated to me what I already knew and what I have seen hundreds of times. Duse will not make me forget Duncan!

"I implore you: work for art and, believe me, your work will bring you joy, the best joy of your life.

"I love you, I admire you, and I respect you (forgive me!)— great artist.

"Write to me even a short note, so that I may know your plans.

"Perhaps I shall manage to come and be enraptured with you. I implore you to let me know beforehand the day you will give a performance with your school. I should not want to miss that incomparable spectacle for anything in the world, and I must arrange to be free. I kiss your classical hands a thousand times and
au revoir,
Your devoted friend K. S."

A letter dater March 20, 1910.

"Dear Isadora Duncan,

Your true friend and admirer was deeply moved by your letter. It arrived on the first night of a new play, at the very moment when I was about to put on my make-up. I was successful in the part and the performance, too, was a success, which, of course, means that you are still the good genius of our theatre, where your name is always remembered. Thank you for remembering me and for the joy of receiving news of you."

It was just then that the Moscow Art Theatre began its work on *Hamlet* under the direction of Gordon Craig. Stanislavsky wrote to Isadora Duncan:

"... It was you who recommended Gordon Craig to us. You told us to trust him and to create a second country for him in our theatre. Come and find out how well we have carried out your wish.

[1] Nothing came of it at the time, and Isadora Duncan's school was opened in Moscow only in 1921.

35

"...Our whole company is enthralled by the new system and for that reason, as far as our work is concerned, this year promises to be interesting and important. In this work you have played a great part without knowing it. You have suggested to me many things which we have now discovered in our art. I thank you and your genius for that."

When Stanislavsky was in Paris in 1909, he wrote in a letter to Moscow:

"I saw Craig's and Isadora Duncan's little girl. A charming child. Craig's temperament and Duncan's grace. I liked her so much that Duncan promised to let me have her if she (Isadora) should die. So here I am already in a new role of grandfather or daddy. If she leaves me all her future children, too, I can rest assured that I shall spend my old age surrounded by a numerous family."

When the little girl and her brother were drowned, Stanislavsky telegraphed to Isadora in Paris: "If the feeling of grief of a distant friend will not hurt you in your great sorrow, permit me to express my despair at the terrible catastrophe that has befallen you."

On Isadora's third day in Moscow she received an invitation from the Commissariat of Foreign Affairs to be present at a small evening reception in its offices on the Sofiysky Embankment. She came, after her performance, dressed entirely in red, from the turban on her head to the shoes of her feet.

When I asked whether it was necessary so to emphasize her revolutionary convictions when going to her first official party, she exclaimed, striking her chest: "I am red, red!"

The Commissariat of Foreign Affairs was holding the reception in the ballroom of the house which had belonged to the sugar king Kharitonenko: gilt furniture on spindly legs, Gobelin tapestries, painted ceilings, shepherdesses and marquises. In one of the drawing rooms, a young actress accompanying herself on the piano was singing "Fiammetta" or some other such song. She was applauded and there were cries of "Bravo!" All the people at the reception were well dressed and spoke to Isadora Duncan in excellent French. Somone called her "Mademoiselle Duncan." She corrected him— "Tovarishch Duncan"—and rose from her seat with a glass in her hand:

"Comrades," she said, "I want to make a speech. Comrades, you have made a revolution. You are building a new, beautiful world, which means that you are breaking up all that is old, unwanted, and decayed. The break-up must be in everything—in education, in art, in morals, in everyday life, in dress. You have succeeded in throwing the sugar kings out of their palaces. Why do you preserve the bad taste of their buildings? Throw out of the window these fat-bellied, thin-legged armchairs and these fragile little golden chairs. On all your ceilings and pictures are Watteau's shepherds and shepherdesses. That girl sang very charmingly, but during the French revolution she would have had her head cut off. She's singing a song of Louis XVI! I hoped to see something new here, but it seems all you want are frock coats and top hats to be indistinguishable from other diplomats."

She sat down. They tried to explain the real position, which did not quite correspond with her romantic ideas about the reconstruction of society and her revolutionary state of exaltation that took no account of the difficulties of the reforms and processes, nor of the time they would require to be put into operation.

Isadora returned home looking very upset. It was after this incident that Lunacharsky published his article under the heading of "Our Guest," in which he wrote among other things:

"Isadora Duncan herself is still full of militant communism, which sometimes induces an involuntary and, of course, an extremely kind, and, if you like, even an affectionate smile. So, for instance, Isadora, invited by our communist comrades to a small, almost family party, felt it necessary to rebuke them for their insufficiently communist tastes, for their bourgeois surroundings, and, generally, for the inconsistency of their behaviour with the great ideal which she had conjured up in her mind.

"The incident might have developed into a rather regrettable scene had not our comrades realized the special charm of the naïve, but in the main quite correct, reproof, for our daily life is still permeated with the remnants of middle-class style."[1]

[1] *Izvestia*, No. 186, August 24, 1921.

V

Isadora Duncan was restless by nature. During the day she was eager to get out of the house and go for walks, and in the evening she wanted to go out and see people. Every day she waited patiently for me to come and take them all off for a walk to the Vorobyov (later Lenin) Hills, with which she fell in love at once. The three of us—Isadora, Irma and I—usually took a cab to the Novo-Devichy Monastery. From there we walked through some kitchen gardens to the bank of the Moskva River, where we were rowed across on a ferry. On the other side of the river we wandered along the overgrown avenues and lawns of Neskuchny Park.

"When teaching children, I always tell them," Isadora said in her sonorous voice, " 'Notice how a little bird flies up into the air, how a butterfly flutters, how the wind sways the trees, how it ripples the water. Learn movement from nature. Everything that is natural is truthful. Everything that is truthful is beautiful. What is beauty? Beauty is truth. Truth is nature.' "

One evening as it was getting dark, we were standing near an old colonnaded summer-house in Neskuchny Park, at the very spot where the sparkling horseshoe of the Moskva River curved round its dark green bank. On the other side of the river, the Novo-Devichy Monastery glowed pink and golden in the sunset. Isadora turned her gaze slowly from the monastery to the river, to our bank, and, turning round, looked for a long time at the huge green slope which descended in the shape of an amphitheatre and above which a great stone building towered.

"It is here," said Isadora, "amid this greenery, that a great popular theatre without walls and without a roof ought to be built. There," she pointed, "is the natural ancient *orchestra*, the platform of the ancient Greek theatre, on which the performance would take place. And there," she pointed at the green slope, "is a natural amphitheatre—seats for thousands of spectators."

She had picked the very place where, about ten years later, was founded the open-air theatre of the Gorky Central Park of Culture and Rest with seats for twenty thousand spectators.

"And there," she said, pointing at the stone building at the top of the slope, "is a good building for my school."

"Comrade," a loud, high-pitched man's voice attracted my attention, "may I speak to you for a moment?"

I saw a man in a long, well-fitting cavalry greatcoat with scarlet tabs in the corners of the collar. The peak of his military cap set off the transparent and almost translucent pallor of his oblong face with its small golden beard.

I went up to him.

"Tell me, is that Isadora Duncan?" he asked, adding, "I am Podvoysky. Translate for me please, and say...I'd like to talk to her."

Podvoysky—the friend and companion-in-arms of Lenin—who, in the days of the October Revolution, was the chairman of the Military Revolutionary Committee in Petrograd and who was in charge of the attack on the Winter Palace.

Their conversation began quickly. Taking part in it myself, I scarcely had time to translate their exciting dialogue and the many questions they asked each other. They seemed to feel a kind of spiritual affinity, a similarity and identity of ideas, especially in the sphere of physical education.

"The last few years," said Isadora, "all my thoughts have been of Russia and my soul has been here. Now that I have got here, I feel that I am following the paths which lead to the kingdom of universal love, harmony, comradeship, brotherhood....I despise riches, hypocrisy, and those stupid rules and conventions I had to live with. I want to teach your children and create beautiful bodies with harmoniously developed souls, who, when they grow up, may show their worth in everything they do, whatever their profession. It is stupid to try to predetermine the future profession of a child who cannot discuss it or make his own choice. I want to teach all children, but not to make them into dancers. A free spirit can exist only in a free body, and I want to set free these children's bodies. My pupils will teach other children, who, in their turn, will teach new ones, until the children of the whole world will become a joyous, beautiful, and harmonious dancing mass. . . ."

Night was falling. Podvoysky led us along paths that he alone seemed to know.

Isadora began to complain that, as far as she could see, rebuilding had not begun in all spheres of life, and she repeated the reproaches Lunacharsky had dealt with in his article "Our Guest."

"Isadora, Isadora," said Podvoysky, "you were born a hundred years before your time. You've come into this world too soon. . . . We are still cutting the marble blocks and you already want to give shape to them with your fine chisel. It is not enough to want to devote your labour, your knowledge, your acquired skill, and your experience first of all to the children of workers. You will have them, of course, they will come to you, but you must go to the workers yourself, to the workers' districts, to the workers' clubs, where you could start teaching separate groups of children and showing their parents the results of your work. Afterwards you can open your large school and many workers will then bring their children to you. Make the workers realize the importance of your work first. Find your way to the high road by using the byways— through the workers' districts!"

It was now very dark. We had climbed a high hill and could no longer see any paths; big boulders and debris of a demolished building barred our way.

"There," said Podvoysky, "it's along such a difficult road that you have to travel towards recognition and success. I brought you here on purpose. These are the ruins of the old world upon which something new and joyous will be built. These are the ruins of Krymkin's restaurant, blown up by the workers, where old Moscow's debauched revelries used to take place. By the by-ways, Isadora, through the workers' districts, on to the highroad."

"*Michatelno* [*zamechatelno*—marvellous]," said Isadora in her broken Russian, a word she had picked up during the last few days.

"All this is well and good," she said presently, "but how are we to get down in this darkness?"

Indeed, to climb up, scrambling over the rubble, was still possible, but to get down in the pitch darkness was not to be thought of.

Podvoysky laughed. "I'm afraid," he said, "that's my fault. But we'll find some way to get down."

That, however, was not so easy. Far away, below us, we could see some flashing lights and soon we also heard voices. A man was shouting something. He got nearer and nearer and soon we could hear him quite clearly calling: "Comrade Podvoysky! Comrade Podvoysky!"

"That's Mekhonoshin," said Podvoysky, and shouted: "We are here!"

Podvoysky was at the time the head of compulsory universal military training, and Mekhonoshin was his deputy. Worried by Podvoysky's long absence—he had, it seems, gone out for a walk for the first time after a serious illness—Mekhonoshin organized a search all over the Vorobyov Hills. Learning from some passers-by, who had seen us, that we were going up to the ruins of the restaurant, he went to look for us with some Red Army men, taking with them torches and ropes, which were needed for our dark descent.

Having got to the top, Mekhonoshin introduced himself and began heatedly to reproach his chief. The doctors had forbidden Podvoysky to go out, especially after sunset, because of the mist which rose over the river. The descent began.

Isadora was quite delighted by Podvoysky and especially by her outing.

Podvoysky said to me: "Tell her that difficulties do not stop people but merely urge them on, and that there are no difficulties which cannot be overcome. She will, I'm sure, come up against many difficulties, not simple ones like these, but she must not lose courage, she must not complain, and she must not be surprised. She will be helped, as we, too, were helped just now. As for her—we need her."

After that day, we continued with our daily walks in the Vorobyov Hills, and we always met Podvoysky there. He was busy with the project of building a Red Stadium in the Vorobyov Hills.

One day Isadora told him that she would like to live in the Vorobyov Hills for a little time, at least until the autumn. Podvoysky at once arranged for her to have a small, unoccupied summer cottage, and the next day I took Duncan, Irma, and Jeanne to their cottage in the Vorobyov Hills.

One day, before they went to live in the cottage, as we were walking down the endless wooden steps to the river, we noticed a huge samovar standing on one of the landings. A bluish smoke, smelling of fir cones, rose from its chimney. A number of athletes, who were wearing only shorts and were very sunburnt, were busying themselves round the samovar, throwing fir cones, blowing up the fire. . . .

"I don't suppose you've ever seen such a huge samovar," I said to Isadora.

When I got down to the river, I looked up: Isadora was still standing high up near the platform with the samovar. I shouted a few times for her to come down quickly, for the ferryman was waiting for us, but Isadora was so interested in the samovar that she stopped several times on the steps and looked up at the landing. . . . At last she came down.

"Didn't you see that the boat was waiting for us?" I grumbled. "What did you want to look so long at the samovar for?"

"*Aber so ein schöner Samovar,*"[1] Isadora said, smiling.

Irma winked at me, gave a knowing look and wrinkled her nose.

Isadora continued to express her admiration for the samovar and kept looking up at the landing, where a tall athlete of fine physique stood, never taking his eyes off her.

"*So ein schöner Samovar hab' ich nie gesehen!*"[2] laughed Isadora.

Podvoysky was greatly interested in Isadora Duncan's plans and was indignant with the Commissariat of Education for taking no steps to make it possible for her to start her work. He offered her the services of his organization, promising to help her organize her school and lessons with children in workers' clubs. I kept Lunacharsky informed about all our affairs, including the move to the Vorobyov Hills, the different problems Duncan raised, and the necessity of finding quarters not only for the school but also for Isadora herself, for winter was approaching, and he took the necessary steps for the organization of the school.

Later, after Duncan had moved to Moscow and was becoming fretful with her inactivity, and there was still no school, Podvoysky, who had met us again in the Vorobyov Hills, again proposed that she should start work with him and, pointing to the house at the top of the green slope, said:

"Your school will be there."

---

[1] "But what a beautiful samovar!"
[2] "I have never seen such a beautiful samovar!"

Seeing the realization of her hopes and dreams so near, Isadora at once agreed.

"You are well informed about all her plans, projects, and needs," Podvoysky said to me. "I don't suppose you would refuse to help Duncan and me in our work, would you?"

I of course promised to help them. Next morning, Mekhonoshin came to see Duncan and reported to her in military fashion that the heating of the building of her future school in the Vorobyov Hills had begun. He also handed me a warrant, signed by Podvoysky, authorizing me to organize the school and the expedition to the Volga region that Duncan had proposed to him and with which he was in enthusiastic agreement. The famine in the Volga region, which the Soviet Government was doing its best to combat and which excited the attention of the whole world, demanded immediate aid. Duncan's project was somewhat fantastic and Utopian. She wanted to go there with a group of film cameramen to make a film with a large group of children of the local population, which might be much more convincing than any of the appeals which had so far appeared in the foreign press and which had had a rather poor response.

Lunacharsky later succeeded in dissuading Duncan from so risky an undertaking by pointing out that the children of the Volga region would, in their present plight, hardly be interested in taking part in such a generous, but rather ill-conceived, project.

As for Podvoysky's proposal in regard to Duncan's school, Lunacharsky immediately issued an official statement to the effect that Isadora Duncan was the guest of the Commissariat of Education, which considered itself responsible for the organization of Isadora Duncan's work in Soviet Russia.

Many, many years later Nikolai Podvoysky still took a personal interest in Isadora Duncan's Moscow school and the theatre-studio that arose from it. Together with Podvoysky, I organized regular classes for six hundred children of two workers' districts, which were under the direction of instructors who had graduated from the Duncan school. They were held in the sports arena of the Red Stadium, which he had established next to the present Central Park of Culture and Rest. During those early years, however, Podvoysky also tried to interest the workers themselves and their grown-up families in Isadora Duncan's theories. As a result, classes in dancing and athletic displays for workers and their families took place in the Vorobyov Hills under the direction of Isadora Duncan. They usually ended in a performance of the *Internationale* in song and movement. More than a thousand students of these classes later took part in such a festival. They were dressed in light red tunics which Podvoysky had made popular. Indeed, Podvoysky did not hesitate to wear such a tunic himself, and he got himself photographed wearing one for a Moscow journal before the festival. But what we did not know at the time, and what was revealed twenty-five years later by Podvoysky at a conference of women athletes, was that Lenin had greatly admired the work of Isadora Duncan in the Vorobyov Hills. The question of whether Duncan should be invited to come to Russia to assist in the work of cultural revolution had been discussed at a meeting of the members of the Soviet Government presided over by Lenin. After Duncan's arrival, Lenin, Podvoysky declared, "was very interested in her work and even offered certain suggestions. He liked Isadora Duncan very much. He appreciated Duncan's demonstration at a mass open-air meeting of how music should be understood and of how it could be readily used for self-education." "As for her quite uncalled for actions," Lenin added, "let us put her right about them, for the more attention we pay to what she is doing, the better the results will be."[1]

After the foundation of Isadora Duncan's school, the question of the transfer of a number of schools and institutes from Moscow to Petrograd was under discussion. Duncan's school was, for some reason, included among those marked for transfer. She was promised good quarters in Petrograd, which was deserted at the time. I at once went to see Podvoysky in the Comintern.

Podvoysky rang me up constantly, questioned me, gave me instructions. He used to summon me to his office, make me sit down, and then, pacing the room, he would say:

"Write it down. Tell them—Isadora and Irma—to get ready at once to prepare, for their artistic work with the children, a demonstration of heroism, a demonstration of the class struggle and of the difficulties of achievement. There should also be something joyful, but tell them that our happiness is of the stern sort, happiness at the stake...."

Podvoysky had made a deep impression on Isadora. She spoke enthusiastically of him. After her regular meetings with him, she

[1] Shorthand report of the section of the conference for promoting gymnastics among women on December 7–10, 1945.

44

used to spend a long time absorbed in thought. Then she would ask me about what he had been saying. Once she said thoughtfully: "I want to write about him. Let them know *there* what sort of man he is!" She then sat down at the table, picked up a few sheets of paper, and wrote the title of an article: "A Commissar." When she had finished the article, she sent it off to the London *Daily Herald*, in which it was published. That was in October, 1921.[1]

After spending a few more weeks at her summer cottage, Isadora Duncan became bored. It rained continuously and a cold wind was blowing. I was busy organizing performances for a group of young ballet dancers at the Bolshoi Theatre. We chose *Coppelia,* with the young ballerina Abramova in the leading part of Swanhild. I produced the first two acts of the ballet, leaving out the final, third act which was not important for the development of the plot. The performers themselves did the choreography. I was, therefore, busy for several evenings. Isadora did not resent my absence on the day of the performance, for she knew that I would come in the evening with a parcel, the contents of which she also knew perfectly well beforehand. She had got tired of the dietetic rolls, the *confitures*, the biscuits and sweets she had brought from England, and she wanted something much more substantial. "Rations" ordered for her and Irma by the Council of People's Commissars from England having not yet arrived, Isadora valued very highly the sausage omelette (a very expensive luxury at the time), the appearance of which on our table depended on *Coppelia*, for I received my rather substantial pay packet as producer and organizer after every performance of the ballet. Irma, who was no less antagonistic to the classical ballet than Isadora, would sometimes ask me:

"Well, how soon will you have another performance of your *Coppelia?*"

One morning, when I had spent the night at the cottage after a performance of *Coppelia*, through the window of my room I saw someone's hand pumping the Primus stove rather clumsily, then I

[1] In the course of a great many years, I later often met Podvoysky at meetings of the All-Union Committee for Sports and Physical Culture and at all sorts of athletic events. The last time we met was at the celebration of the thirtieth anniversary of the October Revolution in the Red Banner Hall of the Central House of the Soviet army, at which members of the Isadora Duncan Studio appeared and were photographed with Podvoysky on the stage.

In 1948 Nikolai Ilyich Podvoysky died. He was buried in the cemetery of the Novo-Devichy Monastery opposite the Lenin Hills, where he had so ardently dreamed of the eventual construction of the Red Stadium.

heard the sound of a small explosion and saw a bluish flame appear over the Primus, followed by a regular hissing noise.

"Michatelno," I heard Isadora say, as her hand put the frying pan on the burner. This was followed almost immediately by the sizzling of a sausage and the hissing of an omelette.

The weather was getting terribly cold. There was still no vacant apartment for Isadora Duncan. At last I suggested to Lunacharsky that he should try to get her some of the empty rooms in the ballerina Belashova's house in Prechistenka Street. Lunacharsky was delighted with my suggestion and quickly made all the necessary arrangements. Shortly afterwards I took Isadora and Irma to the house in Prechistenka, with its large, sparkling plate-glass windows. It was in this house that we were all to experience periods of joy and sorrow of varying degree and duration.

VI

Two streets, Ostozhenka and Prechistenka, one of which began at Crimea Square and the other at Subovsky Square, ran in the same direction but became closer until, at the bottom of the hill, they merged into the green square near the Prechistenka Gates on which stood the huge white cathedral of Christ the Redeemer with its shining golden dome.

In Prechistenka, almost at the corner of Dead Lane, whose ominous name goes back to the time of the Moscow Plague, stood a sturdy, two-storeyed, detached house with rows of plate-glass windows, tall on the top floor and smaller on the lower floor; there was a balcony in the centre of the façade, and on the roof a dome, crowned with an urn and two matching urns at the corners. Next door to this detached house was the old building of the former Khamovnitsky police station with its ridiculous fire tower, above the window from which the young Alexander Herzen looked wistfully on to the yard on the morning after his arrest.

Belashova's house is supposed to have been built on the site of a house and garden that belonged to a foreign doctor by the name of Lander, a great believer in the curative power of mineral waters, which he dispensed to his aristocratic patients, after which the patients were prescribed a "constitutional." The house was built by the vodka distiller Smirnov, who sold it to the millionaire Ushkov, ballerina Belashova's husband, who liked the house so much that he built an identical one in Kazan.

The entrance to the house was flanked by two squat columns; in a recess was a heavy oaken door. The lower floor had a large entrance hall, with two huge, cold, marble benches along the walls. It was impossible to sit on these either in summer or in winter, nor was it possible to move them! A wide staircase of white marble led to the upper hall, with balustrade and rosewood pillars.

Straight ahead and to the right were the two "Napoleonic" ballrooms, an oblong one with columns of grey marble, and a large square one with a balcony looking out on to Prechistenka. On the walls of the two rooms hung huge, heavily framed battle paintings with full-length portraits of Napoleon in the foreground. Next to the square ballroom was the north drawing room, its walls covered with flower-embossed pink satin. Next to it was the "oriental" room, the walls and ceiling of which were decorated with stucco mouldings.

All the doors of the house were high, mahogany double doors with bas-reliefs of Napoleon and Josephine, and bronze ornaments. To the right of the hall was the dining room: a sombre room with ebony-panelled walls, a similar ceiling, and a high musicians' gallery. Through the "Gobelin corridor" (as the "dunclings" were to christen it later) was the entrance to the boudoir.

After the February Revolution, I had to go to see Belashova in connection with a charity ball at the Bolshoi Theatre. I remember Belashova showing me round the house, including her bedroom, which was the size of a small ballroom, and her dressing room.

This ballroom-bedroom later became Isadora Duncan's room. It was then that I saw the beautiful mahogany sofa with its extraordinary arms in the shape of huge golden swans. It was on that sofa that Isadora spent a whole night talking to Sergei Esenin after their first meeting.[1]

"He has just been reading me his poems," Isadora told me after Esenin had gone. "I did not understand a word, but I could hear that it was music and the poems were written by a genius!"

On entering the house for the first time, Isadora Duncan made a wry face at the sight of the beautiful women painted on the ceilings, the gilt columns, and the bas-reliefs of Napoleon and Josephine on

---

[1] Not wishing that sofa to sink into oblivion, I bought it from the Government Fund. A sombre-looking appraiser arrived, who turned out to be the former owner of a Moscow furniture factory. He showed me a mark inside the back of the sofa.

"It's one of my sofas," he said. "A 'Paul the First' sofa. The original is in the palace of Prince Yusupov. The prince asked me to make a copy of it. I made several but sold only a few for 450 gold roubles each. These swans were turned for me by Archangel wood-carvers at twenty-five roubles a pair. I alone know the amount of gold that went into the making of them."

all the doors and cornices. Walking into her room, she sank into an armchair, shaking with uncontrollable laughter.

"A quadrille!" she cried. *"Changez vos places!"*

It turned out that the ballerina Belashova, on escaping from Soviet Russia, arrived in Paris and, looking for a house she would like to lease, got to 103 Rue de la Pompe. The house belonged to Isadora Duncan, who was letting it prior to her departure for Moscow. The house consisted of a large studio, the walls of which were hung with blue curtains, and two rooms—a bathroom and a hall. The plain carpets and curtains, a few good pieces of antique furniture and a marble bath could not be expected to satisfy the owner of the detached house in Prechistenka. Duncan equally did not appreciate the taste of the ruthless businessman who had so impressed Belashova.

Isadora covered the lamps and the brackets in her room and in Irma's with shawls, and "life in Prechistenka" began, though most of the house was still occupied by various government offices.

Visitors came. For want of glasses and saucers, tea was served in large wine glasses. Foreigners thought that Russians, who were great tea-drinkers, preferred to drink that aromatic beverage from wine and beer glasses. The Russians, burning their fingers, were annoyed at the inconvenient foreign custom. . . .

Isadora was bored. Official visits ceased. A few acquaintances came to see her in the evening: Dr. Paul, the Australian ambassador, who later resigned his diplomatic post and stayed in Soviet Russia (he became the managing director of a large German publishing house in Moscow). Lunacharsky called occasionally. Once, after giving notice of his visit in advance, Leonid Borisovich Krasin arrived. Krasin was a great lover of music and an admirer of Duncan's art. Duncan decided to give him a pleasant surprise and dance Schubert's *Ave Maria,* which Krasin was very fond of, at his next visit.

"I'll make him sit on the sofa with the golden swans and dance that piece for him," said Isadora. "But who'll play the music for me on the piano or a violin?"

When the time came, I decided to ring up Yuri Feier, a young violinist of the Bolshoi Theatre Symphony Orchestra, who was a friend of mine and who was to become a well-known conductor and People's Artist of the USSR. He arrived promptly with his violin.

Towards the end of his visit, Krasin, as Duncan anticipated, asked her to dance *Ave Maria* for him. The moment Feier began to play, a radiant Madonna suddenly appeared before us.

Isadora was not religious, though she did give a performance abroad of a mystery a few weeks before Easter, in the finale of which she, as the Madonna, slowly ascended a great staircase to Golgotha at the foot of the Cross, formed by spotlights against a black background. She was transformed into Isolde; she was Leda in the *Grotto of Venus*; she flew menacingly and tempestuously in the *Ride of the Valkyrie*; she created stupendous images in the *Slavonic March*, Liszt's *Funeral March*, and Chopin's *Marche Funèbre*; she was a fiery tribune in *Marseillaise*; the image of spring in Botticelli's *Spring*; she led martial legions in the Scherzo of Tchaikovsky's *Sixth Symphony*.

Now, she was once more the Madonna of Leonardo da Vinci.

Krasin applauded. I was deeply moved. I had seen Isadora dance several times in the hall of the art school, which we had fitted out luxuriously with her curtains and carpet. But I saw *Ave Maria* for the first time. Irma, who never took her eyes of the dancing Isadora, fell silent. The composer, Benediktov, who spent most of his time buying and selling antiques and who was also there, kept muttering something under his breath. The visitors stayed late. After Krasin had left, I went to see my friends off. Benediktov stopped as soon as we had got out into the street.

"Is this Duncan? Why, the whole thing's nothing but an immense fraud!"

Feier and I were dumbfounded.

"Yes!" shouted Benediktov. "There's nothing there! It's a fraud! I could not understand a thing!"

We felt so indignant that we nearly hit him, but he continued to stand up for his view: "An immense fraud!"

"You admit yourself that you didn't understand anything," I said. "Now I can see why you sell pictures and don't compose music. I'm sorry I introduced you to Duncan. It's impossible to pretend and cringe before her. It was my fault you were there...."

"Well, I didn't understand anything," the composer cried excitedly. "I have a right to my opinion, haven't I? I am ready to express it to Duncan herself!"

"So you don't mind my telling Duncan what you said about her?"

"I don't," he shouted, and walked away.

50

Isadora looked sad when Irma and I told her what Benediktov had said.

"He mustn't come here again," she cried. "It is important that I am surrounded only by friends and people who understand me. I can foresee great difficulties. The Tsarist ballet is still supreme here and will fight to retain its archaic forms and to defend its strong position. It will be like that until a fresh wind starts blowing. . . ."

On November 7, 1921, Duncan gave a performance at the Bolshoi Theatre. She danced Tchaikovsky's *Slavonic March,* his *Sixth Symphony* and the *Internationale.* In the *Internationale,* Duncan brought on the stage for the first time a hundred and fifty children dressed in red tunics and moving in an endless spiral—a beautiful living background for the dancing Isadora. Every wave of her hand inflamed the audience like the words of an impassioned Roman tribune.

This first small result of her work with Russian children demanded great preliminary efforts. Her school seemed to have been created already: nearly all the Government offices had moved out of Belashova's house, and beds, mattresses, and bedding for the first forty "dunclings," crockery, pots, and pans, etc., were all brought into the school, which already had a service staff of sixty people. It included "instructors," that is to say, women teachers of general subjects, as well as a doctor, an assistant doctor, nurses, cooks, kitchen maids, washerwomen, a doorkeeper, porters, stokers, plumbers, secretaries, typists—and, finally, a whole "organization committee." The committee held its meetings in one or the other ballroom and heatedly debated any question that arose, the minutes of the meetings being carefully kept by the secretaries.

There was feverish activity in the house on Prechistenka. Isadora was still extremely worried by her tedious inactivity in her huge cold room, where she tried to keep warm by wrapping herself in her thin silk shawls, curled up in a corner of the sofa with the great gold swans. She was worried because, in her intensely busy school, there was not a single child: the children she wanted so passionately to teach and for whose sake she had left Europe, America, and "art that is so inextricably tied up with commerce."

Every day the committee promised her that they would announce the admission of children, but for some reason they kept putting off the moment that was so very important to Duncan.

Lunacharsky had refused to give Duncan permission to work within the military educational system, and after that I took no direct part in the organizational work of the school, but merely kept up my contact with Lunacharsky himself.

Isadora said to me, with growing irritation:

"I don't mind if I only have black bread and black porridge, so long as I get a thousand children and a large hall. . . ."

To ask for a thousand children and a large hall was, of course, a utopian demand. The fuel situation was very precarious. All Lunacharsky could promise was a small school of forty children.

Isadora was becoming gloomier and gloomier. I tried to convince her that the small group would become "a phalanx of enthusiasts," future instructors. Isadora agreed with me, but she did not give up her dream.

Lunacharsky then sent one of his officials, M. D. Eichenholz, who had an excellent command of French, to see Duncan. Eichenholz spoke with her for three hours. A few days later he sent her a statement in French, summarizing her ideas and what her Moscow school was to accomplish.

While Duncan was studying it, I left the room so as not to interrupt her reading, but she quickly called me back and held out Eichenholz's statement to me.

I am still at a loss to understand how such an erudite person as Eichenholz—who, incidentally, wrote an introduction to Flaubert's novel *Bouvard et Pecuchet*, demanding an encyclopaedic knowledge of the subject—could have failed to grasp Duncan's fundamental idea and how he could have overlooked the most important point in her aims and demands: "the close approach of the life of the children to beauty and happiness"; how he could have overlooked the whole educational significance of her idea, her most vital and realistic dreams, which Lunacharsky understood so well and which Eichenholz reduced almost to the rules and regulations of a ballet school.

Across the first page of Eichenholz's manuscript, which Duncan held in her outstretched hand, was written in red ink her annihilating verdict, Idiot. . . .

Eichenholz did not appear again, but Isadora Duncan exploded: she demanded children, she demanded work. The committee rushed all over the house, but carefully avoided Isadora's room.

In the evening I went to the editorial offices of *The Workers' Moscow*. I wrote a short notice announcing the opening in Moscow of Isadora Duncan's school for children of either sex between the ages of four and ten, and added the footnote: "Preference is given to children of workers."

The same evening Isadora, Irma, and I, armed (without the committee's assistance) with a hammer, nails, and a step-ladder, hung Isadora's sky-blue curtains in the "Napoleon ballroom," covering up Napoleon and the Battle of Austerlitz in the process, and laid a plain blue carpet over the parquet floor.

"Now the light, the light!" cried Isadora. "It's impossible to remove that chandelier! It must weigh a ton! But we shall transform it. If it's going to be a revolution, then let it be a revolution! *A bas Napoleon!* The sun! The sun! Let us have the warm light of the sun and not this ghastly white!" she kept crying, unable to compose herself.

I understood Isadora Duncan's exacting demands. Her art required the fullest harmony of music and light.

"You do not imagine, do you, that anyone could dance Chopin's *Nocturnes* in a red light or Schubert's *Marche Militaire* in a blue? Remember John Locke's famous blind man in his *Essay Concerning Human Understanding*. He imagined purple light as the sound of a trumpet."

Duncan's dislike of white light was based on her penchant for everything natural, including sunlight. She categorically refused to allow a spotlight to follow her movements on the stage.

"The rays of the sun do not run after a man," she used to say.

I lowered the only lighted, big electric bulb from the otherwise unfunctioning chandelier and Isadora wrapped it in one of her orange-pink shawls. The ballroom grew warm at once.... Near the wall we put a small electric heater that had been sent for Isadora. I screened it with a piece of blue stuff, and in the magic pink light there appeared something looking like a blue sea or a southern sky.

Isadora informed the committee that she expected everything to be ready for the enrolment and examination of the children the next morning. Next morning, shortly after their parents had read the notice in the paper, the children arrived: a large number of girls and a few boys. The committee, it would seem, did not waste its time worrying about the status of the school: the parents brought their children to "the school of dancing."

The doctor examined the children, while we helped to enrol them and explain matters to their parents. I watched the Tamaras, Lucys,

Manyas, Ninas, Julias, Lidas, standing by themselves, or whispering to one another, or tearing themselves away from their mothers to run up the white marble staircase. I did not suppose that for many, many years to come I should be a witness of their lives, with all their joys and sufferings, their creative work, their happiness, their grief at bereavements, their love, successes and dramas, their victories in art and their defeats in life.

The school had started: the only thing wanting now was "music."

In all her performances Isadora Duncan gave pride of place to music. She tried to communicate the spirit of the music and not to "dance to its accompaniment." Isadora's own repertoire, and that of her school and, later, of the theatre-studio which bore her name, consisted mostly of such works of the great composers as concert pianists play at their concerts.

When she performed with a piano and not with a symphony orchestra, Duncan demanded that the grand piano be moved on to the stage in full view of the audience. Anxious to show that the pianist appearing with her was not an "accompanist," she insisted that his name be printed on the playbills in the same type as hers, and the same applied to the conductor. Nevertheless, famous concert pianists as well as certain conductors refused to appear with her, for they thought that they would be playing a rather inferior part in such concerts and be reduced to mere accompaniment, though Isadora Duncan never dictated tempos and did not ask a conductor to signal her entry with his baton.

All this created certain difficulties in the choice of pianists for Duncan and her school. She was glad to see any musician who cared to come, skilfully avoiding any hint of an official "audition."

My own view of the pianist was determined by Isadora's eyes: if she listened to the music with unseeing eyes, sunk into a kind of trance, the pianist was first-rate. If she sat with open eyes expressing complete indifference, I knew I could take a polite leave of the pianist and, having thanked him for his playing, not enter into unnecessary negotiations with him.

The first to arrive was Peter Lyuboshitz, a young pianist with an established reputation. As a rule, Peter always appeared with his two sisters: Leah, a violinist, and Anna, a cellist. The Lyuboshitz trio was well known.

Isadora listened to Lyuboshitz's playing with unseeing eyes, as though looking somewhere deep inside her. So she looked at the children, at the Kremlin, at the golden crowns of the trees on the Vorobyov Hills, at the rapt people who surrounded her at the end of a performance.

Lyuboshitz came every day, and with his arrival the house was filled with music: the majestic chords of Liszt's *Funeral March*, the victorious chariots of a Chopin polonaise, the desperate *Etude in D sharp Minor* of Scriabin, in which Isadora, for some reason, seemed to detect the tragedy of the Volga famine.

In the evening Isadora worked in her studio, which had been specially equipped for her. It occupied the former spacious dining room. The walls of the studio were draped with dark red curtains Isadora had brought from Greece. The floor was covered with a smooth, thin, soft carpet of the same colour. A large concert grand piano, a stove, and a leather-covered sofa with a high Gobelin tapestry hung over the back completed the furniture of the studio.

During her first winter in Moscow, I remember, Isadora was especially interested in Scriabin. She seemed to have quite a special kind of attitude towards him.

One day she suddenly said to me: "Please come and sit with me in the studio while I'm working on Scriabin. I'm afraid of being there alone."

"But isn't Lyuboshitz there with you?"

"He's at the piano. I don't see him. I don't feel him. You can't imagine what's happening: Scriabin is crushing the two of us. During my first visit to Russia, Scriabin came to see me. I did not understand him then. I was much too inexperienced. Before leaving, he said to me: 'I'll come to you again and then you will understand me.'"

She seized me by the hand and dragged me to the studio, from which came the thunderous chords of Scriabin's *Etude*.

"And now," she whispered, stopping at the high doors of the dining room, "now that I have grasped Scriabin, I keep hearing his voice in the studio: 'I'll come to you again'... I'm afraid he will come in now, Scriabin will... I'm afraid to be there alone...."

VII

Georgi Yakulov, the well-known Moscow artist, stopped me in the street one day. He had achieved great popularity with his designs for the scenery of many new plays in the theatres of Moscow. Yakulov, incidentally, designed the memorial to the twenty-six Baku Commissars. He worked on this design when Esenin was in Baku. Esenin's *Ballad of the Twenty-Six* is dedicated to him.

"I'm giving a little party at my studio tonight," said Yakulov. "Do come, and bring Duncan, if possible. It would be interesting to introduce her into the circle of Moscow artists and poets."

I promised to do my best, and Duncan agreed at once. Yakulov's studio was on the top floor of a tall house, somewhere in Sadovaya Street.

The appearance of Duncan, that evening, produced an immediate hush, which was followed by an inconceivable hubbub in which the name of Duncan could be heard again and again.

Yakulov beamed with pleasure.

Suddenly I was nearly knocked down by a man in a light grey coat. He kept turning his head this way and that and shouting: "Where's Duncan? Where's Duncan?"

"Who's that?" I asked Yakulov.

"Esenin," he answered, laughing.

I had seen Esenin a few times, but only in passing, and I had not recognized him just now.

A little later, Yakulov and I went up to Isadora. She was reclining on a sofa. Esenin was kneeling beside her and she was stroking his hair, scanning: "Za-la-ta-ya ga-la-va" (golden head).[1]

[1] (This is the only genuine episode in Anatoly Marienhof's sensational *Novel Without Lies* which deals with the Duncan-Esenin love affair.)

Yakulov introduced me. I looked attentively at Esenin. In spite of the Russian proverb "Ill-fame runs and good fame lies down," he seemed to be haunted by both sorts of fame at one and the same time: the fame of his poems in which there was genuine poetry, and the fame of his brawls and eccentric behaviour.

He was rather short and, for all his elegance, a little stout. His eyes were unforgettable: blue with an almost embarrassed look. There was nothing harsh about him, neither in his features nor in the expression of his eyes. Of all the sculptures and portraits of him, Konenkov's wooden bust is perhaps the most life-like.

Without rising from his knees, Esenin turned to us and said: "I was told Duncan was at the Hermitage. I rushed off there ..."

Isadora again buried her hand in "the gold of his hair"...that was how, afterwards, they "talked" with each other all through the night, apparently with full understanding.

I was feeling tired and at last asked Isadora whether she would come home with me. The other guests were already leaving. Isadora rose reluctantly from the sofa. Esenin followed her down into the street. When we got outside it was getting light. I looked round: there was not a cab to be seen anywhere. Suddenly we heard the clatter of a cab in the distance. Luckily, it was vacant. Isadora sank into the seat as though it were a luxurious carriage driven by two horses harnessed one behind the other. Esenin sat down beside her.

"Very nice!" I said. "And where am I going to sit?"

Isadora gave me an embarrassed and guilty look and, smiling, tapped her knees. I shook my head. Esenin fidgeted. He did not know me, nor why Isadora had come to the party with me, nor why we were leaving together.

I squeezed in, standing with my back to the driver. Esenin fell silent but never once let go of Isadora's hand. Lit by the first rays of the sun, the cab clattered slowly along Sadovaya Street, then, having passed Smolenskaya Street, turned left and drove past a large church standing in the middle of a cobbled street, as though on an island. We were driving along very slowly, but my fellow passengers did not seem to care. They were happy and did not even trouble me with requests to translate what they were saying to each other.

I remember driving much later in a cab with Isadora. She could not stand slow driving and she asked me to tell the cabman to drive faster, which I did. The cabman jerked the reins, smacked his lips, uttered his famous "gee-up," and soon relapsed into his former languid state. Isadora asked me again to hurry him up. I did so with the same result.

"You're not telling him properly," Isadora cried angrily. "Now, Esenin always says something which makes them drive fast at once."

I tried all the traditional ways of urging cabbies to speed up, but it was no good.

"No, no," explained Isadora, "those are not the words he used. Esenin says something very short and very strong, just as in a game of chess. I can't remember it. But whatever it is it makes them drive off at a spanking pace."

I did not care to repeat Esenin's vocabulary in Isadora's presence.

On that first morning, however, neither Isadora nor Esenin paid any attention to me, who could not help watching them, nor to the dozing cabby: we had driven round the church in the middle of the cobbled street several times already.

"I say, Father," I cried, touching our old driver on the shoulder, "you're not marrying us, are you? You've driven round the church three times just like going round a lectern!"

Esenin gave a start and, on discovering what was happening, burst out laughing.

"He's married us!" he cried, shaking with laughter, bending over and looking with glowing eyes at Isadora.

Isadora wanted to know what was the matter. When I explained, she said slowly, with a happy smile on her face: "Marriage!"

At last the cabby arrived in Prechistenka and drew up at the entrance to our house.

Isadora and Esenin stood on the pavement, but did not take leave of one another. Isadora looked guiltily at me and said pleasingly, motioning towards the door with her head:

"Ilya Ilyich, te-ea?"

Afterwards, Isadora and Esenin talked "all through the night," sitting on the sofa with the golden swans. The night was long in Duncan's room thanks to the drawn curtains and shaded lamps. Outside the autumn sun was shining brightly.

With Esenin's appearance in Prechistenka, the Imagist poets began to pay visits at Isadora's house. Among them, more often than the rest, came Anatoly Marienhof, a tall, handsome young man, Vadim Shershenevich, and Ryurik Ivnov. There were many of these Imagists, and they all swarmed round Esenin, like midges in a shaft of sunlight. Not only Imagists, though. There was, for instance, a certain Grisha Kolobov, whom the poets nicknamed "How Much for the Salt?" He was the representative of the evaluation commission and had his own railway carriage. On arrival at a place, his first question was: "How much for the salt?" and he would buy several sacks of salt and bring them to Moscow in his own railway carriage.

Esenin joined the group of Imagist poets in 1919. He believed then that their literary positions were practically identical, for, like them, he too considered the image to be the basis of all art. The Imagists needed Esenin badly: his name was a good advertisement. The moment Esenin broke with them, Imagism was dead. The Imagists, incidentally, were good businessmen: their bookshop in Nikitsky Street, their publishing house, their poetry readings, and their café, "The Stall of Pegasus" on Tversky Boulevard, all of them profitable enterprises, were part of the Imagist "programme."

"The Stall of Pegasus" played a tragic part in Esenin's life: he could always get his vodka free there, and vodka had a disastrous effect on him.

One evening Duncan happened to have quite a few visitors. Among them was the poet Rukavishnikov, who wore a very long goatee. Lunacharsky was also expected. I was busy in the school downstairs and did not go up, although Isadora had sent for me twice. At last a third messenger arrived: she wanted me urgently.

On entering Isadora's room, I saw the following scene: Esenin was sitting on the sofa in a tense, bellicose posture and with an angry, resolute expression on his face. Next to him, Rukavishnikov was stooping quietly. Esenin was holding him firmly by the beard.

"Why didn't you come?" Isadora whispered. "He's been holding him like that for twenty minutes."

When I went up to the sofa, Esenin smiled and, letting go of Rukavishnikov, got up and greeted me joyfully.

For some reason he usually restrained himself in my presence. I never heard him utter a harsh word. He somehow quietened down at my appearance. Isadora made use of that. It was impossible to be angry with Esenin: his face suddenly beamed with an angelic, child-like smile and there was an embarrassed look in his blue eyes. . . .

All the same, I did say to him quietly:

"Sergei Alexandrovitch, what on earth made you do it?"

59

"My dear Ilya Ilyich, why does he write poetry? Tell him not to."

But it was not only Rukavishnikov's bad poetry: it was Esenin's "fans" who interfered with his work. A few months later, in March, 1922, Esenin wrote to a friend:

"I live roughly, somehow, without a place I can call my own, because at home I am constantly disturbed by all sorts of good-for-nothing loafers, including Rukavishnikov. They, if you please, drop in for a drink with me! I simply don't know how to get rid of these stupid fools and I'm getting thoroughly ashamed of burning the candle at both ends."

I believe he was friendly only with Marienhof. They lived in one room in Bogoslovsky Lane, next to Korsh's theatre. When visitors arrived in the evenings, Esenin was usually asked to read his poems. He liked to read them, especially *The Hooligan's Confession* and Khlopusha's monologue from his long poem *Pugachev,* which he was writing at the time. In the intimate circle of his friends, he used to read in a low, rather husky voice, which sometimes fell to a whisper. . . .

Under the influence of his bohemian surroundings, the rebellious theme in Esenin's work at one time took the form of the idealization of hooliganism and rough play. Hence his *Hooligan's Confession,* his *Poems of a Brawler,* and his *Drunken Moscow,* all of them proof of his mental breakdown, the serious creative crisis he was going through at the time. But one can also detect alarm, confusion, and exhaustion in his hooligan poems.

Esenin was engrossed in writing his *Pugachev.* While working on the poem and trying to have it published in a single volume, he kept running to his publishers and printers, and telephoning them. One day he burst into Prechistenka looking triumphant and with a bundle of thin paperback volumes with brick-red covers on which, in straight, thick letters, was printed the title of his poem—*Pugachev.* He wrote a brief and moving inscription on one of them and presented it to me. . . . On the copy of *Pugachev* which Esenin gave to Isadora he wrote: "For everything, for everything, for everything, for everything I thank you . . . !" and underlined the last line: "My dear one, my good one, my beautiful one."

All sorts of things have been written and said about Esenin: that he wrote his poems while drunk, that he never corrected a line, that he wrote without thinking or working hard at his poems. The truth is that he worked very hard at a poem. He spent a long time maturing his poems in his mind, or, rather, not the poems themselves, but the thought behind them. The lines of a poem took shape in his head in an almost finished form. That is why he found it so easy to put it down on paper afterwards. I cannot remember his exact words in this connection, but their sense was: "They say I write without making corrections. Sometimes there are corrections. I do not write with a pen. I merely put the final touches on with a pen."

I saw Esenin writing a poem only once. It was during the day. He sat at Isadora's large mahogany desk, quiet, serious, rapt. He was writing *A Wolf's Death*. When some time later I went into the room again, he got up from the armchair without his characteristic jerky movements, but as if he were carrying a heavy weight, and, holding a piece of paper in his hands, he asked me to listen. Incidentally, the poem has been printed several times under the title of *A Wolf's Death* but in his last autographed copy Esenin crossed out this title, and now its first line is used as its title: "Mysterious world, my ancient world..."

Esenin loved the Russian language passionately. He knew many local sayings and dialects as well as Old Slavonic.... He was keen on the purity of Russian, and any careless mistakes he came across in print made him angry. It was not an accident that Esenin did not learn any foreign language. He once told me that it would have "interfered" with him. In a letter from America, he wrote: "I do not recognize any language except Russian, and if anyone wants to talk to me, he'd better learn Russian."

Esenin's enthusiasm for "triptychs of the Virgin," his cult of the "illiterate, best-shoe-wearing peasant," which left such an imprint on his early poetry, was the result of the influence of Nikolai Klyuev, his "spiritual father" and "master." Esenin spoke a great deal about Klyuev and liked to read his poems. One day he came to Prechistenka with Klyuev and the sculptor Konenkov, a tall, broad-shouldered, youngish-looking man with a large grey beard. Klyuev wore his usual long-waisted peasant coat, a Russian blouse, and top-boots. His hair was thickly oiled and he had an unctuous expression on his face. Esenin did not treat Klyuev as a "son" might do, but with condescension and hidden hostility. Isadora asked Klyuev to read some of his poems, Klyuev read many and readily. Isadora, who knew no Russian, liked his poems nevertheless because of their music.

"I wish," she said, "Klyuev would teach the children Russian literature."

I tried to explain to her that that was forbidden by the rules of the Commissariat of Education. Suddenly Esenin shouted:

"You must not allow it. You don't know Klyuev's political views. And, besides, it's nonsense."

Klyuev, too, though he fawned on Esenin, sometimes snarled at him. I remember Esenin saying on one occasion, when discussing Klyuev's outlook: "It's old! The dogs don't even bark at it any more. You won't devour us!"

At first Klyuev bristled, then, casting a look at Isadora, he smiled sweetly and, pointing a finger at Esenin, who was born in Ryazan, sang out venomously: "In Ryazan pies have eyes, they are eaten, but they keep on looking." Duncan, of course, did not understand a word. (Later I found the same phrase in one of Klyuev's letters to Esenin.) Esenin leapt from the table. There was hatred in his darkened eyes. Klyuev remained sitting meekly. Isadora began worrying me to explain what they were talking about.

It was Klyuev who was responsible for the stories which have misled such an experienced writer as V. S. Rozhdestvensky, who repeated the false statement about Esenin's "pyjamas," Duncan's "laces," and, finally, the legendary "samovar." ("He wore striped, light flannel trousers and a coat of the same kind—red and black— well, just like a convict," Klyuev described Esenin's "pyjamas" to Rozhdestvensky, though Esenin never had such pyjamas.)

According to Klyuev, Duncan poured him "a glass of very strong tea" from the samovar. Klyuev "took a sip" and "black spots" appeared before his eyes. The "tea" was brandy. "Very well," the story according to Klyuev goes on, "so I thought to myself—clever! So they get their drinks straight from the samovar before breakfast! What are they going to do at lunch?" (In fact, Isadora never had a samovar.)

There were many "legends," Rozhdestvensky writes, about the first meeting of Esenin and Duncan. And he goes on to describe something that never happened and in this way creates a new legend: "She lived in Povarskaya in a detached house and opened a studio for rhythmic exercises there."

The big house, in which Duncan occupied only one room, was, as is well known, not in Povarskaya but in Prechistenka. Duncan abhorred the "rhythmic" and "plastic" studios for they adopted only her "bare feet" and tunics, and forgot the chief thing—the naturalness of movement, its simplicity and expressiveness.

And here is Rozhdestvensky's description of "the first meeting": "The pupils of the famous dancer were giving a performance. One girl after another, wearing ancient tunics and barefoot, performed her rhythmic dances, which reproduced the black figure drawings on the Greek vases. Esenin watched them without interest. The supple and severely rhythmic movements seemed to say nothing to his soul...."

The author of these reminiscences does not even suspect that on the day of "the first meeting," which took place in the autumn of 1921, the girl students had not even crossed the threshold of Duncan's school, which they entered in winter towards the very end of the year, and that their ages varied from four to ten. At the time, needless to say, their movements were neither "supple" nor "severely rhythmic."

Rozhdestvensky goes on to describe how Isadora "began her dance" after her pupils and how "Esenin opened wide his enraptured eyes...jumped up from his seat and, with the sharp stone of his ring, cut three words—I love Duncan—on the huge mirror on the wall, putting three huge exclamation marks after those words. Spoiled by her incessant successes, the world celebrity had seemingly never before experienced such a rapturous avowal. She demanded a translation of Esenin's words, and she was struck by their meaning no less than the manner in which Esenin chose to express his feelings. When she learnt that before her was a famous poet, who had so recently been a simple village shepherd, Duncan was herself no less enraptured."

The first meeting of Esenin and Duncan took place, as I have already described, not in Prechistenka, but in the studio of the painter Yakulov in Bolshaya Sadovaya Street, and, at the time there was neither a school nor pupils. There was not only no "huge mirror" on the wall, such as is usually found in classrooms and rehearsal rooms of the classical ballet, but there was no studio, and, anyway, Duncan did not have any mirrors in her studio, which was draped with plain, austere curtains. The incident with the mirror was quite different and took place six months after their first meeting. The inscriptions were made by both Duncan and Esenin, and the meaning of the three words written by Esenin (not with "a sharp stone" but with a stick of soap) was diametrically contrary to that mentioned by Rozhdestvensky.

As for the story of the brandy in the morning, what happened was this: Isadora woke me at about seven o'clock one morning by knocking on my door. When I went and entered her room, she was standing at the window. It was drizzling outside and it was still rather dark.

"Do you know the tale of the azure bird?" she asked.

"You didn't wake me to ask me that?"

"No. I got up very early, went round the school, and found a great many things that have to be put right."

"For instance?"

"Well, lots of different things. The cat jumped on to the dresser and knocked these eggs on the floor. They broke. So you don't know the tale of the azure bird?"

"By Maeterlinck? The Blue Bird?"

"No, the azure one. I'll tell you. A very poor peasant was told: 'If you succeed in catching the azure bird, happiness will come to you. But the bird comes flying to your field very early and it flies away at five o'clock in the morning.' Every day the peasant got up at dawn but, though he waited till five o'clock, he never once caught sight of the azure bird. However, as he was already in his field, he started working early in the morning and soon his work began to bear fruit. He had plenty of everything, life was good to him and so happiness came to him. That, you see, is what it means to get up early. You are asleep and you don't see what's happening in the school."

"But I shan't have any sleep at all if I get up at six o'clock. I usually go to bed very late."

"Tell me," Isadora said, changing the subject, "is it true that Russians start drinking vodka in the morning?"

"I have never heard of it. Drunkards, I suppose, start drinking in the morning, but they also drink in the day, in the evening, and at night."

"No, no!" Isadora insisted. "I was told about it. There's some secret here. The Russians are a very clever people, and if they do that, there must be some hidden meaning in it."

"It's called taking a hair of the dog that bit you. They say that to get rid of a hangover one must drink a glass of vodka in the morning after a drinking bout the night before."

"No, that's different," Isadora insisted. "There must be something in it. Vodka must stimulate one in the morning in the same way as, for instance, music you hear at some resort early in the morning. Come, let's try it."

And she got a bottle of vodka and two glasses out of the cabinet.

"I won't drink," I said. "Vodka in the morning!"

"That's not polite. A lady asks you to drink with her and you refuse. We have to find out what effect it has."

We drank.

"Let's go for a walk," she said suddenly.

"Certainly not," I cried angrily. "You wake me at daybreak to catch an azure bird, you make me drink brandy, and now you want me to go out for a walk in the cold and rain...."

"Well, in that case, let's have another glass. Only you mustn't refuse. We have to find out what effect it has."

The glasses were filled and emptied again.

"Let's go for a walk," I heard her say again.

"It's hardly worthwhile," I said, but my reply had no note of confidence in it.

"Very well, another glass, then."

And the bottle gurgled again.

"Well, how do you feel?" asked Isadora.

"Oh, well, it does wake you up a bit, doesn't it? I'm no longer sleepy and I feel a little more cheerful."

"Of course! I was sure there was something in it. It doesn't weaken you, but gives you a burst of energy. Well, are we going for a walk? I shall work afterwards! Only we must take a last helping of this elixir."

We drank.

"Into the fresh air! Into the fresh air! It isn't such a bad idea to go for a walk now, is it?"

"Very well," I replied, willingly enough. "It's not raining very much now. Coming?"

The rain had stopped. As we went down Prechistenka we saw the golden dome of Ivan the Great glitter suddenly. Duncan quickened her steps. We walked along the Volkhonka and Mokhovaya. It was a glorious morning. Isadora laughed at our experiment and no longer tried to convince me of its usefulness. She walked along and enjoyed the morning.

"How lovely it is, even in cities," Duncan was saying, walking with her inimitable light step. "And yet they played their part in destroying the natural beauty of man. The span of man's life gets shorter from century to century, from epoch to epoch people lost height, health, and naturalness of movement, influenced by their absurd clothes: crinolines, corsets, high heels, jabots, hard shirt-fronts and collars and everything else that disfigured the human body and interfered with the freedom of man's movements. Religion, too, was responsible for this by making the dance a mortal sin in the past."

"In Russia," I said, "Paul the First banned the waltz as 'an immoral dance.'"

"The waltz?" Isadora cried in surprise and went on: "Moscow is not such a 'stone sack' as London, New York, and Paris. Here there still is some vegetation, but there children grow up without air, without sun, without trees, without water. I know it sounds incredible, but in those great 'stone sacks' there are tens of thousands of children who have never seen the country, or know what a field or a wood looks like except from books and pictures. Plant a flower in a cellar, in which no ray of light ever penetrates and it will grow, but its leaves will be almost white. From one generation to another, children grow up sickly, pale, awkward...."

We were approaching the riding school. On crossing Vozdvizh-enka, Duncan stopped. Straight across the street, the Kremlin gleamed white and golden. Isadora fell silent and gazed at it for a long time.

"How beautiful!" she exclaimed. "What a miracle man can create, and yet he degenerates himself. To give back to man his lost beauty—that is the aim of my life. I am thought to be a utopian, but I am far from Fourier's 'phalanx' or some sort of 'direction of man.' Here, in this country, the foundation has been laid for a new life, a new morality, a new way of living. I was anxious to come here because I realized long ago that my reform can be only part of a general reform of schools, everyday life, and life as a whole!"

When we returned home, Duncan asked: "Are you still displeased because I woke you and took you out for a walk?"

"No...."

Konenkov and Esenin were friends. They had known one another since 1918. In the evening, Esenin would start pestering everybody: "Let's go to Krasnaya Presnya! Isadora, Konenkov!"

Konenkov's small studio was in Krasnaya Presnya. It was freezing there in spite of two stoves. In the studio you were greeted by a whole gallery of Russian Pans, carved out of wood: forest gods with the kindly, warm, smiling faces of cunning little old peasants looking steadily at you with shrewd and clever eyes. Konenkov stroked these faces lovingly, and they became even warmer and came to life under his quivering fingers. They seemed to be listening to the affectionate characterizations he gave every one of them as he introduced them to us, calling them "forest spirits."

There was a smell of the forest in the studio, which was full of tree stumps and blocks of wood.

Konenkov used to come to Isadora's studio and watch her dancing for a long time. He would ask her about Rodin and she told us how Rodin went to see her the first time in Paris, and she danced before him. After one of her dances, Rodin rose and moved towards her with outstretched hands and unseeing eyes. He kneaded and pounded her body as though it were clay.

"I was too young and stupid then. I was offended and pushed him away. Rodin! I was very sorry afterwards. I should not have pushed him away...."

Esenin refused to understand it, but Konenkov apparently understood. He carved two wooden statuettes of Isadora dancing and gave them to her. She took them with her to France. What happened to them after her death I do not know. They were beautiful.

VIII

On the tall, narrow mirror that reached from floor to ceiling in Isadora's room could be seen the unwiped trace of the joke Esenin and I played on Isadora: a few broken lines made by a piece of soap created the illusion of a broken cheval glass. The soap lay on the marble sill. One day Isadora picked it up and quite unexpectedly wrote in block letters on the glass in broken Russian: *Ya loobloo Ezenin* (*Ya lyublyu Esenin:* I love Esenin). Picking up the little soap pencil, Esenin drew a line under the letters and quickly wrote: "But I don't love Isadora."

Isadora turned away, looking sad. I took the piece of soap, which Esenin had kept in his hand with a malicious smile, and, drawing another line, drew a conventional picture of a heart pierced by an arrow and wrote: "That time will come."

How many times afterwards, when Esenin was under the spell of his love for Isadora, did he remember those words! Isadora did not wipe them off, and for a long time they remained there silently declaring, denying, and foretelling their love for one another. Only before leaving for Berlin did Esenin wipe off the offending words and quickly write: "I love Isadora."

Isadora was engrossed in her work. One hundred and fifty children came daily to their classes. Forty had to be selected from them.... The dream of a thousand children in a large hall still remained a dream. Podvoysky kept looking for such a hall and from time to time sent his car for us. But we returned disappointed: the halls were too cold.

One sunny day in late autumn, Isadora and I were on our way to inspect one of the halls Podvoysky had found for us. Our chauffeur was driving at a crazy speed. On one of the lanes children scattered in all directions at the approach of our car, but one of them, taken by surprise, first stopped dead then rushed across in front of the car, which hit him. I seized the chauffeur by the shoulders. He braked. Isadora, her body pressed against the back of the seat, was paralysed with horror, her face deathly pale. We got out of the car with an anguished feeling that nothing could be done to save the little boy, when suddenly we saw him get up silently from the ground, dash across the road, and disappear through a gate into a yard.

"He's alive, alive!" people cried around us. "Only scratched."

"What luck! What luck!" Isadora whispered. "Let's drive to a confectioner's," she said. "I can't look at that chauffeur, the murderer! How could he drive so fast in a street where children were playing?"

At the confectioner's, we put a cake and boxes of chocolates and sweets in a big box and went back to the lane, where a perky little girl led us to the basement room where the boy lived. It had almost no furniture, but there were five or six children in it. On a bar table in the middle of the room sat a tiny child, no bigger than a doll, with a sallow face and a pair of solemn eyes, who stretched out his arms to the little girl who brought us in. There, too, was the little boy who had been knocked down. He had not yet recovered from his fright, but he was already eyeing us and the box with interest. His injuries had evidently been seen to; the little girl, his sister and the eldest of the family, dipping a bit of cotton wool in a saucer and wiping his cut forehead carefully.

"A miracle!" exclaimed Isadora. "This boy is my mascot. I want him in my school."

As I untied the box, the baby stretched out his toy-like hands for a sweet which he began sucking solemnly. The little girl, speaking very fast, told us that their mother was the caretaker of the house, that she was out and knew nothing of what had happened. Turning to her brother she said severely, "Just let me catch you running about in the road again!"

I wrote down the address of the school and asked her to tell her mother to take the boy there in the morning. The children saw us off to the car, only Isadora's "mascot" and the baby staying behind. Looking round at the baby as she was leaving the basement room,

Isadora said: "There will be no more such children in this country! My mission is to help to make it so."

Sitting down sideways in the car so as not to see the chauffeur, she exclaimed: "To come to this country for the sake of the children and nearly kill one! If that had happened, I'd never have wished to see the light of day again!"

Next morning, a little woman came with Isadora's "mascot" but, for all our persuasions, she could not make up her mind to part with her boy and send him to the school. The four years that had passed since the October Revolution were not enough to transform her way of thinking and convince her that the doors of all schools and university lecture rooms would be open to her children. She stole furtive glances at the painted beauties on Belashova's ceiling, the marble balustrade, the rosewood columns with their gilt stucco mouldings, and repeated stubbornly that she would not give up her son to those who "lived" at the school. Isadora followed her distrustful gaze sympathetically and, when she had gone, remarked:

"I've been saying for a long time that we ought to tear off all this gilding together with the Romans and the Greek women and whitewash it all!"

The hundred and fifty children who attended the school for the preliminary course loved Isadora, loved the dances in which they whirled round to the lovely music of Schubert's waltzes and Rachmaninov's playful *Italian Polka*; they loved the blue ballroom with its patches of sunrise and sunset and the intrusion into its pinky light of a bit of blue sea or southern sky, gleaming with a mysterious sapphire glow. There was a four-year-old girl among them, who was always the first to arrive, who knew her place in the first row at the gym lesson, where the smallest children were drawn up, and who treated these exercises with droll seriousness. There were boys and girls of different ages, but none over the age of ten, who were shy and clumsy when they first came, but who in a remarkably short time revealed the natural and beautiful movements with which nature had endowed them.

Isadora soon knew every one of them and devoted a lot of affection, warmth, and patience to these little Muscovites. During the lessons they watched Irma with bated breath when she demonstrated the different movements, gliding unbelievably lightly and noiselessly over the blue carpet. Isadora was greatly upset when the time approached for parting from the majority of these children, the time when she would have to select only forty of them for her future "phalanx of enthusiasts." She prolonged her lessons and included all the children in the *Internationale*, with which she decided to conclude her first performance at the Bolshoi on November 7, the fourth anniversary of the October Revolution. The programme included Tchaikovsky's *Sixth Symphony* and *Slavonic March,* and the *Internationale*.

"From the chaos of sounds, from the countless number of their combinations, composers, by an incomprehensible process of work, create the great harmony of music," Duncan said. "I have always been of the opinion that composers do not belong to the category of ordinary men, but when I hear the *Sixth Symphony* my conviction grows into infinite admiration. I try to penetrate into the mystery of this great creative process, but cannot grasp where this great music originates, where in Tchaikovsky, why it is in him that I suddenly begin to hear what later becomes the highest achievement of symphonic music that amazes the whole world. The music of the gods descends only on such geniuses as Tchaikovsky," she continued, pensively. "We ordinary people cannot hear it while it is still drifting about in the ether, we do not possess the quite inconceivable potentialities of hearing what they later preserve for humanity in catching those sounds in five staves."

I remember Isadora's telling me how Richard Wagner's widow, who was one of the dancer's great friends, spoke to her of something that struck her most forcibly in Duncan's work.

"Richard," she said, "always saw the music he composed in plastic images, but how did you so grasp his ideas and images as to be able to embody them?"

It is not surprising that when Arthur Nikisch saw Duncan for the first time, he exclaimed: "*Sie macht die Musik klar!*"

In her interpretation of the *Sixth Symphony* Duncan approached the musical work not as a musician but as a musicologist: she looked for the revelation of the image through her great creative intuition, and that is perhaps why she succeeded in embodying so exactly the essence of the composer's intention in her movements.

Duncan, however, never insisted on her own treatment. She said and wrote many times that, as one who belonged to the old world, she could only indicate to her pupils the ways along which they themselves could achieve their aims.

71

Every evening Isadora worked at the *Sixth Symphony* and the *Slavonic March* in her studio. The French Communist Henri Gilbeau, who was in Moscow at the time and who often went to see Duncan, was horrified when he learnt that twice in the *Slavonic March* there occur snatches from the Tsarist national anthem, "God Save the Tsar."

"It's unheard of," he thundered, "it shouldn't be allowed! It's insulting and provocative!"

"*Vous êtes fou,*" Isadora replied.

"*C'est une sottise!*" he cried. "Snatches from the Tsarist anthem on November 7 at a performance celebrating the October Revolution! It's a political mistake. It will be interpreted as a provocation. Lunacharsky will never permit it."

"You don't understand anything," Isadora replied. "Everything depends on the treatment, on the plastic image which I give of the *Slavonic March* in my composition and on the particular moment when the bit of the anthem is played.

"*Vous êtes fou,*" she repeated, and she decided to invite Lunacharsky and Krasin to her rehearsal at the studio.

They came. They sat through the entire *Sixth Symphony* in silence.

"It's shattering!" Lunacharsky said after watching the *Slavonic March*.

Duncan never agreed with the conventional treatment of the *Slavonic March* and even less with the well-known idea of Tchaikovsky, who wrote it in memory of the liberation of the Bulgarians from the Turks by Russia.

"I can't believe," she used to say, "that a great man like Tchaikovsky, whose thought is so philosophically profound, would have been satisfied with only one single idea in that great composition. A man like that could not but be a revolutionary at heart. He would have laughed at all of them and would have put into his march infinitely greater thoughts, hopes and faith in the future."

To the hollow beat of the first bars of the *Slavonic March*, Duncan, in a dark-red tunic, which looked like a Russian shirt, appeared from the wings at the back of the stage, stooping, with hands that seemed to be tied behind her. She seemed to walk for a long, long time, with heavy steps, like someone who has risen from the bottomless depths of dark mines, someone who is no longer used to bright light, someone crushed and enslaved, who is leaving the darkness for the light. On reaching the centre of the stage, Duncan is still fettered, but no longer bent. She listens to the sounds of the distant, rousing march, she hears the rhythm of footsteps, heralding liberation. She—a born slave with trembling limbs— listens painfully to those approaching sounds, still unable to believe them. Then she begins, timidly but also joyfully, to tap a foot in rhythm with the march, which becomes louder and louder. But, in another instant, her face becomes distorted with horror: the trumpet is calling to others! She has been deceived. The brass voice of the accursed anthem pierces her like a sword. She collapses on her knees as though pressed down to the floor, her scattered hair sweeping the ground, her whole body swaying with grief and despair. But next moment she rises, stern and terrible. You can see the invisible fetters, you are drawn forward with her in an intense superhuman effort. You shudder at the deafening sound with which the fetters are torn asunder and the chains fall clattering to the ground.

Man has freed his hands which have been fettered for ages. He stretches them out before him. They are distorted, disfigured by slavery, their fingers twisted and contorted. Duncan's body, too, trembles convulsively with disgust at itself, at those disfigured, twisted hands. The tremor seems to shatter her, and you begin to shudder and tremble with her. Once more the brassy voice of the Tsarist anthem resounds and Duncan is transformed: her feet seem to find some firm ground, she bends forward as though ready to fight, ready to battle for her life. She flings up her arms, her eyes look upwards, fixed at the two-headed bird hovering above her. There it is! The trumpet utters a dying cry. Duncan seizes and strangles, strangles that bird of ill omen. Then, suddenly, her arms drop exhausted at her sides. A sigh of joy and great relief escapes her. There is an expression of the triumph of victory and liberation on her face, tears of happiness gush from her eyes....

I am well aware how difficult it is to put into words the powerful impact of Duncan's art in the *Slavonic March*. The story of the creation of the dance is interesting. It owes its existence to a spontaneous idea. Duncan was giving a performance in New York when news of the revolution in Russia was received. The orchestra was billed to play the *Slavonic March* after Isadora's appearance in the *Sixth Symphony*. In the interval she summoned the conductor and told him that she meant to appear in the *Slavonic March*.

"Good Lord," he exclaimed, horrified, "without a rehearsal?"

"There's no need for me to rehearse it," she replied. "It has been fermenting inside me for a long time. Today when Russia has achieved freedom, it is about to burst out of me."

Duncan generally disliked dress rehearsals. A morning rehearsal had been arranged at the Bolshoi shortly before a first-night performance. The large Bolshoi orchestra was conducted by Nikolai Golovanov, who had often been in Prechistenka and taken part in Isadora's discussions with Henri Gilbeau. At first he hesitated to express his final opinion, but after attending a rehearsal in the studio, he came over unreservedly to Isadora's side.

At the morning rehearsal the whole of artistic Moscow turned up. Duncan arrived after everything on the stage was ready.... She went up to the footlights, bowed to the orchestra, and exchanged greetings with Golovanov. She then put a chair straight in front of the conductor and asked him to start the *Sixth Symphony*. She sat without moving through the whole of the first movement of the symphony in her short fur jacket and dark Spanish felt hat. The disturbing waltz of the second movement began. Everyone waited: was Duncan going to wait for the orchestra to go through the whole of the symphony a second time and merely listen to it the first time? But as the last chords of the *Lamento* died away, Duncan got up, thanked Golovanov and the orchestra warmly, and then said: *"Je vous prie Marche Slave,"* and sat down again. She then stayed to hear the orchestra rehearse the *andante cantabile* and the *1812 Overture* of the second part of the concert.

The audience was in a terrible state of agitation: was she not going to dance at all? What kind of rehearsal was it?

What had happened during Isadora's first visit to Petersburg in 1905 was repeated now: Golovanov alone remained calm: he had foreseen it.

On November 7, the theatre was so crowded that the barriers separating the boxes were broken down. Even the corridors were packed with people. At the time we did not know that Lenin was expected to be present. When Lenin appeared in one of the boxes accompanied by Dzerzhinsky he was greeted by a storm of applause. Before the beginning of Isadora's performance, Lunacharsky came on stage and gave a brief account of the work of "the world-famous dancer, Isadora Duncan," and a brief résumé of the content of the dance. At the end of the *Slavonic March,* Lenin got up and cried in a loud voice: "Bravo, bravo, Miss Duncan!"

Lunacharsky again appeared on stage. He announced that Duncan had agreed to repeat the last scene of the dance if the audience would sing the *Internationale* with her. When Duncan came on stage, the whole audience, including Lenin, rose and sang the *Internationale*. . . .

Esenin never missed a single performance of Isadora's either in Moscow or in St. Petersburg. At her first performance at the Bolshoi, the poet brought many of his friends. He was very fond of the *Slavonic March* and sometimes watched it from the wings. He was particularly impressed by the speeches Duncan made during and after her performances. Esenin himself had no talent for oratory, though he used to read his own poems with shattering force. The ability to make a speech without hemming and hawing or pauses aroused his admiration.

"Do you really translate from the stage all that Isadora says, or do you add something of yourself?" Esenin tried to find out from me after one performance, smiling excitedly, eyes shining. "I know she loves to talk. But how do you remember those long periods?" And, becoming serious suddenly, he added, shaking me by the shoulders with his strong hands: "Take the *Slavonic March*. Isadora hated the Russian Tsarist regime. So did I. Always. I was even punished for it and sent to join a penal battalion."

One day Esenin said to Isadora: "You are an Imagist."

She knew what he meant but, raising her blue eyes to him, asked in broken Russian: "Why?"

"Because in your art the image (*obraz*) is the main thing."

"What is *obraz*?" she asked, turning to me.

I translated: "Image." Esenin laughed.

"Isadora," he said, with an abrupt negative gesture of the hand, pointing a finger at her, "Marienhof is not *obraz*, your *Marche Slave* is *obraz*."

She did not understand. Nor could I explain to her what Esenin meant because there was much I did not know at the time. In his article "Life and Art," Esenin wrote of the Imagists: "My fellow poets were carried away by the figurativeness of the verbal form. They seem to think that the word and the image are one and the same thing."

Esenin gazed at Isadora with laughing eyes.

"Why not explain to me, if not to Isadora?" I said to him.

He dismissed this with a wave of the hand.

"I'm sick to death! Another time. To hell with them!" And, looking thoughtfully at Isadora again, he repeated:

"You are an Imagist. But a good one. Understand?"

She nodded.

"You are—*revolution*! Understand?"

This conversation took place shortly before Esenin's departure abroad with Duncan, which marked the beginning of his break with the Imagists.

IX

On the day when she had to select forty children from the hundred odd children who had been attending the preliminary classes, Isadora walked into the "blue ballroom" with a heavy heart.

"How am I to do it?" she asked. "I can't look at those children's faces and tell them that they've not been admitted."

She was given a batch of green and red tickets which she had to distribute among the children during their last trial lesson. There were forty red tickets. The lesson began as usual with a slow step to the slow Schubert march. Then the leaps began. The children rushed, leaping into the air in a large circle.

"Up! Up!" Isadora cried in English. "Stop! Manya, what are you doing with your hands?" she asked a pretty little fair-haired girl with dark eyes and a frightened look on her face. (For the last six weeks, the children had learned to understand Isadora's short remarks addressed to them. When she talked to them at some length, I used to translate.) "Once more!" Isadora carried on with her lesson, and again she went on repeating: "Up! Up!"

The movements followed one after another. The children flew about like a flock of birds, spreading their arms like wings, quickly moving their legs and bending their bodies up towards the ceiling and down to the floor, imitating the flight of birds. In the difficult "fast run," the restriction and constraint of their movements, which they could not have overcome in so short a time, became particularly obvious.

"To become as nature created him," Isadora always said, "a

77

person, it seems, must go through a whole school, must become completely artless, which is an art in itself."

Many, many years later, when some of these children who had become studio teachers rushed along the green sward of the stadium in the "fast run," spectators, even those who were near, were under the impression that they never touched the ground but rather, were floating through the air.

The children danced Rachmaninov's *Polka* by rushing past each other like the wind, twisting into a spiral and then forming two joined circles moving one after another in opposite directions around the four-year-old Lida, whom Isadora had placed in the centre. From time to time Isadora would call some child to her and give her a red or green ticket, after which the child ran into the adjoining room, where they were divided according to ticket by the "women instructors," who later told their parents, gathered nervously downstairs, the results of the test.

"These tickets make it even more painful," Isadora said. "They grasp the green and the red tickets with the same expression of joy, without suspecting their significance."

On December 3, 1921, forty children crossed the threshold of the school for the first time. Some of them later worked in the studio and the Duncan theatre-studio. Thereafter, December 3rd remained an important day in their lives and we always observed its anniversary wherever we happened to be—on tour in Byelorussia, on an English boat sailing from Changchun to Shanghai, in wintry Kislovodsk, in warm Tashkent, in Moscow and New York, at the twenty-fifth anniversary of the foundation of the school, the twentieth anniversary of the studio at the Central House of Artists in Moscow, and at the jubilee performance in the Stanislavsky Theatre, when we appeared in Tchaikovsky's *Sixth Symphony* in a revival of Duncan's production.

Forty children lived at the school, but the school did not lead a normal life. The time-table drawn up by Duncan was not adhered to. Of all the subjects, only the morning gym and the evening dancing lesson were carried out as planned. The general education was in a muddle. Only two of the teachers that had been engaged had any teaching experience and were acquainted with the curriculum of the new school. But the curriculum, too, was doubtful, for during these as well as subsequent years, it kept changing from the Dalton plan to the group method. The "organization" committee was at a total loss, for it was not able to organize even the day-to-day running of the school, though the staff exceeded the number of children by 150 per cent.

The school was in a constant uproar.

"The children come to their dancing lesson," Duncan declared, looking upset, "excited and unable to concentrate. In such a state they are also unable to listen to music as they should."

Lunacharsky came to see Duncan one evening about a fortnight after the opening of the school. Irma and I took part in their conversation in Isadora's room. Duncan said it was very difficult for her to work—the school needed the services of a headmaster. Lunacharsky agreed, but he said one had to be very careful in making such an appointment, for what they wanted was not only a good organizer, but also a man who understood art as well as Duncan's ideas and the aims for such a school.

"Here's your headmaster," said Duncan suddenly, pointing at me.

I could not help being surprised. Duncan knew that such a man would have to devote all his time to the school and that I did not want to part with the theatre or with journalism. Besides, I did not know how to run a school.

"Well, why not?" said Lunacharsky. "I know Comrade Schneider very well, but . . ." He leaned towards Isadora and I caught the end of his sentence: "*mais c'est un jeune homme.*"

I still objected because I did not want to give up my work in the theatre.

"Hasn't my school any relation to art?" asked Isadora with a smile.

We went on to discuss the organization of the school. I told them what I thought of its present state and enumerated the things I considered necessary for the normal running of the school and for Duncan herself.

"What's today? Monday? Well then, come to see me at the Commissariat of Education and we shall decide what has to be done. I shall sign all the necessary orders and issue the announcement of your appointment tomorrow."

Nothing was decided on Wednesday, nor on Thursday, nor on Friday, but I did accept the headmastership of Isadora Duncan's school all the same. The real trouble, it seemed to me, lay in the attitude of the Commissariat of Education towards the school.

Lunacharsky several times complained of "the stupid resistance of people who thought that it was a luxury."

One day Duncan asked me: "Why am I Eye-sedora? Why have they given me such a funny name in Russia instead of Isadora? I am Isadora Duncan. If you pronounce my name 'Eye-sedora Dooncan' in any other country, no one will realize that you are speaking about me. I quite understand that in Russian Duncan may sound like Dooncan, but why 'Eye-sedora'? Please give me back my name."

I had known why for some time. When, at the beginning of the century, the first telegram arrived in Petersburg with the news of the appearance of a new star in the European world of art, the translator carefully transliterated the name and surname of the new celebrity according to the pronunciation of single letters of the alphabet. The letter "I" therefore became "Eye," and "sa" was transformed into "se."

Once I issued a poster in Moscow advertising a performance by Isadora Duncan, her name properly transliterated, and many people were convinced that it was quite a different person.

"I'm afraid," I said, "you'll have to remain 'Eye-sedora' in Russia."

Isadora spent every evening working alone in her "red studio." One could hear Scriabin, Liszt, Beethoven (the *Fifth Symphony*) being played on the piano in the ballroom. One day Duncan let the pianist go home and danced without music. I saw two absolutely perfect compositions. The absence of music was compensated for by quite an extraordinarily clear rhythm, accentuated by the dull taps of the foot on the floor. The other dance, while preserving the same rhythmic punctuation, was perfectly comprehensible thanks to the expressiveness of Duncan's movements, the gradual deceleration of tempo, and the same kind of gradual transition of movement from light and gay to painful, heavy, and burdensome.

"These are dances without music," said Duncan. "*Death and the Maiden* and *The Burden of Life*."

She repeated the two dances. In the first one could feel the sharp dividing line between life and death, which the maiden approached only occasionally. But in the finale there was a moment so strong and expressive that I felt that the mysterious door had opened wide before the maiden and she "entered" there and again "saw" everything. Isadora never performed these dances on the stage.

Esenin came every day. Isadora hardly ever left the house: she preferred to be alone with Esenin. There was, also, a secret reason for that: when visitors came, drinks were served, and Esenin became difficult. . . .

Duncan kept repeating that by running away from Europe, she was running away "from art that was inextricably bound up with commerce." She therefore categorically refused to appear before an audience that paid for its tickets or to accept any payment for her performance. At her insistent demand, I declined any requests for public performances. But Lunacharsky succeeded in persuading her not to deprive the public of the chance of seeing her performances under conditions generally accepted throughout the country for theatrical shows.

Duncan gave in, and we announced four appearances with a symphony orchestra at the Bolshoi Theatre, after which she received an invitation to give several performances in Petrograd.

Early in February, leaving Irma to look after the school, Isadora, Jeanne, and I set out for the Nikolayevsky railway station. Esenin saw us off. There was no proper railway timetable. There was no sale of tickets, seats being reserved without payment by applying for them beforehand. I had reservations for four seats in a compartment of the international express.

Having found a place for Jeanne in the waiting room, the three of us took a table at the buffet. It was announced that the train would not leave before midnight or even before two o'clock in the morning. Isadora was happy: there was no need for her to part with Esenin as yet, and she did not seem to mind waiting for a wearisome hour in a cold and unheated restaurant. No drinks were sold there, but we had brought two bottles of wine with us. We were warmly dressed and, warmed by our talk and the wine, we did not notice that it was long past midnight. Taking my notebook, Isadora became absorbed in drawing the plan of an ancient Greek theatre and explaining to Esenin the part played by the chorus in it. After boldly sketching the semi-circle of the amphitheatre, she closed up the *orchestra* and, drawing a tiny circle in its centre, wrote under it: "poet." Then she quickly drew a large number of lines radiating from the circle towards the spectators.

"We shall appear together," she said to Esenin. "You will take the place of the Greek chorus. The poet's word and the dance will create such a harmonious spectacle that we ... *wir werden die ganze Welt beherrschen!* [We shall be the masters of the whole world.]" Isadora laughed. Then, suddenly leaning towards me, she said softly in an imploring voice:

"Please, persuade Esenin to come with us to Petrograd."

"Why, it's not necessary to persuade him. Sergei Alexandrovich, do you want to go to Petrograd?"

He nodded joyfully and, turning to Isadora and speaking in their verbless dialect, cried with feeling:

"Isadora! You ... I ... Isadora—Esenin—Petrograd!"

We cheered up. Isadora began drawing caricatures of herself and Esenin. I kept that notebook for a long time. Isadora sketched human figures in two or three lines and that was how she drew herself and Esenin.

In Petrograd, we stopped at the Hotel Angleterre. We arrived in the evening and, tired from the journey, went to bed. Duncan and Esenin occupied a large room on the first floor. The room was very cold. Several times a day either Esenin or I climbed on to the writing desk and felt the top of the pipe of the radiator on the wall. It was quite cold near the floor. In the end, I summoned the hotel manager and asked for another room.

Duncan and Esenin left room No. 5, the room in which, almost four years later, Esenin committed suicide by tying the rope of his trunk to the pipe which had been stone cold in February, 1922, but which was so hot in December, 1925, that it scorched his swinging dead body....

Petrograd awaited Isadora Duncan's first performance with keen interest. Great impatience was shown by the ballet world and the Russian followers of the school of Duncan, the so-called "plastic" dancers, whom Duncan treated with unconcealed contempt, preferring even the classical school of dancing to them.

But it was not the world of the ballet, which filled the boxes of the former Marinsky Theatre to overflowing, that worried Duncan, but the crew of the *Aurora* and the Petrograd workers, who formed the great majority of the spectators in that huge playhouse.

I was even more worried than Duncan, for she asked me to enlighten the audience in my introductory speech about the idea of her school, the reasons for the failure of her schools in Europe, the social roots of her desire to come to Soviet Russia, her work there and her creative aspirations.

"But," I objected in dismay, "that'll take at least half an hour!"

"More if necessary," she replied.

"But they won't want to listen to me. They came to see your performance, not to listen to my speeches."

"These people," Duncan interrupted me, "want to know and have a right to know many things. When I came to Petersburg when Russia was under Tsarist rule, they were not admitted to theatres. The government was afraid of them, they were killed in the streets for fear of what was to come. I came to Russia for the sake of these spectators. Do you mean to say they won't want to know why I am here? Look, I'm trembling myself, like a beginner...."

She poured out half a glass of champagne, drank it and, filling it to the brim, held it out to me:

"Drink it. I understand the state you are in."

I recoiled.

"Why," I cried, "if I drank it, I wouldn't be able to say anything at all."

"I shouldn't have offered it to you," she replied, "if I didn't realize how nervous you are. Drink it. I know from experience: it will give you the necessary courage."

Esenin came into the dressing room. He wanted to get a pass for someone. Isadora clung to him. He patted her on the shoulder encouragingly, covering his hand with powder, smiled, and gave me his "blessing." I wrote out his pass and went out in front of the curtain.

The audience was very attentive, and that gave me courage. Isadora was greeted with thunderous applause. Every movement of the *Sixth Symphony* was followed by rapturous shouts. During the second part of the performance, the stage was suddenly plunged into darkness. The orchestra stopped playing. People in the auditorium began striking matches. I brought out a lantern and put it near the footlights. In its light Duncan, who remained standing motionless in the middle of the enormous stage, was barely visible. She asked the audience not to strike any matches, but to wait until the electric lights had been repaired.

A hush fell over the audience. It did not seem possible that there were thousands of people in the theatre. The flame in the lantern blazed away quietly, throwing feeble flashes of light on the frozen figure of Duncan, who was still painfully conscious of the music of the symphony which had come to such a sudden stop.

The light failed to reappear. It was chilly on the stage. I picked up Isadora's red cloak and put it over her shoulders. Duncan set her cloak straight, walked up to the lantern, which burned with a reddish light, and raised it high over her head. In her red cloak with her head raised challengingly, she looked like some revolutionary symbol. The audience responded with a thunder of applause. Duncan waited for it to subside. Then she took a step towards me and turned round. I realized what she wanted and came up to her.

"Comrades," she said, "I'd like you to sing some of your folk songs."

The audience, filling the huge theatre to capacity, began to sing. In darkness, without a conductor, without accompaniment, amazingly keeping time and tune, and with harmony, they sang one Russian folk song after another.

Duncan remained standing with the lantern raised high over her head, and her outstretched hand did not falter for a single moment, though I could see that it cost her an immense exertion of will and a great physical effort.

"If I had let my hand fall," she explained to me later, "the singing would have stopped and its spell would have been broken. It was so beautiful that not even the most famous choirs would stand comparison with that inspired singing."

This went on for about an hour. Duncan did not drop her hand and the audience sang on and on.

"There is one more of your songs that I once heard," said Duncan during a short pause. "It is a sad song, but it tells of the dawn of a new life. In the finale, the dawn breaks and the song resounds with terrible force and faith in victory."

I had barely time to translate the words when, as though by the wave of the hand of an invisible conductor, the audience burst into the old revolutionary song of a martyr who died "for the people's cause" without knowing that "from our bones a stern avenger will arise, who will be much stronger than we."

Tears ran down Duncan's cheeks as the song grew louder and increased in intensity. Light gradually returned to the chandeliers of the auditorium and the projectors and spotlights on the stage. Reddish at first, then yellow, sunny, and, finally, blindingly white, it flooded the huge theatre and the gigantic chorus, which rose slowly with the light, and shook the auditorium with the last refrain: "Will be much stronger..."

At the same time, Duncan flung off her red cloak and the curtain slowly descended. Not even the most talented producer could have thought of such a climax.

X

We returned to Moscow. Life, it seemed, went on as usual in the predetermined sequence of schooldays. But Isadora could not bear monotony in anything; she invariably got excited by some new idea that came into her head, the next inevitable *grossartige idee.* . . .

She was now all agog over a new project that came into her head: to organize "a brilliant festival" in the school which might, incidentally, improve the school budget. She drew up a plan for the festival. It would start early in the evening with a "demonstration lesson" with the children of the school in the "blue ballroom." Next there was to be a concert performance. Isadora would dance Chopin and Scriabin in the "red studio." Since she considered pancakes and gipsies to be indispensible parts of Russian merry-making, she insisted on the inclusion of these ingredients in a "cabaret" which, according to her plan, was to open immediately after the end of the concert and her dances.

I tried to persuade her to give up the idea of the cabaret, pancakes, and a gipsy choir, but she was counting on the large number of Americans, members of the American Relief Organization, who were greatly interested in the festival.

"Otherwise they won't pay a million for their tickets," Isadora told me. (Even for those days of ridiculously inflated prices, the cost of the tickets was high.)

"All America wants is money, money, money," Isadora kept repeating, "so let them spend money themselves. You will never attract them by the charm of dancing children, nor by Chopin and Scriabin."

She insisted on carrying out her plan, but as soon as the notices were posted, Lunacharsky 'phoned me: "The notices you issued have met with an unfavourable reception by our Party leaders. I must warn you that everything you do should be kept within the limits of the strictest decorum. I shall hold you personally responsible for any cases of drunkenness within the walls of the school."

Fortunately, I fell ill. I was laid up with a high temperature and insisted on the cancellation of the festival. But Isadora immediately wrote the following letter to Lunacharsky:

Dear Comrade,
The words "within the limits of the strictest decorum" do not exist in my vocabulary. Will you, please, explain what you mean.
Yours,
ISADORA DUNCAN.

Lunacharsky answered in a detailed and very mild letter (regrettably not preserved), which he addressed to me and which he asked me to translate carefully to Isadora. He explained very patiently that Isadora was ignorant of the old habits of the Russian public, which invariably associated gipsies and pancakes with vodka, and that no one could possibly guarantee that someone would not bring vodka with him.

Isadora gave in, but nevertheless, could not reconcile herself to the idea that "one of the most progressive men in the world, one of the most prominent Bolsheviks, should talk about the 'limits of the strictest decorum'!"

I must add that, far from supporting Isadora's idea, Esenin objected to it, using the same arguments about "the association of gipsies and pancakes with drink."

Isadora again became engrossed in her work with the children. The school had only boarders. Duncan refused to admit any day pupils.

"At first," she said, "we must stick severely to 'the principle of isolation from the family.' For the time being, every back of a chair smells of the old education even in the most communist family."

She insisted that her children be given every opportunity of listening to symphonic music and seeing the plays performed by the Moscow Art Theatre. (Stanislavsky always gladly put a box at our

87

disposal.) The children also saw Davydov at the Maly Theatre, and enjoyed the piano recitals of Egon Petri. They pricked up their ears like hares at the sound of the grand piano. But Duncan was adamant in her refusal to take the children to see the ballet at the Bolshoi Theatre.

"They will be enticed by those fairy-tale spectacles, the wonderful orchestra, the extraordinarily colourful scenery and costumes, the wonderful virtuosity with which the natural balance of the human body is overcome. They are not yet able to distinguish between spectacular and natural, beautiful movement."

Isadora disliked the cinema and was always telling people how her pupils were surprised after a visit to the cinema. "We did not know Africa was grey," they said. Later on, their escapes to the small magic cinema in Prechistenka and their visits to the big Kolos and Art cinemas were real holiday occasions for them.

On Isadora's desk lay Jean-Jacques Rousseau's *Emile* in a bright yellow cover and a tiny volume of Plato. After she had been reading the Plato, she often became lost in thought for a long time.

Once I caught a glimpse of her sitting up in bed with this book, putting it aside and, bending down to the floor to put on a slipper, shaking a fist at the three angels with lutes eyeing her from a picture on the wall.

This gesture may have had its reason: Isadora maintained that one of the angels was the spitting image of Esenin. The likeness was indeed remarkable.

I saw Esenin, sitting alone at the desk in Isadora's room in a funny sort of mood, blow a few times at the flame of the table lamp and extinguish it with a vicious flick of a finger at the chimney. He was generally given to unexpected actions. He would bring some people to Prechistenka who had absolutely nothing to do with him, or take it into his head to go to—Persia.

The announcement of his intention to go to Persia came suddenly. Isadora took to her bed. She did not get up for several days and finally refused to eat or drink for two days. Late in the evening I went into her huge room, which was dark except for the small lamp on a bedside table.

"There," Isadora indicated a place behind the low, nickel-plated foot of the bed, "Esenin was standing there a minute ago."

"Of course," I tried to explain to her in a very calm tone of voice,

Isadora Duncan and her children, Deirdre (5) and Patrick (3). Paris 1913

▶

The car in which Isadora's young children and their nanny drowned, being lifted from the Seine

Isadora and Walter Rummel, 1919

Isadora Duncan in Paris, 1920 ▶

The building which house Isadora's Moscow school at Prechistenka

Sergei Esenin (top row, second from left) with others associated with Sytin's publishing house, Moscow 1914. Anna, Esenin's first girl friend, is in the front

Podvoysky, friend and companion-in-arms of Lenin, with members of the Duncan school on the Vozobyov Hills, 1924

An early picture of Sergei Esenin, in 1914 ▶

Alexander and Tatiana Esenin, father and mother of the poet

Esenin with Nikolai Klyuev, a poet who had a great influence on Esenin's early work

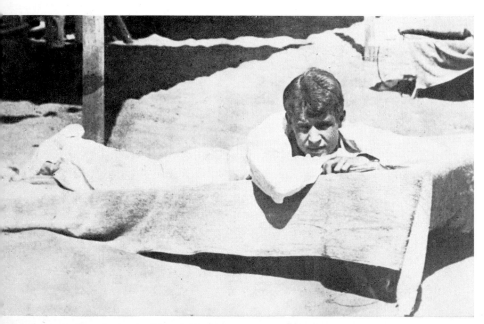

Esenin on holiday in Italy

Three pictures of Isadora and Esenin, 1922

"if you go on refusing to eat and drink, you'll start having not only visual, but also aural, hallucinations."

Then I myself clearly heard Esenin's voice calling me by name. The voice seemed to come from somewhere beyond the "oriental" room. Running through that room and the pink satin one, I saw in the embrasure of the arch in the dark "blue ballroom" a white figure moving towards me....

"Alive! Alive!" he cried.

It seemed that Grisha Kolobov, the representative of the evaluation commission ("How-much-for-the-salt"), had to go to Rostov-on-Don in his railway carriage and promised to take Esenin with him. (He may have counted on Esenin helping him with the sacks of salt.) "Rostov is practically North Caucasus, and Transcaucasia and Persia are just a stone's throw away"—so apparently thought Esenin, who, for some reason, was always hankering to visit the native land of Omar Khayyam and Hafiz.

But in Rostov Esenin had got tired of his friend's commercial deals, and he had quarrelled with him and taken a train back to Moscow. That was the end of Esenin's "journey to Persia," to Isadora's great delight. That, also, explained his sudden appearance in Prechistenka.

I was once asked by someone what I thought of Esenin's suicide —whether there was more fear of life in it or courage before death. By nature Esenin was no coward, if one overlooked one strange aberration: his inexplicable fear of—the militia. Mayakovsky wrote:

"My militia guards me" ...

But Esenin was scared of it. The appearance of the militia had the same effect on him as a jet of water on a flame.

Esenin's natural courage was revealed to me when mysterious things began to happen in Belashova's former house. Strangers with electric torches penetrated into the building through unknown passages at night. They vanished instantly at the slightest alarm. We kept watch, but one night the affair took a serious turn: having opened the front door with a skeleton key, the thieves entered the children's bedroom by a back staircase. One little girl woke up: "Keep still!" one of the bandits hissed at her. But she screamed with fright and, jumping out of bed, ran straight to the door, past the intruders. The house was instantly in an uproar.

Esenin, all of us, including some of our visitors, rushed off to

Isadora and Esenin, whom she married in May 1922

investigate. Near the marble staircase downstairs was a small room where I used to receive the children's parents. In a corner of the room was a low door through which one could crawl to a dark box-room under the stairs. The box-room had a similar door which led into the corridor near the children's dining room. It was in that box-room that, led by Esenin, we all gathered. We opened the door. I struck a match and, suddenly, something stirred in the darkest corner. I lit several matches at once. Esenin rushed forward so impetuously that he extinguished the burning matches. But he crawled fearlessly through the little door, waving a log:

"Come out! Come out! It's too late! We've got you!" he shouted.

The figure stirred again and crawled obediently straight at Esenin. It was then that we recognized our doorkeeper, Pavel Vasilyevich. He lived a long way from the house and he had not gone home that night, thinking of spending the night in the box-room.

The incident was, of course, somewhat comical, but if one of the bandits had happened to be in the box-room, Esenin could have been knifed. A little later we discovered a large hole in the wall behind the wood panelling of the children's bedroom, probably where Belashova had hidden her jewellery. Someone from her "retinue" seemed to have known about it. We informed the authorities, who discovered that the chief "treasure hunter" was the former manager of the Belashova household and who lived in the neighbourhood. The nocturnal visits ceased after his arrest.

A few days later, Esenin showed us an excellent hara-kiri knife which he had bought somewhere. Its slightly curved blade was beautifully polished. Attached to the large sheath was a smaller one containing a sharp, thin stiletto. "When committing suicide," Esenin explained, "the Japanese cut open the stomach with the large knife and when the bowels fall out cut off the last gut with the little dagger. What self-control and what barbarity!" he added.

Esenin soon lost interest in the knife. He did not like to see it. He hid it away and later gave it to me. It disappeared mysteriously some time after.

One day I heard the clatter of horses' hooves, which stopped at our front door. I went up to the window and saw Isadora, who had arrived in a cab. She saw me and waved. I noticed something flash in her hand. Running up the marble staircase two steps at a time, she stopped before me. She looked radiantly happy and excited.

"Look," she said, showing me a large, shining gold watch in her gloved hand, "it's for Esenin. He'll be so glad he has a watch now."

Isadora rushed to her room, picked up a pair of scissors, and cut one of her small passport photographs in a circle. She then opened the back lid of the watch and put it in.

Esenin, who had no watch of his own, was delighted with his present. He kept opening his gold watch, putting it back in his pocket, and taking it out again, happy as a child.

"Let's see," he would say, pulling his watch out of his waistcoat pocket. "What's the time now?" And, having satisfied himself, he would shut it noisily and then, biting his lip and prying open the back lid with his finger nail, he would whisper mischievously: "And who have we in here?"

A few days later, when I got home from the Commissariat of Education, I entered Isadora's room just as that watch, with a flash of gold, was hurled the short distance from Esenin's hand to the parquet floor and was smashed to bits with a loud bang.

Torn bits of pistachio-coloured paper were scattered on the large mahogany grand piano, all that remained of the two large five-million-rouble notes which Esenin had torn up. Duncan, who was completely indifferent to the money she kept receiving from her many American and European contracts, did not look as if she cared about the destruction of the notes, though she had been very pleased when I had brought them to her that morning. "I'll go shopping with Esenin in Petrovka and cook a lovely dinner for him in the evening," she said, looking at those strange notes which had only just been issued.

But now, pale and haggard, she looked sadly at the smashed watch and her photograph, which had fallen out of its lid. Esenin was still in a highly excited state. He kept looking round the room, twisting and turning without moving from his place. My arrival, which usually made him behave normally again at once, had no effect. I picked him up by the shoulders and knees and carried him a few steps to the door of Isadora's bathroom. He did not offer any resistance, though, he seemed to be terribly heavy. Because of some misunderstanding on the part of the Commissariat of Education, our water rates had not been paid and we were threatened with having our water supply cut off. I had therefore ordered all the baths, tanks, and tubs in the house to be filled with water.

After pushing through the door with my burden, I found myself immediately beside a tub filled to the brim with water. Esenin gave a violent jerk, thinking that I was going to plunge him fully clothed into the cold water (he seemed to have recovered his senses and was well aware of what was going on). I set him down in front of the wash basin and, pushing his head down, turned on the faucet. I then wiped his head thoroughly. Throwing aside the towel, I saw a smiling face and deep blue eyes, which did not look at all embarrassed.

"What a damn silly thing to do," Esenin said, combing his hair with his fingers. "Very stupid, I'm afraid. Where's Isadora?"

We went into her room. She was still in the same pose, her eyes fixed on the white face of the gold watch which had rolled up to her feet. Not far away lay her photograph. Esenin rushed forward, picked up the photograph, and pressed Isadora to him. She dropped her hand on his head, which was still wet.

"Cold water?" she asked, raising a pair of frightened eyes at me. "Are you sure he won't catch cold?"

Neither Esenin not Isadora could remember what had started the quarrel that led to Esenin's outburst.

Life went on as usual. The school demanded a great deal of work every day from Isadora and her entire staff.

As I said earlier, the parents had brought mainly girls. It is true that Lunacharsky had sent us a group of children of parents who had returned to Russia, among whom were a few boys from England and America. But they did not stay long. We were not particularly sorry to see them go, for a separate boys' dormitory and additional staff to look after it would have complicated our budget too much.

That is why the theatre-studio, which later evolved from the school, was of necessity composed entirely of women.

Duncan did not permit any punishment in the school. Those who were guilty of misbehaviour were sent to bed immediately after supper.

"Useful but boring," Isadora explained to me.

A graver misdemeanour was "punished" by exclusion from a
dancing lesson, which we found to be the most effective penalty.
The children made quite astonishing progress. They danced
waltzes, Schubert marches, Rachmaninov's *Polka,* Gluck's Amazons
from *Iphigenia in Tauris,* and the charming little scene from
Iphigenia in Aulis: Chalcidian maidens throwing dice on the seashore.

The short Schubert waltzes seemed to acquire a new life and a
new sound in the children's dances.

In the old days Vienna had gone crazy over the new dance, the
waltz, just as a century later the whole of Europe went crazy over
the tango. The waltz descended on Vienna from the mountains with
the bands of strolling musicians who carried with them a violin, a
trumpet, and a drum. "*Waltzen, rollen, drehen* . . . [Roll, turn round,
rotate]." That was the origin of the "waltzer"—the waltz. The
fashionable dance became the rage in Vienna. Dancing halls com-
peted with each other, delighting their clientele with their "brilliant
illuminations of a thousand wax candles" or with their "new
parquet floor." One dance hall inveigled clients by including "a live
giraffe" in its show. But the young girls of "good society" were not
allowed to go to dance halls while the waltzing craze was growing.
It was then that waltz balls began to be given in private houses.
Visiting these balls, Schubert was always ready to sit down at the
piano and improvise waltzes, which he noted down on returning
home late at night. The finale of one of these waltzes, later ex-
panded by Liszt, gives an almost visual picture of the end of the
ball. There is hardly a single Schubert waltz that Duncan did not
use in her school. One of them, *The Three Graces,* remained for a
long time in the repertoire of the studio. It began with a pose
showing the famous sculptural group, which also appeared in the
finale. Other waltzes included *Reflection, Sunbeam,* etc.

There were also many dances from "Schumann's album." I particularly liked *Blindman's Buff* and *The March of the Toy Soldiers.*
The children coped brilliantly with the difficult gymnastic movements. At the finale of the scene the whole formation fell down
instantly, just like lead soldiers drawn up in a row falling at the flick
of a finger. They also danced *The Waltz with a Scarf* to the music of
Schubert. A very fine crimson woollen scarf flew up in a light arch
in the hands of two little dancers, looking like a miraculous cloud
and not dropping till the other children had passed under it.

93

There was a touching spontaneity, simplicity, and naturalness of movement in their performance. The freshness of a spring breeze, the light and warmth of sunbeams, the tremulous motion of leaves, clear skies and joy of living—all of this found expression in the dances of those children.

It is true that because of her headstrong fancy Isadora nearly destroyed all the results achieved by her school.

Among the Prechistenka visitors was Alexander Rumnev, an actor of the Kamerny Theatre. He was tall and quite handsome, but affected, with the angular gestures of a Pierrot, and rather effeminate. In the Kamerny Theatre he acted, sang, and, most of all, danced. He was young, gay, and witty. Duncan was nice to him and thought him a capable dancer.

Duncan believed that in a gym class music was quite unnecessary or should be limited to a minimum.

"It would be even better," she said, "if the lesson were given to the beating of a drum. A physical training instructor ought really to conduct such a class, or, better still, a Red Army man. He would give them vigorous movements, good breathing, strong muscles. We would come to an understanding not to get in each other's way."

But before I could do anything about it, Duncan came into my office one day and, exclaiming in English, "It's a lovely idea!" proposed that I should engage Rumnev as our physical training instructor. Irma usually had the gym class.

I objected, but Isadora was obstinate.

"Why make things difficult for Irma?" she said sympathetically. "The poor girl has to get up before seven in the morning, and she goes to bed so late."

Rumnev began his work as physical training instructor. Two weeks passed. Isadora began to show signs of nervousness, especially after coming from the dancing lesson she gave from five to seven o'clock in the afternoon.

"I'm always telling them at the lesson," she cried at last, "that if they keep thinking of their arms and legs, their arms and legs will be all that people will see. Listen to the music and dance! They understood it so well. What's the matter with them now? For the first time I cannot find the reason. The children have acquired a sort of affectation, their movements have become so unnatural. What's the cause of it?"

94

Irma and I had known "the cause of it" for some time, but we had waited for Isadora herself to talk about it.

"What's the cause of it?" she again asked wistfully.

I said nothing but just gave a jump à la Rumnev. Isadora burst out laughing and seemed unable to stop for a long time.

Next morning I had to get up at six, wait for the arrival of Rumnev, chat amiably with him for a while, then, handing him his half-monthly fee, inform him that Irma had decided to take on the gym lessons once more.

The children sang Russian folk songs and Grechaninov's songs beautifully. The rather daring idea occurred to me to invite Grechaninov, who lived in Moscow at the time, to work with the children. Grechaninov at once agreed. Under his direction, the children's choir sang as delightfully as they performed the dances inspired by Duncan.

Later, Grechaninov's songs, transferred to the stage and accompanied by movement and dancing, became a regular feature of the repertoire of the still youthful studio, and were as successful in Russia as in China and America.

"That's my reward," Isadora said one day after a dancing and singing lesson. "Before my departure for Moscow, the European and American papers were sceptical about my 'Bolshevik venture' and prophesied its failure. If only they could see these Russian children now! I always knew that Russians are very musical, and their aptitude for dancing has been known the world over for a long time.... If only the world could see these children! We should deal another blow to the old and the obsolete!"

She became worked up about a new idea. Isadora never put anything off, and a day or so later she came into my office with a little piece of paper on which she had written a telegram addressed to the well-known American impressario, Hurok, who always organized Isadora Duncan's tours.

The telegram read: "Can you organize tour with participation of my pupil Irma, twenty delightful Russian children, and my husband, the famous Russian poet, Sergei Esenin? Cable immediately. Isadora Duncan."

The reply from New York arrived without delay. "Interested. Cable conditions and beginning of tour."

The Soviet Government gave its permission for the tour, and Duncan began making preparations for the first performance of her

95

school in Moscow and for her departure abroad, intending to carry out all the necessary preliminary work there before the arrival of her school.

The hall of the Bolshoi Theatre was placed at our disposal for the initial performance of the school. The matinée performance was to be accompanied by the symphony orchestra of the theatre. A rehearsal was to take place the day before. The children, who were accustomed to dancing to the accompaniment of a piano, were at first a little confused by the orchestra and the rehearsal took longer than expected.

After one of the dances, the members of the orchestra suddenly rose from their seats and began putting away their instruments. Duncan looked inquiringly at me. Apparently the orchestra was about to leave, the two hours allotted to the rehearsal being up. Duncan asked me to tell the members of the orchestra that she had only two or three Schubert waltzes left to rehearse, but they went on putting away their music and their instruments.

"I am happy to work with Russian children," she said to the orchestra, "without asking anything for it or receiving anything in return. Can't you give another ten minutes of your work to these children?"

"We know what you received," a man shouted from the orchestra.

"What did he say?" Duncan asked me. I translated.

"What did I receive?" asked Duncan.

"A sable coat!" the violinist shouted resentfully.

"Here's my fur coat," said Isadora, pulling at the short fur jacket she was wearing, "and I've been wearing it for many years."

There was a noisy scene in the orchestra. The musicians crowded around the embarrassed violinist. Duncan asked for the curtain to be drawn and rehearsed the remaining dances to the accompaniment of the piano.

"Personally, I have nothing against that young man, who must have been misled by some malicious people," Duncan told the members of the orchestra who came on the stage to express their sympathy. "But this attack might compromise my whole mission here. All sorts of slanderous rumours may be spread in Moscow and may get into the foreign press. And that's all that's needed to discredit my stay in Russia. No one can accuse me of feathering my own nest, and I do not intend to defend myself. Let Comrade Lunacharsky investigate the matter."

There was a whole story behind the "sable coat." When the cold weather came, Lunacharsky had asked me whether Duncan and her companions were prepared for the Moscow winter. I told him that only Duncan had a short fur jacket. A few days later, Lunacharsky telephoned to say that I could take the three of them to the fur warehouse, situated at the refrigerating plant of the former fur dealer Mikhailov in Bolshaya Dmitrovka Street.

We drove down there. In the huge refrigerated rooms hung rows of fur overcoats for which any woman would have given her eyeteeth. There were gorgeous sable coats, black astrakhan coats, silvery chinchilla coats, and even regal ermine coats. . . . Among them were some second-hand coats, left behind and confiscated from the émigrés.

Duncan chose a fur-lined cotton coat for Jeanne and two very modest simulated "mink" overcoats. She also chose three warm reindeer fur caps with ear-flaps. We left them in the refrigerating plant, for we had first to get an official authorization from the Commissariat of Education.

A few days later I was summoned to see Lunacharsky. There were some papers on his desk and he was examining them with a perplexed air. They were the bills for the fur coats, which cost a sum that was enormous even at the fantastic prices of those days. The three reindeer caps alone were comparatively cheap.

Lunacharsky did not know what to do: the Commissariat of Education did not budget for such "purchases." On being told about it, Duncan at once refused to accept the coats and asked only for the fur caps to be sent. The whole affair merely made her burst out into irrepressible laughter.

But because of the stupid and hostile attack of the violinist, it was no laughing matter.

The legend of "the sable coat" spread all over Moscow. Lunacharsky took the necessary steps and the president of the county court was appointed to investigate the matter. The violinist was threatened with very unpleasant consequences, for the County Court had taken the view that his "diversion" was an attempt to slander the measures of the Soviet Government. A young and very beautiful, though rather inexperienced, woman was put in charge of the case as prosecutor. She dragged out "the case of the sable coat" at a time when we had other, more urgent things to think of. There was the impending departure of Isadora for America, for one thing.

Feeling sorry for the violinist, Isadora asked me to get the case quashed.

The violinist's outburst was not the only case of hostility towards Isadora Duncan from people who did not understand or did not accept her art. They could not forgive Isadora her revolutionary zeal in art, nor her sympathies with the young republic, nor her arrival to work in Moscow.

S. Y. Levik, a former opera singer and editor of *The Herald of Art and the Theatre*, mentions in his memoirs a case of sabotage by the orchestra of the former Marinsky Theatre during a performance by Isadora Duncan in Petrograd.

"In the winter of 1921–22 [Levik writes] it was difficult to maintain discipline in the theatres. But on February 13, 1922, an incident occurred which was quite out of the ordinary: the orchestra which played the *Tannhäuser Overture* as an accompaniment to Isadora's dances quite deliberately mixed up the major and minor keys, sometimes entering incorrectly, sometimes slowing down too much or, on the contrary, 'running away' from the conductor. Realizing that it was a case of sabotage, Nikolai Malko, the conductor, kept turning from right to left to make both sides of the orchestra play in unison, but without success. On February 22nd I published in my paper an article under the heading 'Orchestra Players, Come to Your Senses,' in which I wrote, among other things: 'It is a terrible thing that you should transform yourselves from artists into riotous savages' and 'come to your senses before the bog into which you are sinking begins to appear to you as a purifying font.' "

Isadora and Esenin decided to regularize their marriage in accordance with Soviet laws, particularly in view of their forthcoming visit to America, for Isadora knew only too well the danger of falling foul of the "police morals" there.

Early one sunny morning the three of us went to the Registry Office of the Khamovnichesky Soviet, which was situated quite near in one of the Prechistenka side-streets.

The Registry Office was dull and bureaucratic. When asked what surname they would like, both said they would like the surname of Duncan-Esenin. So it was written down in their marriage certificate and in their identity papers. Duncan had not even brought her

American passport with her, she had left for Soviet Russia with some useless French "scrap of paper" with a small photograph of her on the last page. She looked extraordinarily beautiful in that photograph, with vivacious eyes, full of moist brilliance and deep feeling. In the spring of 1940 I handed this little book to the Literary Museum, together with Esenin's letters.

"Now I'm Duncan," shouted Esenin when we went out into the street from the Registry Office.

The day before, Duncan had come to me looking embarrassed. She held her French "passport" in her hand.

"You couldn't correct something in it, could you?" she asked, looking even more embarrassed.

I did not understand. Then she pointed to the date of her birth. I laughed—before me stood Isadora looking slim and beautiful, much thinner and much younger than the Isadora Duncan I had met for the first time a year earlier.

It was not without good reason that on their arrival by air in Berlin the same month everyone found that Isadora looked much younger and, indeed, "scarcely older than Esenin." It was shortly after her arrival that she told reporters at the Hotel Adlon in Berlin: "I love the Russian people and intend to go back next year. Nevertheless it is very comforting to return to a place where one can have warm water, napkins, heat, etc. One has other things in Russia, but poor weak humans that we are, we become so accustomed to luxuries that it is very difficult indeed to give them up. Not that the Russians believe in giving up luxuries. On the contrary, but they believe in luxuries for all and if there is not enough to go around, then everyone should have a little less."

In Brussels, replying jokingly to the rapturous expressions of surprise at her "Moscow rejuvenation," she said that it was apparently "the lack of nourishment" in Russia that was responsible for it, and advised "those who suffered from obesity to go for a pilgrimage to Moscow" if they wished to achieve "airy proportions."

But on the day before her marriage she stood before me, with a smile of embarrassment, her finger pointing to the date of her birth written in black ink on her French passport.

"Well," I said, pretending not to notice her embarrassment, "I have Indian ink but, believe me, it's not necessary."

"It's for Esenin," she replied. "We don't feel this difference of fifteen years in our ages, but when it's written down here and we

99

hand our passports to strangers, it may make him feel uncomfortable. I shall soon have no more use for this passport. I shall get another."

I "corrected" the date.

The flight from Moscow airport was to take place very early in the morning. All the children wished to see Isadora off, and I applied to the Comintern, which owned the only bus in Moscow, to let us have it to take the children to the airport. It was a big red Leyland bus. (We were to be given this bus many times afterwards for trips around the city. These were the so-called "propaganda trips." The children wore a special uniform, and the side of the bus bore the legend: "A free spirit can exist only in a free body!" and it was signed: Duncan School.)

It was Esenin's first flight, and he was perceptibly agitated. Duncan prudently took some lemons and two bottles of champagne on board the plane with her.

"He may be sick," she said, "but if he sucks a lemon and drinks some champagne, he will be all right."

"In bumpy weather the champagne may have the opposite effect," I retorted.

But she assured me that she had found the combination of lemon and champagne an excellent remedy for any mishap during a flight.

In those years, air passengers were given special tarpaulin coats to put on. Esenin, looking very pale, arrayed himself in the sack-like garment, but Duncan refused to put one on.

Before boarding the plane, while we were still sitting on the grass of the airport, Duncan suddenly remembered that she had not made a will. She asked me for my notebook and quickly filled two pages with her short will. In the event of her death, she appointed her husband, Sergei Esenin, as her sole heir.

She showed me her will.

"But you're flying together," I said, "and in case of an accident you will both be killed."

"I never thought of that," she said, laughing, and quickly added: "and in the event of his death, I appoint my brother Augustin Duncan as my heir." Then she put her sprawling signature at the bottom of the page, and Irma and I put our signatures under hers as witnesses.

At last, Duncan and Esenin boarded the small aeroplane, which deafened us with its motor as it moved off along the field. Suddenly

Esenin's pale and agitated face appeared at the window. He was banging on the glass with his fists: they had forgotten the basket with the lemons and the champagne. I rushed to the bus, but the driver was running towards me with the basket. I snatched it from him and rushed after the plane, which was hobbling along the uneven field, caught up with it, and, running under its wing, handed the basket to Esenin.

The motor revved up, the light aeroplane ran swiftly along the airfield, rose into the air, and soon became a small black speck on the sparkling blue sky.

I was sorry we had taken the children to the airport. They had never seen a plane leave the ground before and they looked rather dispirited, pale and unusually quiet, with raised heads and wide-open eyes.

The bus driver was busy with the motor, which would not start. We all sat down on the grass in silence. I squatted down on some telegraph poles which were lying near us, took out my blue notebook, and began my report on the departure of Duncan and Esenin by air for Berlin, which the theatrical journal, *The Worker-Spectator*, had commissioned me to write.

The sky became overcast, it began to drizzle, and then raindrops formed inky smudges on the pages of my notebook. I shut it and put it away between the papers in my briefcase. I forgot all about it, not suspecting that five years later the papers of Europe and America would be writing about this notebook.

Sergei Esenin died three years later. Isadora died a year and a half after Esenin. We learnt about the fatal accident in Nice during our tour of the Don Basin with the studio. I at once applied for permission for Irma and myself to fly to Isadora's funeral.

We got the permission, but it was Saturday and, while there were no difficulties so far as Irma was concerned, for she was a foreigner, I, as a Soviet citizen, had to get a passport for travelling abroad. It was impossible to get through all the formalities in one day. Irma flew off alone.

A few days later I received a telegram from her: "Send Isadora's will immediately."

During the six years since the foundation of the school, a great mass of papers had accumulated. In addition, the large desk, which had been in Isadora's room before, had been transferred to my office and all its seven drawers were filled with all sorts of papers—

Isadora's and mine. I began to look for the will and, surprisingly quickly, found my small notebook among the papers. I immediately recognized the violet ink smudges made by the rain. But Isadora's will was not there. A number of pages in the middle of the notebook had been torn out. I could only suppose that on her return with Esenin from abroad in 1923, Isadora accidentally found my notebook and, either in that year or after she and Esenin had parted in 1924, destroyed her will.

I telegraphed to Paris that there was no will and, by return, received another telegram: "Will must be found. Raymond claims to be her heir. Forbids use of Duncan's name without permission. Threatens its removal from Moscow school."

But all I had was my blue notebook with its middle pages torn out. I replied: "Will apparently destroyed by Isadora."

Two weeks later I was very much surprised by a telephone call from Charles Recht (a legal authority on the USSR), whose name I had heard mentioned a few times by Isadora. He was a Russian who had emigrated to America before the revolution and lived in New York. He introduced himself to me as Isadora's legal adviser. He spoke Russian fluently, though with a slight English accent. Recht told me that he had flown to Moscow to get Isadora's will.

"But I've already telegraphed twice to Paris that I have not got her will."

"Please don't say anything about it to anyone," he said, "but I have already told the Soviet reporters that you are in possession of Isadora's will."

"Why did you tell them something that isn't true? Who were the reporters?"

"They were from *Izvestia* and *Ogonyok*."

"There is no will."

"But there was one. And I want a confirmation of that to be published in the Soviet press. This would stop Raymond Duncan's action."

"But the will was written in pencil on the pages of a notebook and would hardly have any legal validity."

"By American law it is valid. There was the case of a dying man who, left alone in his room, crawled out of bed and wrote his will on the door with a piece of chalk. The door was produced in court and the will was declared valid."

"When did you arrive?"

"I've been in Moscow for three days."

"When did the reporters see you?"

"On the first day of my arrival."

"There has been no report published in *Izvestia* and I'm sure no such report will be published because it is of no importance. As for *Ogonyok*, I shall inform them of the real situation myself."

Recht looked offended. Our talk took place in the evening. Next morning he must have flown back to America.

I was sitting at Isadora's desk. The arch leading into the next room, the so-called "blue ballroom," had been bricked up at my request and the niche filled with bookshelves which I covered up with a curtain. Suddenly I heard something drop on the floor. I looked under the desk. There, on the floor by the curtain, I saw a blue notebook.

"Where did it fall from?" I wondered. "Did I not put it in the middle drawer of the desk?" But, on opening the drawer, I at once saw the notebook. It was lying on top of the papers where I had put it.

Startled at the appearance of its double, I bent down, reached for the second blue notebook, and, opening it, saw Isadora's will.

It was then that I remembered I had several of those cheap notebooks. On the day I saw Duncan and Esenin off at the airport, I must have had two similar notebooks in my briefcase. In one Isadora wrote her will, and in the other I began to write the report on which the raindrops had left the violet smudges.

I at once sent a telegram to Irma: "Will found."

When Irma and some members of the studio left for America the following year, the validity of Isadora's will was being decided by a Manhattan court. Lunacharsky later sent me the pro-Soviet paper *Rusky Golos* (Russian Voice) published in New York. A large headline immediately caught my eye: "Isadora Duncan's will declared valid by Manhattan Court."

"The story of the will" has made me anticipate events that occurred more than five years later. In the meantime, Isadora Duncan and Sergei Esenin were flying over the plains of the Baltic provinces and Poland towards Europe and America.

I was told about the year they had spent abroad by Duncan herself, as well as by Esenin, Isadora's brother Raymond, and her sister Elizabeth. I also learned a great deal about it from Mary Desti during her stay in Moscow in the autumn of 1927.

Who is Mary Desti?

Isadora did not talk about her a great deal. I saw that name for the first time on the first day of Isadora's arrival in Moscow. It was printed on the label of the cigarettes *Aromatique* with "the vamp." I noticed the same inscription: "Mary Desti factory" also on Isadora's scent bottle.

Desti had known Isadora since 1901, when Duncan's art was beginning to be appreciated in Paris. It was in Paris they first met and it was there that their friendship, which lasted for over twenty years, began. Desti told me that she worshipped Duncan, and there is no reason why one should not believe her. But what bound Isadora to Desti? Desti was not an artist, nor a writer, nor even a businesswoman. She could, therefore, be of no help to so unbusinesslike a woman as Isadora. Mary travelled, tried to become a dancer, started small industries which she grandly described as tobacco or perfume factories. Her most successful enterprise was the production of batik fabrics. She employed a whole group of painters to produce very attractive designs. She presented Isadora with one of the finest works of her atelier. It was the fatal crimson scarf with the spread-eagled bird and blue Chinese asters which caused Duncan's death.

It was to Desti that young Isadora confided her first feelings of love for a man.

"Everything seems different since the revelation of love," Isadora told Desti. "I was born for love."

Dancing wildly round Desti, Isadora cried: "Why didn't you tell me what love was like?"

Desti was the witness of Isadora's first being a mother when, on her second return to Paris, she saw little golden-haired Deirdre jumping about beside Isadora on the bed. She was also the first in the Paris morgue where "on a little white marble slab . . . were our two little angels." Desti was also present at Isadora's tragic end.

Before her marriage, Isadora had often travelled with Desti. With her she visited the Bayreuth Festival at which Isadora's friendship with Wagner's widow Cosima Wagner, and her family began.

Some of Mary Desti's activities came to an end with lightning speed at the instigation of Isadora, as, for instance, Desti's choreographic ambitions. According to Desti, an "extraordinary thing" happened at a rehearsal in Bayreuth, something that concerned her "dream" of the stage. At that particular rehearsal she had danced Isadora's part in *The Three Graces* with two young German ballerinas. Cosima Wagner was so "enraptured" by her dancing that she said in a loud voice to Isadora: "How beautiful! But she resembles you!" This, according to Desti, so infuriated Isadora that she rushed on to the stage and, shaking Desti by the shoulders, shouted: "Don't ever do it again! Never!" Desti was so surprised that she could scarcely breathe. On the way to their hotel, Isadora, Desti writes, kept repeating: "It's awful! Even the very expression of my eyes! No, I will never teach anyone again. They only succeeded in making an imitation of me!" So ended Desti's stage career.

When Desti came to our school, the children who were expecting her shouted as soon as they saw her walking up the staircase: "You're like Isadora! You're just like her!"

But that was only the first outward impression. Desti tried to imitate Isadora in everything. She wore the same kind of cloaks and hats, she had the same kind of hair style as Isadora, she even tried to imitate Isadora's way of walking, which was extraordinarily harmonious and wave-like; the way she carried her head and arms, and her whole bearing, were quite wonderful and inimitable. Desti never quite managed to copy them.

Isadora put an end also to Desti's perfumery business. Desti opened her "perfumery studio" (or, more simply, shop), which Paul Poiret, the arbiter of Paris fashion, had decorated himself. The studio was patronized by the beautiful French actress Cécile Sorel, a friend of Isadora and of the Spanish king, the former Bavarian Prince Rupprecht, the Grand Duke Alexander Mikhailovich, and other "persons of high rank." Desti's perfumery shop did not prosper, though. Duncan had always taken a dim view of it and advised Desti to throw all the scent bottles out of the window and wind up her "business." Afterwards, however, Isadora changed her mind, for that, she explained, would merely be "a grand advertisement." Instead, she told Desti simply to close her shop and leave all the scent bottles behind. Such advice was very characteristic of Duncan, but Desti could hardly be expected to accept such a drastic way of liquidating her "perfumery studio."

At first I had no idea that Desti intended to write a book about Duncan. She constantly asked me about Isadora's life in Moscow and about her tours, but her intention became clear to me when she began writing down not only a few facts but whole episodes, and spent a long time rummaging among the large heap of newspaper cuttings which Duncan and Esenin had brought with them from abroad and which I had kept.

It was with a feeling of inexpressible vexation that in Desti's book I later read accounts of some of the episodes I had told her about, which she so distorted that I could scarcely recognize them (for instance, Duncan's performance before the sailors of the *Aurora* in Petrograd, and many others). I partly blame her "literary secretary" for the distortions of the truth and misleading her readers, for it was really he who wrote her reminiscences, sitting by the bedside of the dying Desti in a New York hospital.

Desti asked me to let her take away some newspaper cuttings. As I had quite a few duplicates, I did not refuse, particularly since she courteously shared her "material" with me, telling me of Duncan's and Esenin's travels across Europe and America. When telling me something, Desti consulted her small leather-bound diary, each day of which was covered in small handwriting. Comparing the episodes I had written down from her dictation with the same episodes in her book, I again and again came across terrible distortions, introduced deliberately or by the all too flowing pen of the secretary.

I talked to Desti, standing at the large plate-glass window looking out on Prechistenka covered in the white cotton-wool peignoir of winter. The house porters were shovelling the snow from the road into long heaps on the sidewalk.

"What were the songs Esenin liked to sing?" Desti asked. "The words 'many times' were often repeated in them," she said, pronouncing the Russian words *mnogo raz* (many times) with an effort.

Esenin did sing *Gypsy Girl*, though it would hardly be right to call it singing. It was rather what is known as *parlando*, the style of the *diseur* or *diseuse*, introduced I believe, by Mistinguette.

Esenin would begin to sing:

> "*Evening, a train, a road, lights,*
> *My road is far away....*"

Then he would go over to *parlando*, raising his voice a few notes higher almost to *falsetto*:

> "*My heart's heavy with anguish,*
> *My soul's full of alarm....*"

But the expressiveness and the anguish in his voice and on his face tugged at one's heartstrings and one could not help being seized with a feeling of shivering anxiety. You *felt* the evening, the train, you saw the twinkling lights and the road disappearing in the distance.

"When one of Esenin's riotous scenes was about to take place," said Desti after listening in silence to my remarks about the *Gypsy Girl*, "he should be calmed down by a suggestion that he should sing something. Sometimes he also danced. But that was absolutely terrible. Once Esenin and his friends were dancing like demons and jumping up to the ceiling. But Isadora liked very much to see Esenin dance . . ."

"I am surprised at your prejudiced attitude towards Esenin," I said. "But I think I understand the chief reason for it: Esenin's outward elegance, his shapely figure and his charm, made people like him quickly. Those who disapproved of him, knowing him only from the various stories about him, became his closest friends the moment they met him."

XI

Duncan and Esenin arrived in Berlin on May 12, 1922. They stayed at Berlin's most fashionable hotel, the Adlon. There a whole crowd of journalists was waiting for Isadora. The arrival of Isadora Duncan from "Bolshevik Moscow," accompanied by a young, well-known Russian poet whom she had married, was a sensational event and therefore grist to the newshounds' mill.

Before her first departure for Moscow, Duncan had been attacked by the journalists of Paris and London. The journalists had fired hundreds of questions at her and her answers were published in a great number of interviews interspersed with exclamation and interrogation marks.

"Aren't you afraid to go to Soviet Russia where there is nothing to eat?"

"I'm afraid of spiritual, not physical hunger. The dream of my life must be realized. Only in Russia is there any hope of creating such a school."

"But there are lots of schools in America which apply your method."

"In America numerous schools are opened by people who apply my method without understanding it and who teach their pupils things they should not do."

"What contract have you signed with the Soviet Government?"

"I'm going to Russia without any contract. I'm sick to death of contracts. People have a wrong idea about Russians. They may not have enough food, but they are determined that art and education must be available to everybody."

"Do you know the conditions under which you will have to work?"

"I'd like to find out whether there really is a place in the world where people do not worship the spirit of commerce more than the mental and physical development of their children. America has rejected that. Child labour still exists there."

Now that Duncan had spent a whole year in Moscow, questions were fired at her like bullets from a machine gun.

"In spite of privations," Duncan replied now, "the Russian intelligentsia carries on with its heavy task of rebuilding their whole life. My great friend Stanislavsky, the director of the Moscow Art Theatre, and his family eat bean porridge, but that does not prevent them from creating great works of art."

During the first months of her life in Moscow she gave a number of answers which were published in *Humanité*:

"Dear Comrades, you ask about my impressions of my journey, but all I can tell you is only the impressions of an artist, for I am too ignorant of politics myself

"I left Europe where art is suppressed by commerce.

"I am convinced that one of the greatest miracles in the history of mankind is taking place in Russia, a miracle that only happens once in two thousand years. We are too near to it to be able to see more than merely its material consequences, but those who will live during the next century will realize that through communism mankind has decided to take a big step forward.

"The martyrdom of Russia, the sufferings for the sake of the future, will be as fruitful as the martyrdom of the Nazarene. Only the brotherhood of the workers of the whole world, the Internationale, can save mankind. As for hunger, I'm not afraid of it. My mother, a poor piano-teacher who had to provide for her children, often had no food but she was always successful in alleviating the pangs of our hunger by playing the works of Schubert and Beethoven, to the accompaniment of which we, the children, danced instead of eating. It was thus that I made my debut as a dancer."

During the summer of 1922, Muscovites walked about in light white canvas shoes with rubber soles. Esenin had flown from Moscow to Berlin in such a pair of shoes and a blue suit.

This surprised and greatly amused the Berlin reporters. But Desti writes in her book that Esenin, who was very fond of clothes, "had himself decked out in a blue suit and white canvas shoes," thinking that "with his lovely mass of yellow golden hair, that stood out like an aureole around his head, it really didn't matter what he wore: he always looked beautiful."

However, in her description of Esenin's stay in Berlin, even she, who was always prejudiced against him, admits that he was "entirely occupied with the publication of his poems."

In the Berlin "House of the Arts" there were many Russians who sympathized with Soviet Russia, including some émigrés, who published the paper *On the Eve*. They were very interested in Esenin.

On the first day after his arrival in Berlin, Esenin went by himself to the café "Leon," where he immediately began reading his poems. He was received with great acclaim. As soon as he sat down at a table after his reading, a waiter came up and told him that Isadora Duncan had arrived. Esenin at once got up, went out to the vestibule, and returned arm in arm with Isadora, looking happy and smiling. They were given a noisy ovation. Isadora proposed that they should sing the *Internationale* in honour of Esenin. She and Esenin began to sing and they were joined by many people in the café. But some White Guardsmen who were also there began shouting, "Down with them!" and interrupted the singing by whistling. Esenin jumped onto a chair and shouted: "You won't stop us by your whistling," and went on singing. Afterwards he recited his poems again.

Such incidents occurred again and again.

Back in Moscow, Esenin declared many times: "Did I raise hell there because I was drunk? Was it so bad? I raised hell for our revolution!"

Soon after his arrival in Berlin a big reception was given in his honour at the Hall of the Society of Dentists. At the previous reception in the House of the Arts he was still wearing his Moscow suit and canvas shoes. This time he wore evening dress, a top hat, and a black cloak with a white lining. He was very nervous and kept smiling superciliously. But when he began reading his poems, he was transformed and his reading produced a tremendous impression.

Maxim Gorky and Alexey Tolstoy lived in Berlin at the time. Tolstoy invited Esenin and Duncan to dinner. Gorky was also invited. It was about this meeting with Duncan and Esenin at Tolstoy's that Gorky wrote his well-known article.

Duncan had met Tolstoy before, in Smolensk. I had to leave for Moscow on some urgent business and I had asked Alexey Tolstoy, who was in Smolensk at the time, to introduce Duncan before her performance. She met Gorky in Berlin for the first time. She was very excited about this meeting and very happy for Esenin to be sitting at the same table as Gorky and Tolstoy. Gorky saw before him not Isadora Duncan, a great artist and a reformer of the art of dancing, but a woman who was no longer young, red in the face from drinking too much, who was dancing with a bunch of wilted flowers and making a fool of herself by representing, to the accompaniment of a gramophone record, a Paris apache strangling his mistress. The mistress was represented by a scarf, which writhed and twisted in Isadora's expressive hands.

"This famous woman [Maxim Gorky wrote in his article] glorified by thousands of European aesthetes, subtle connoisseurs of plastic art, sitting next to the small, boyish, wonderful Ryazan poet, was the perfect personification of what he did not want. There is no question of any prejudice here, of something that has occurred to me on the spur of the moment. No. I am speaking of my impression of that painful day when, looking at that woman, I thought: how could she feel the meaning of such sighs of the poet as:

It would be nice, smiling at the haystack,
To munch hay with the snout of the moon....

"I had seen Duncan on the stage a few years before that meeting, when they used to write about her as a miracle, one journalist declaring quite astonishingly: 'Her exquisite body burns us by its blaze of fame.' But I don't like and I don't appreciate dancing that is an expression of intellect.... At Tolstoy's dinner she also danced, having first eaten, and drunk vodka. Her dance seemed to me to depict the struggle between the weight of Duncan's age and the constraint of her body, spoilt by fame and love. These words are certainly not meant to be offensive to a woman. They merely speak of the curse of old age...."

By saying this Gorky did not intend to question Duncan's importance in the world of art, as some seem to think. In one of his unfinished stories, Pushkin mentions a banquet given in honour of Mme. de Staël by the aristocracy of Moscow, who, he declares, saw in her only "a fat, fifty-year-old woman dressed not as befits her age." But in his *Contemporary Review,* Pushkin paid tribute to the intellect and feelings of that extraordinary woman whom, he wrote, "Napoleon honoured by his persecution and Europe by her respect."

In his article, Gorky wrote of Esenin:

"Six or seven years later I met Esenin in Berlin at Alexey Tolstoy's. Of the curly-headed, doll-like boy only the very bright eyes remained, and even they seemed to have been burnt out by some too-bright sun. Their troubled look often changed its expression as it slid over people's faces, sometimes challenging and disdainful, and, all of a sudden, diffident, embarrassed, and distrustful. I had the feeling that his attitude towards people was, on the whole, unfriendly. One could see at once that he was a drinking man. There were bags under his bloodshot eyes and the skin on his face and neck was grey, faded, just as though he never went out of doors and slept badly. His hands, too, were restless and limp at the wrists, like the hands of a drummer. Besides, he looked troubled and absent-minded, like a man who had forgotten something very important and could not even remember that he had forgotten. . . .

"Esenin communicated with Duncan by gestures and by touching her with his elbows and knees. When she danced, he sat at the table and drank wine, looking at her out of the corner of his eye and knitting his brows. It was perhaps at that very moment that he put those words of compassion into the lines of verse:

'*They loved you too well,*
They soiled you all over . . .'

"Later Duncan, exhausted, knelt down and gazed at the poet's face with a languid, drunken smile. Esenin put his hand on her shoulder, but turned away abruptly. And again I cannot help thinking that at that very moment the cruel and pitifully desperate lines must have flashed through his mind:

'Why do you look with blue splutters?
Or do you want me to bash your face in?
...Darling, I weep
Forgive... forgive...!' "

Esenin was asked to read his poems. Gorky writes:

"The impression produced by Esenin's reading was quite over-powering. It was painful to listen to him, painful to tears.... It was impossible to believe that such a little man could possess such enormous power of feeling, such perfect expressiveness. ...He thrilled me so much that a lump rose to my throat and I felt like sobbing. I remember I just could not say anything nice to him. Besides, I don't think he needed my words of praise. I asked him to read his poem about the dog whose seven puppies were taken away and thrown into the river. 'If,' I added, 'you're not too tired.'

"'Poems do not tire me,' he said, and asked mistrustfully, 'Do you like my poem about the dog?'

"I told him that, in my opinion, he was the first poet in Russian literature to write about animals with such sincere love and with such skill.

"'Yes, I love animals very much,' said Esenin quietly and thoughtfully.

"I asked him if he knew Paul Claudel's *Paradise of Animals*. He did not reply, felt his head with both hands, and began to read *The Song of a Dog*. When he uttered the last lines—'The dog's eyes rolled like golden stars onto the snow'—his eyes too filled with tears."

I received several letters from Esenin from Germany and Belgium. (In the spring of 1940 I turned them over to the Literary Museum, along with his letters from Ostend and Brussels.)

Esenin began almost all his letters with the salutation: "Dear, dear Ilya Ilyich, greetings and kisses..." He was always worried about the material position of his sister Katya, who was studying in Moscow, and asked me to force the "Writer's Shop" to let her have some money or try to borrow some money somewhere and give it to her, and, he wrote, "I'll send you a cheque in a letter."

But it is highly questionable whether Isadora and Esenin could have sent me a cheque. Living on a grand scale and always spending more than they could afford, they were often very hard up themselves.

Here is one of his letters from Wiesbaden, June 21, 1922:

"Dear Ily'a Ilyich, greetings and kisses. I am sorry not to have written to you for so long. The Berlin atmosphere has played hell with me, my nerves are in such a terrible state now that I can just manage to drag my feet about. I am undergoing a cure in Wiesbaden. I stopped drinking and am beginning to work.

"If Isadora had not been so crazy and had let me sit down quietly for a moment, I should have earned a lot of money. I have just received over one hundred thousand marks, while I can hope only for another four hundred. Isadora's affairs are in a terrible state. In Berlin, her solicitor sold her house and got only ninety thousand marks for it.[1]

"The same thing may well happen in Paris. Her property, her library and furniture, have been pilfered and her money in the bank has been impounded. She has just sent off a trustworthy man there. The famous Paul-Boncour[2] not only did nothing for her but he even refused to give her his signature for a visa to Paris. This is what her affairs are like.... But she doesn't seem to care. She is off by car to Lübeck, to Leipzig, to Frankfurt, to Weimar. I follow her with tacit obedience, for every time I disagree, she becomes hysterical.

"Germany? We'll talk about it later, when we meet, but it isn't much of a life here. Life is in our country. There is really the slow, sad decline here that Spengler[3] talks about. We may be Asiatics, we may have a bad smell, we may scratch our bottoms shamelessly in public, but we don't stink of putrefaction as they do. There can be no revolution here. Everything is in a deadlock. The only thing that can save them is an invasion by barbarians like ourselves.

"An invasion of Europe is needed....

"However, serious thoughts in a letter do not become me at the

---

[1] The German mark was practically worthless at that time.

[2] Paul-Boncour, very active in French politics from 1906, when he was a member of the Chamber of Deputies.

[3] German philosopher, author of *The Decline of the West*.

moment. To business. For God's sake find my sister through the shop[1] and see that she gets money for this cheque. She is probably very hard up. The cheque for Irma is just to find out whether she could get any money on it. If she can, Isadora will send her as much as she wants.

"If my sister is not in Moscow, write her a letter and give it to Marienhof. Let him send it off to her. Also, before you leave for London, ask her to come to see you and make a note of her proper address to which we can send money, for without it she'll be helpless.

"Give my greetings and my love to Marienhof. I have sent him two letters to which for some reason he has not replied. I could tell something really remarkable about our Berlin friends (especially concerning some denunciations they sent to the French police to make sure that I am not allowed to go to Paris. But of all this later, I must take care of my nerves.) Don't forget before leaving to take all my books and Marienhof's and everything they have been writing about me during this time.

"I press your hand.

"Hope to see you soon, your loving Esenin.

"My humblest regards to Irma. Isadora married me a second time and now she is no longer Duncan-Esenin, but simply Esenin."

A letter from Belgium:

"Brussels, July 13, 1922

"Dear Ilya Ilyich,

I have written to you at length about our adventures and travels in three long letters. I don't know whether they reached you.

"If you could see me now, you would probably not believe your own eyes. It will soon be a month since I stopped drinking. I've taken the pledge not to drink till October. I could do it all because of a painful attack of neuritis and neurasthenia, but now that too has gone. Isadora is very worried about you. Though we thought in Moscow that we might be able to send you money, it is impossible to do so from here.

"On Saturday, July 15th, we are flying to Paris. It will be easier to send it from there.

[1] The Writer's Bookshop, founded by Esenin and Marienhof in 1920. It was closed in 1923.

"In a parcel we sent you by air mail through Krasin's office,[1] we put two cheques for ten pounds each, one for Irma and the other for my sister. Have you received them?

"We did it in order to find out if it were possible to send you money that way.

"Dear, dear Ilya Ilyich, you will of course create a sensation with your school in Europe. We are waiting for your arrival with impatience. I, in particular, am waiting for it, for Isadora has no idea of practical matters, and I find it very painful to look at all that pack of bandits that surround her. When you arrive, the air will become cleaner.

"I have a very, very great request to make of you in the same words as in my former letters: please, give some money to my sister before you leave. If you haven't any, or if your father or someone else hasn't any either, ask Sashka and Marienhof and find out how much they give her from the shop.

"This is my greatest request. For she has to get on with her studies, and when you and I are up to our necks in it in America, it will be quite impossible to help her from there.

"Best wishes and a thousand greetings to Irma. We were told here by someone that you've joined the Commissariat. Is it true?

"Do come. We'll have a celebration. We sent you a telegram to urge you to come. You have first to go to Berlin, and from there you'll be sent by 'express' to Paris or Ostend.

"That is all. We'll talk things over at greater length when we meet.

"Come! Come!

"Let my sister have some money. Take poems from Marienhof, his address, and many new books. It's devilishly boring here.

"Your loving

"S. Esenin"

Before her arrival in Soviet Russia, Isadora had danced in Brussels and was highly indignant at some philistine remarks in the Belgian press about her costume on the stage. As she simply could not resist making speeches, she gave in to her weakness at her last performance in Brussels. She addressed an angry speech to the Belgians, whom she accused of being enemies of art. She told them about her departure for Soviet Russia, where, she declared, art was

[1] The Soviet Foreign Trade Commissariat.

free. Her speech aroused general resentment, and such scandalous attacks on her were published in the press that some expressed the opinion that Duncan would never dare to show herself in Belgium again.

These misgivings were shared by Isadora Duncan's impresario, who nevertheless took the risk of announcing her performances in Brussels, having first made sure of his commission by taking a high percentage of the gross receipts. However, to the surprise of the sceptics, Duncan danced to full houses in Brussels, her public showing the same love and the same rapturous appreciation of her art.

In Belgium she received an offer from Paris, from her friend Firmin Gémier, and at once telegraphed me:

"Gémier, director of the Trocadéro Theatre, invited me to give ten performances in Paris with Moscow school. Ask Government's permission for school's tour. Telegraph. Love. Isadora Duncan."

I showed this telegram to Lunacharsky, who did not raise any objections to the school's departure, but that Paris visit wrecked all the difficult arrangements I had made for the school to go to America. This I telegraphed to Isadora. But she would not give up her idea, and soon I received a telegram from her with a proposal to leave with the school for the Ostend festival.

I sent her another telegram and persuaded her to give up this "lovely idea" of hers too. Besides, she entirely overlooked the fact that such a tour would have entailed enormous expense, while we would be able to go to New York without any preliminary expenditure, having received in Moscow from the steamship company, the White Star Line, the tickets paid for by Hurok in New York.

From Brussels Duncan and Esenin intended to go to Paris but were suddenly faced with all sorts of serious difficulties. Duncan was used to obtaining visas from all consulates and embassies without any trouble or delay. Now everything had become highly complicated. The diplomatic representatives were scared off by the Moscow visas on Duncan's passport, by Esenin's "red" passport, and by the hubbub which their travels had caused in the press.

At last, at the end of July, 1922, thanks to the good offices of Duncan's friend Cécile Sorel, Isadora and Esenin arrived in Paris, having been warned against any political activity and told that they would be under police surveillance.

The next two months were quiet. Esenin and Duncan travelled.

They visited Lübeck, Frankfurt, Weimar, Wiesbaden, Venice, Rome, Naples, and Florence.

Esenin continued working on the publication of his old poems and writing new ones. These volumes of his poems were published in Berlin. Isadora told me that in Weimar Esenin spoke in whispers, gazing reverently at the witnesses of the life of great poets—old hornbeams growing among young fruit trees. He looked for a long time at a page left unfinished on his desk by Goethe.

They left for Paris without any special adventures, little suspecting how much they would have to live through there on their return journey. In October they sailed from Le Havre to New York on the big liner S.S. *Paris*.

XII

Duncan and Esenin arrived on the S.S. *Paris* without any complications, but they were not allowed to disembark. The immigration inspector informed them that they would have to spend the night in their cabin and go to Ellis Island in the morning for examination. The inspector gave no explanation of why they had to be detained on Ellis Island, and only inadvertently let slip the information that he was acting in accordance with instructions received from Washington.

In her white felt hat, a pair of red Russian boots, and her long cape, Duncan stood on deck arm in arm with Esenin and surrounded by a crowd of reporters. The New York Jewish daily *Forward* published a photograph taken by its correspondent; Isadora and Esenin, their heads tossed back, laughing at the statue of Liberty in New York harbour. Under the photograph, the paper quoted Isadora's words: "That is the American goddess of liberty. It is in her name that the two of us have been detained on the island of tears."

Esenin, who, as he later declared, had prepared a statement, was contemptuously silent. (In his statement he was going to say that it was his belief that "the soul of Russia and the soul of America are about to understand each other" and that they had come "to tell of the Russian conscience and to work for the rapprochement of the two great countries.")

The American journalists remained true to form: they fired idiotic questions at Duncan about her dances, about Moscow, about Esenin, about Ellis Island, about visas, about her attitude to Americans, and even "what she looked like when dancing," to which Isadora quite reasonably replied that she could not tell them that because she never saw herself dancing.

Addressing Americans through the reporters, she said:

"They have detained us only because we came from Moscow, although the American consul in Paris, who issued us our visas, assured us that there would be no trouble with the immigration authorities."

All the New York evening papers that day came out with large headlines: "Arrival of Great Artist."

Meanwhile, Duncan and Esenin were sitting in their cabin, wondering whether they would be incarcerated on Ellis Island. The New York *Times* wrote: "Isadora Duncan held at Ellis Island. The Gods may well laugh! Isadora Duncan, to whom the school of classical dancing in America owes its foundation, put in the class of dangerous immigrants."

Even so patriotic an American as Desti, recalling many years later with a feeling of indignation this shameful episode, commented in her book on the fact that Isadora had been refused admission to her own country—Isadora, "to whom every country in the world," she wrote, "had thrown open its doors, thinking no honour too great to crown this wonderful American! The artists of the world had bowed before her; the students and thinkers of all countries agreed that she was the highest expression of art in our day; and yet at the threshold of her own country, for whose freedom her grandparents had fought and died, where even the scurviest foreigner with the most mediocre talent was received with open arms, Isadora found the door closed in her face."

In spite of the fact that the Department of Labour, under which the Immigration Bureau operates, had not issued any order, Duncan and Esenin were told that the order for their detention had been issued by the Department of Justice in view of Isadora Duncan's "long residence in Russia." It was suspected that she might be serving as a courier for the Soviet Government.

After his return from the United States, Esenin wrote of Ellis Island in his article "The Iron Mirgorod": "After we had sat down on a bench, a fat gentleman wearing a round hat came out of a side door. His hair was brushed back from his forehead in a crew cut and for some reason reminded me of Pichugin's illustrations in Sytin's edition of Gogol's works.

" 'Look,' I said to my companion, 'it's Mirgorod. A pig will come running presently, seize a document, and we shall be saved!' "

"They made me sign a paper promising not to sing the *Internationale* as I had done in Berlin. . . ."

After a two-hour interrogation, Duncan and Esenin were set free. Isadora told the reporters who were waiting for her: "It never occurred to me that people could ask such incredible questions."

Isadora's friends gave her and Esenin a friendly welcome at their hotel. Duncan looked happy, she told them of her impressions of the Soviet Union and refused to talk of anything else. She could not wait to tell the whole of America about it, as she put it. The reporters had to write down the sentence with which she concluded every interview: "Communism is the only solution for the world."

The three performances given by Isadora Duncan in Carnegie Hall were highly successful and ended without incident in spite of Isadora's speeches on Soviet Russia. But the consequences of her speeches soon became apparent: her appearances in Philadelphia were cancelled, and the mayor of Indianapolis got frightened of Isadora's "Bolshevist speeches" and did not permit her to enter the city. Isadora's manager had assured the mayor that Duncan would refrain from making any speeches, but after her very first performance Duncan, as a local paper expressed it, "made one of her most inflammatory speeches about Communist Russia." Next morning the reporters told Duncan that she had been forbidden entry into Indianapolis "for ever." Duncan received that "sensational" piece of news with the utmost indifference. But her manager was nervous and he warned Duncan that the first incident, however insignificant, would lead to the cancellation of her tour.

In Milwaukee he allowed reporters to interview her, but at a banquet given in honour of her and Esenin she again made a speech. In Boston her speech to the audience ended in a riot. The tour was cancelled. But Duncan went on to give performances and, as she and Esenin told me, twelve times after her performances, which invariably ended with the *Internationale,* a Black Maria took Duncan to the police station.

The papers became furious and published violent attacks on Duncan and Esenin. They accused Esenin of debaucheries even if there weren't any and exaggerated every statement made by him, such as his expressed dislike of American customs and his disappointment in America. Esenin's nerves were on edge.

There was another reason for Esenin's "explosive" condition. (Duncan told me about it.) He thought that America neither recognized nor appreciated him as a poet. Lunacharsky laughingly showed me a cutting from a New York paper which stated that "three departments, the Departments of Justice, of Labour and the State Department, had begun a court inquiry to find out the relationship of Isadora Duncan to the Soviet Government." Later the following report appeared in the official organ of the Central Committee of Art Workers. "It is reported from Washington that the Departments of Labour and Justice and the State Department are collecting evidence about the propaganda of Bolshevik ideas carried out by the well-known dancer Isadora Duncan which had allegedly taken place during her performance in Boston. Officials of the above departments state that though they find the appearance of the dancer 'in a state of nakedness' to be 'offensive,' they can do nothing about it, but if she carries on 'red propaganda' she will soon find herself on Ellis Island for deportation to Russia. . . ."

The inquiry of the above-mentioned departments was begun after a report had been received that at her performance in Boston Duncan took off her red scarf and whirling it over her head shouted: "I am red!"

Finally Duncan was deprived of her American nationality for her "red propaganda" and she and Esenin were invited to leave the United States.

On leaving America Duncan told the journalists: "If I had come to this country as a great financier to borrow money, I would have been given a great reception, but as I came as a recognized artist, I was sent to Ellis Island as a dangerous character, a dangerous revolutionist. I am not an anarchist or a Bolshevik. My husband and I are revolutionists. All geniuses worthy of the name are. Every artist has to be one to make a mark in the world today."

This statement was published in the papers on the morning after Duncan and Esenin had sailed away from the shores of America.

Some reporters could not deny themselves the pleasure of publishing their shorthand notes on what Duncan had said to them after her official statement:

"Freedom here—— Pah!" Duncan exclaimed angrily, pulling at her scarlet scarf. "When I got up the other morning I read a story in a newspaper that my beloved Sergei had given me a black eye in a

Bronx flat. It's a lie! I don't even know where the Bronx is. I never was there in my life."

After his return from abroad, Esenin wrote in *Izvestia*, in his article "The Iron Mirgorod":

"The strength of reinforced concrete, the enormous bulk of the buildings, have compressed the brains of the American and narrowed his sight. The customs of the Americans reminded me of the never to be forgotten customs of Ivan Ivanovich and Ivan Nikiforovich in Gogol's story. Just as for the heroes of Gogol's story there was no better city than Poltava, so for the Americans there is no better and no more civilized country than America.

" 'Listen,' an American said to me, 'I know Europe. Don't argue with me. I have been all over Greece. I saw the Parthenon. But all that is not new to me. Do you know that in the State of Tennessee we have a much better and a much newer Parthenon?'

"Such words make one wish to laugh and to cry at the same time. They characterize America marvellously, especially her inner culture."

In February, 1923, the American ocean liner S.S. *George Washington*, on which Duncan and Esenin had sailed for Europe, arrived at Cherbourg. Duncan told the reporters: "I have been driven out of America. The United States is insane on the questions of Bolshevism, Prohibition, and Ku-Klux-Klan. In that land of the free there is no more freedom! The American papers printed details of my personal life, what I ate, what I drank, the people I associated with, but never once said a single word about my art. Materialism has become the curse of America!"

After Isadora Duncan's death the whole American press spoke quite differently about Duncan, and the New York Russian paper *Golos* wrote during the American tour of the Duncan Moscow Studio: "The time will come when freedom-loving Americans will throw the Statue of Liberty, this symbol of mercenary-minded freedom, into the sea and raise in its place a statue of Isadora Duncan, who was the personification of true freedom and who called for the brotherhood of nations."

XIII

On February 13th one of the Paris evening papers published the following notice: "Today's Mardi Gras was ruined for two reasons: one was rain and the other the disappearance of Isadora Duncan. Her admirers hoped that her presence would be the silver lining to the clouds which for two days have blanketed France. But since her disembarkation from the *George Washington* at Cherbourg she has hidden herself away somewhere in France like a recluse."

Duncan and Esenin were, however, in Paris.

"If you would save my life and reason meet me in Paris. Arriving *George Washington*. Love, Isadora."

Desti received this telegram in London and immediately left for Paris. At the station Isadora had just time to warn her: "Forget that I'm the great artist. I'm just a nice, intelligent person who appreciates the great genius of Sergei Esenin. He is the artist; he, the great poet."

Mary Desti burst out laughing.

"No, no, Mary," said Isadora, "for the love of Heaven, be serious, and do as I ask you or we are all lost."

At that moment an enormous bundle of elegant furs, crowned by a tall fur hat, emerged from the train. It was Esenin dressed in winter clothes and wrapped in Isadora's fur rug.

They stopped at the Hotel Crillon, but did not stay there long. Isadora fell ill, and the French authorities ordered Esenin to leave France.

She decided to send Jeanne to accompany Esenin to Berlin, where he had friends and where there was a Russian embassy, which France did not have at the time. She sent off all her things with him, intending to leave for Berlin herself as soon as she was well again.

Isadora did not get well, she could not sleep, she was running a high temperature. From Berlin, Esenin and his friends bombarded her with telegrams. Finally the following telegram arrived: "Isadora browning darling Sergei lyubish mora darling scurry scurry." Isadora quickly interpreted it as meaning: "Isadora, Browning will kill your darling Sergei. If you love me, my darling, come quickly, quickly."

Isadora said to Desti: "Mary, dear, if you are really my friend, find a way to take me to Sergei or I will die. I can't live without him. I love him and he loves me. The thought that some harm may come to him drives me mad. Find out where we can get a car to take us to Berlin."

"Here we were without a penny, yet she wanted to go by auto to Berlin," Desti exclaims in her book.

Isadora could not go by train because she did not feel well enough for such a journey. She raised sixty thousand francs—a fraction of their real value—on her three Carrière paintings, and, getting a car and a chauffeur who agreed to drive her to Berlin, she telegraphed to Esenin to be of good cheer for she would be joining him soon.

Esenin's forced departure quite naturally whetted the appetite of the Paris papers, and that was why Isadora categorically refused to see reporters. On the night before her departure for Berlin she had dinner with two artists of her acquaintance. Getting into the lift with one of them, her friend Murphy, she was followed by a reporter whom she knew. She pretended not to recognize him and turned to Murphy, whom she addressed as Sergei, and then said something in Russian, pinching Murphy's arm to make him take part in her plot against the reporter. The Frenchman beamed all over on hearing Isadora speak Russian and addressing Murphy as Sergei.

"Miss Duncan," he said to her with a knowing and confidential smile, "you might as well admit that Sergei is in Paris."

"No, no, he isn't," Isadora denied it, pretending to be frightened.

The correspondent smiled maliciously and insisted that everybody had known for some time that Sergei was staying at that hotel.

Isadora begged the journalist to come in and discuss the matter with her. On entering she pushed Murphy into the bathroom and told him in a whisper to make a terrible scene.

While trying to convince the journalist of the awful consequences of disclosing Esenin's presence in Paris, she kept looking apprehensively at the bathroom door and frightened the Frenchman by telling him what a fearless and desperate man Esenin was. At that moment Murphy threw a dinner tray into the bath with a tremendous crash and followed it up by smashing a few bottles on the tiles of the bathroom floor. As a finishing touch to the cannonade, he broke an electric light bulb, which sounded like a revolver shot.

Isadora seized the arm of the frightened reporter and begged him to stay and protect her. After promising not to say a word about it, he tore himself out of her hands and ran out of the hotel, just as Murphy flung open the bathroom door.

"I've revenged myself on all of them for their absurd stories about me and Esenin," Isadora cried, choking with laughter.

An hour later, the car was speeding her away to Berlin.

Next morning the correspondent published a sensational report disclosing Esenin's secret stay in Paris. A few hours later he had to eat his words.

The journey from Paris to Berlin is not really short, particularly in a car. Besides, Isadora was never very lucky in her travels by car, which always ended in some accident (not to mention the tragic death of her children and, later on, of herself). While in Russia, I recall, Duncan had a motor accident somewhere between Pskov and Leningrad, in Moscow we nearly ran over a child, near Batum we were almost precipitated into an abyss, near Moscow our car broke down in a wood, and so on. This time the car took her only as far as Strasbourg, where it broke down. Isadora hired another car, which also broke down after travelling a short distance. The third car was very temperamental and, besides, it had no headlights. It was getting dark. But that did not stop Isadora. She went to Bayreuth.

"I must embrace dear Frau Cosima [Wagner]," she declared. Several more hours were wasted. The car just got as far as Bayreuth late at night and finally gave up the ghost. Isadora did not attempt to get Wagner's widow and her children out of bed at such an inconvenient hour. Instead, she ordered a hundred of the most beautiful roses to be sent to Cosima in the morning. She herself felt a sudden access of energy and accepted a lift to Leipzig from a complete stranger. The man drove like a madman and Duncan, who loved fast driving, urged him to go faster. To make things worse, he fell in love with her and did not hesitate to carry out her wish. He drove at breakneck speed, went through a barrier in the middle of the road, hit a heap of stones and, scattering them in all directions, rushed on regardless, all the time looking at Isadora rather than at the road. After arriving in Strasbourg, Isadora hired another car and two days later, at ten o'clock in the evening, at last drove up to the Hotel Adlon, where she was to met Esenin. A group of people was already waiting for her on the sidewalk.

The moment the car stopped, Esenin leaped over the head of the driver into Isadora's arms. They remained like that, clasped in each other's arms. A crowd gathered, but neither Isadora nor Esenin paid any attention. Esenin's golden hair, lit by the strong electric lights, waved about in the wind (he had dropped his cap as he leaped into the car). It was with difficulty that they were at last persuaded to leave the car. The police, who soon appeared on the scene, tried to disperse the crowd which was gaping at the extraordinary spectacle. The interest in the proceedings was heightened by a lanky long-haired Russian poet in a bright-red shirt with a balalaika. The other poets were no less picturesque.

They all went off to the Palace Hotel, where Esenin's retinue, who went on before the husband and wife, lined up with their musical instruments on the sidewalk and, at their approach, struck up a march. When the manager of the Palace Hotel asked Isadora how many people had arrived and how many rooms they would want, she replied with a regal gesture: "For all of them!"

"Food! Food!" shouted Esenin.

"Yes, yes," Isadora replied in Russian. "Food!"

A table was laid in the middle of the great salon and the whole company crowded round. Isadora ordered "only Russian food and drink" and to the accompaniment of balalaikas and Russian songs, the feast began.

Isadora, Desti writes, was more beautiful than ever. Her eyes were full of happiness. Esenin knelt before her, tears streaming down his cheeks, and he called her "a thousand beautiful, tender Russian names." Then Esenin jumped on to a table and began reciting one of his poems. "An electric shock" ran through everybody at the table. "Although at the time I did not understand one word of Russian," Desti adds, "I too was carried off by the force and pathos of his voice and expression."

Then Isadora and Esenin danced a "Russian" dance. But the merriment soon came to an abrupt end. Isadora overheard Esenin who was talking to another poet utter the name Anna (what he actually said was *ona,* the Russian word for "she," but he pronounced it *ana* in the Moscow fashion). That was enough. Isadora thought that Esenin was talking about some woman he had fallen in love with, and, jealous, told his friend that she had known all about "that Anna" for a long time. It took some time for the misunderstanding to be cleared up, and Isadora and Esenin, both considerably chastened, retired to their rooms. Next morning they had to go to another hotel, where the same company was waiting for them. Esenin sang, Isadora danced a Russian dance. Esenin stopped her, saying that only Russians could perform that dance as it should be done. Again they quarrelled.

Desti took Isadora to her hotel. But Isadora longed to be with Esenin. She told Desti that she could not leave Esenin, for that would be like deserting a sick child. She had to take him back to Russia, where he was loved and understood and where he was treated with kindness by everybody. In the morning Isadora telephoned Esenin. She told him to come to her hotel and bring all his things and all his friends. She proposed that they should all go back to Moscow, but first they had to go to Paris to sell her house in Rue de la Pompe and return to Russia on the money.

But Esenin could not go back to Paris, nor could he possibly hope to obtain a visa on his "red" passport. Besides, Isadora decided to return to Paris by car and take the whole company with her. The only difficulty was that none of them had any money.

Esenin and his friends did succeed in raising four thousand francs and paid in advance for the hire of a car which was to take them as far as Strasbourg.

The large open car which appeared the following morning looked extremely exotic: Isadora and Mary Desti sat on the back seat, the poet in the red shirt sat next to the driver, while Esenin and the musician with the balalaika sat in the two extra seats in front of the back seat. Besides quantities of luggage, there was a basket with thousands of Duncan's press-cuttings collected in Europe and

America. She dragged that battered basket of press-cuttings everywhere with her. She had not had time to read them all, and now they were flying about all over the place, even littering the road to Leipzig. Many cuttings were thus lost, which is a pity, for I learned a great deal of importance from them afterwards, and I have included some in this book.

At one o'clock in the morning the car drew up before a first class hotel in Leipzig, frightening the night porter who, looking at the motley company, was uncertain whether he should let them have any rooms. It was then that Esenin stepped forward: arrayed in his fur coat, topboots, and hung all over with a large camera and a pair of binoculars from which he never parted, he looked so impressive that the porter relented.

On the way to Strasbourg they stopped in Weimar and visited Goethe's house. About ten miles before reaching Strasbourg their driver had refused to go any further because the French, he said, would confiscate his car. It was only then that they realized they were travelling without visas and turned back to a small town where there were an American and a French consul. Isadora told them that she was taking a sick husband back to Paris to see a specialist and received three visas. The "musician" had to return to Berlin, but he did not even protest, for Esenin had broken his balalaika the day before. It was pouring with rain when they left Strasbourg at night in a closed car, a type in which Isadora ordinarily refused to travel: since the accident with her children she could not look at a closed car, let alone travel in one. They had only gone two miles when Isadora declared that she felt faint and must go back. She could not remain in the car a moment longer, for it was like the car which had fallen into the Seine with her children. She was suffocating and she began banging on the windows. In desperation they returned to the hotel. Desti left for Paris alone, promising to send Isadora immediately two thousand francs to cover their travelling expenses. The money arrived the same day and they left for Paris in an open car. On the way, however, Isadora decided that it was quite impossible not to show Esenin the architecturally wonderful "cathedral district," and they spent three days and all the two thousand francs in visiting the cathedrals.

Four days later Desti got word from Isadora that they were in Paris at the Westminster Hotel but that they had no money. They had arrived at night and registered as Mr. and Mrs. Esenin. The concierge had no idea that the new guests were the famous Isadora Duncan and her no less famous husband whom the Paris papers had made such a fuss about not long ago. Having found out who they were, the manager of the hotel informed them next morning that their rooms had been booked by other guests. Desti got them rooms at the Hotel Madrid in the Bois de Boulogne. They were very pleased and hastily left the Westminster. On the way, Isadora had the car stop at the Carlton for dinner. The dinner went on for a long time. They arrived at the Hotel Madrid late at night and found that their rooms had quite naturally been taken. Desti telephoned the Hotel Continental to find out whether the rooms formerly occupied by Isadora were free. They were and she booked them, telling the reception clerk that Duncan and her husband would be arriving immediately.

Early next morning Desti's son looked out of the window and noticed a familiar couple sitting on a bench in the Tuileries Gardens and a man in a red shirt hovering about them. He realized that it was Isadora, Esenin, and the poet who accompanied them. Desti ran out to the Tuileries Gardens and was told that the same thing had happened in the Hotel Continental as in the Hotel Westminster. The concierge knew nothing about them, but in the morning the hotel manager hastened to inform Isadora and Esenin that their rooms had been booked from 2 A.M. by other people.

Esenin had taken no part in all these unpleasant negotiations with the hotel managers. He was very calm, sarcastic, and, like Isadora, worried about the police, since they had deported him from France not long ago. He longed to go back to Moscow and was only waiting for Isadora to wind up her business affairs.

In Paris he was very busy preparing his book *Confession d'un Voyou* (Confessions of a Hooligan) for publication in a French translation by F. Ellenson and M. Miloslavskaya. Although Esenin believed that the study of a foreign language would interfere with his writing, he did spend some time in Paris learning English. In Paris he wrote about his parents' little house:

> *I loved that wooden house,*
> *Stern wrinkles glimmered in its timber,*
> *Our stove so wildly, so strangely*
> *Howled in the rainswept night. . . .*

He had longed to be back in his homeland for a long time. In the same poem he wrote:

> ... *Only nearer to my homeland,*
> *I'd wish to be now....*

But to go back to Moscow they had to have money. Isadora could have raised a little more money from the money-lender on the Eugène Carrière paintings she had left with him, but he refused to see her. Esenin drove with her to the money-lender and made him pay everything he owed her. From there they went to an art dealer, a great admirer of Duncan's art, and told him about the Eugène Carrière pictures kept by the money-lender. Isadora said she was afraid she would never get them back. The art dealer offered to redeem the pictures at once and buy them himself from Duncan at their current value, promising to return them to her without interest or loss when she could take them back.

The art dealer gave Isadora a considerable sum of money. Isadora and Esenin then drove off to have dinner at the Carlton. But on the way Esenin stopped the taxi, his attention attracted by a shop window full of bright-coloured silk kimonos and dressing gowns of every colour. They spent half an hour in the shop, where they left the lion's share of the large sum they had just received. Isadora looked at her husband with adoring eyes, just as if he were a little child excited by a new toy. They had dinner at the Carlton, where they were welcomed respectfully, and Isadora decided to take a suite of rooms there. The manager invited them very cordially to a banquet which was to take place on the following day in the restaurant. Afraid of the publicity, Isadora at first refused, but the manager kept begging them to go, and in the end she agreed. After a rowdy scene at the banquet, she fell ill again. The doctor found her condition serious. Esenin, extraordinarily tender, never left her for a minute, but his nerves were on edge, fearing that the police might turn up again. When Isadora recovered, they decided to move to her house at 103 Rue de la Pompe.

"I decided," Isadora told me later in Moscow, "to get away from all that crazy life and hide myself away with Esenin in my little house with the studio where I could have a rest and get ready for my great work in Moscow."

Their money was gone again and they started selling the things in the house. "Well, what shall we eat today?" Isadora used to ask cheerfully. "The sofa or that bookcase?"

Isadora found that each day her house improved. She hated expensive furniture, especially writing desks, preferring simple things and plain tables, on which she could put papers and books any way she liked. A year later, when I went to Paris, I found the house completely empty.

On the eve of their departure for Moscow they went to have dinner at a Russian restaurant, the Scheherazade. They were sitting quietly at their table under a huge standard lamp. Suddenly a waiter, holding a tilted bottle of champagne in a napkin and filling Esenin's glass, bent over and said to him: "You see, Mr. Esenin, I was aide-de-camp to his Imperial Majesty, and here I am filling your glass with champagne."

Esenin, who could not stand these Guardsmen-waiters, replied: "Don't you talk to me, you dirty toady, just keep on filling my glass!"

The aide-de-camp hit Esenin and, as Isadora told me afterwards, in less than a minute Esenin was all in white: six former Russian army officers hurled themselves on him, pulled off his coat and trousers and, dragging him along the floor, threw him out into the street. Esenin nearly knocked over a policeman who, turning round and seeing in the middle of the night a man in underclothes, caught him by the scruff of the neck and hauled him off to the police station.

The man who started the fight was a certain Zubkov, the head waiter of the restaurant.

So Esenin was again in the hands of the police. Isadora, who had rushed out into the street, could find no trace of him. In the morning she discovered to her consternation that Esenin was in danger of being sent to a lunatic asylum.

That is the origin of the ridiculous story that Duncan put Esenin in a lunatic asylum in Paris. Actually, Isadora rushed off to see the Mayor of Paris and literally went down on her knees before him, imploring him to let her place Esenin in a private clinic, for she could have got him out of it any time she liked and taken him back to Russia.

Anxious to meet her halfway, the Mayor agreed, and they left for Moscow at once.

Hours before their departure for Moscow, a Paris newspaper published an article by Dmitry Merezhkovsky attacking Esenin and

Duncan. In reply, Isadora published an open letter in *Nouvelle Revue* and the New York *Herald*. "I took Esenin away from Russia where the conditions of life are still very difficult," she wrote. "I wanted to save him for the world. Now he is returning to Russia to save his reason, for he cannot live without Russia. I know that many hearts will offer up prayers for this great poet so that he may live to create beauty in future."

Replying to Merezhkovsky, who called Esenin "a drunken peasant" in his article and accused Duncan of "selling herself to the Bolsheviks," Isadora wrote:

"During the war I danced the *Marseillaise* because I thought that way led to peace. Now I dance the *Internationale* because I feel that it is mankind's anthem of the future. Esenin is the greatest living poet of modern Russia. Edgar Poe, Verlaine, Baudelaire, Musorgsky, Dostoevsky, Gogol—they all left immortal works behind them. I can well understand that Mr. Merezhkovsky could not have lived with those people, for men of talent always live in fear of men of genius. In spite of that, I wish Mr. Merezhkovsky a peaceful old age in his bourgeois place of refuge and a respectable funeral, his hearse accompanied by undertakers wearing black plumes and hired mourners in black gloves."

XIV

If you take the old Kaluga road out of Moscow for about twelve miles, you will cross the river Pakhra. Along its banks spreads the large, noisy village of Red Pakhra. Turning left along a country road your way lies through a birch wood rustling in the sun; suddenly you find yourself in a gloomy colonnade of silent firs whose long, sprawling roots toss your car about so mercilessly that you feel as if someone was shaking you by the shoulder saying: "Where have you got to? Where have you got to?"

But a moment later the firs are left behind, a warm wind blows in your face, and the car rolls softly, through shafts of sunlight, along the grassy ruts.

"*Stradan* [suffering]," says the driver, "Krasnoye is not far off."

"Stradan?" every passenger will be sure to ask. "Is that what it's called?"

"They've been through a great deal of suffering, you see. That's where it got its name from. It was called that as far back as the time of Catherine the Great. The country folk had plenty of suffering inflicted on them afterwards by that..." and the driver will point with his whip at the brick country house situated above the village.

"By whom?"

"By a local woman landowner, they say."

"Who was she?"

"Saltychikha."[1]

The red and white house with its great park belonged to Saltychikha, who became widely known for her cruel and inhuman

[1] Mother of Russia's great nineteenth-century satirist Saltykov-Shchedrin.

134

treatment of serfs. Thanks to the old Bolshevik Yemelyan Yaroslavsky, Duncan's school was given the house as a summer holiday retreat.

Tall, broad-shouldered, with a head of curly grey hair, Yemelyan Yaroslavsky lived with his wife Klavdiya Kirsanova and their six-year-old daughter Mariana in a small house near the Prechistenka Gates. He was a member of the Central Committee of the Party and was head of the anti-religious movement.

Mariana had been admitted to the Duncan school, and I remember her telling me after returning from one of the first Christmas Tree parties for Moscow children that she was able to see everything very well because she had been sitting on the knees of "Uncle Lenin."

Yaroslavsky and his wife took Irma and me to Saltychikha's former country house, Krasnoye, which was near a state farm. Having reached an agreement with the farm manager that the schoolchildren should receive free milk in return for work in the market garden, we drove back to Moscow. We were promised that all the rooms in the house would be whitewashed by the time the children arrived.

On the way back Yaroslavsky told me that Mariana was born in Yakutsk, where he and Kirsanova had been exiled.

"She's such a delicate child because of that," said Yaroslavsky after a short pause. "The climate there is cruel and the living conditions of the political exiles were terrible. I remember being sent to the Yakutsk Governor as a representative of the political exiles. He received me in his office, sitting while I stood. Next day *I* was sitting at the governor's desk and he was brought to me as a prisoner under arrest!"

Just then our car suddenly slowed down, slithered slowly sideways, nearly hit a cow, and was on the verge of toppling into the valley far below us. Fortunately it hit a wooden post, and came to rest.

"The steering rod has broken," the driver whispered, white-lipped, and crawled under the car.

Yaroslavsky rose from his seat and looked down.

"I don't think they would have been able even to gather up our bones," he said imperturbably.

"What did happen in Yakutsk?" I asked Yaroslavsky some time later when our car was speeding towards Moscow.

"The news of the February Revolution arrived, and I was elected president of the revolutionary committee."

In Saltychikha's house, into which we soon moved, the talk was of ghosts and the sinful soul of Old Saltychikha, which walked at night. The kitchen staff of the school especially talked a lot about Saltychikha's ghost. In the end the stories about the ghost spread among the children, who woke up in the middle of the night and started shrieking because they seemed to have seen something or heard the shuffle of slippers.

The legend of Saltychikha and her house still persists, but on inquiring among the old inhabitants of Krasnaya Pakhra, I learnt that the house had really belonged to one of Saltychikha's relations—Count Saltykov, whom she often visited. The house had another historic interest, for Field Marshal Kutuzov and his staff spent a day there during Napoleon's retreat from Moscow. The mistress of the house was preparing some special cabbage soup for the Field Marshal when he and his staff had to leave hurriedly because Napoleon had launched a surprise attack on the flank of the Russian army.

But the innumerable commissions of the Commissariat of Education were an even greater nuisance than the ghosts. They contrived to find us in spite of the fact that we had hidden ourselves away in a place without railway connections with Moscow.

The People's Commissariat of Education was heatedly debating the question of which one of its departments should be put in charge of Duncan's school. Was it an institution for social education or a school for professional training? Duncan insisted firmly that her method of artistic and physical education of children was basically opposed to any attempt to predetermine the child's future profession. On the other hand, she accepted Lunacharsky's proposal to create "a phalanx of enthusiasts"—the future instructors and teachers of the school.

But Duncan was abroad and we had to carry on the bitter fights with the different commissions. Besides, quite rightly hating "pedologues," Duncan lumped them all together shying away from any examination by official organizations interested in her method.

The school had excellent relations with the Institute of Social Hygiene, headed by Professor Molkov, a great supporter of Duncan's ideas, and who had a perfect understanding of her methods.

Duncan was a great friend of Molkov and his wife. She gave a party on the birth of their child, conforming with her ritual of 'October' celebrations, and presented it with a tiny red tunic. But she found it very difficult to put up with the different investigations and experiments of the Institute, and it was only after her departure that we began to work in earnest with the Institute, which afterwards organized a whole exhibition on the health of children, dedicated to the Duncan school. Incidentally, it was during one of its investigations that the Institute established as a positive fact that the Duncan method developed 'the length of legs' and facilitated childbirth. (Here Molkov proved right. Many years later all the 'dunclings' who got married had easy labour.)

Duncan had her own secret reason for being frightened of too much scientific interference with art. Having once left her Berlin school in charge of her sister Elizabeth, she had gone on a tour abroad and on her return to Germany saw in the streets of Dresden big, screaming posters advertising an exhibition under the title of *Der Mensch* (Man).

Her interest aroused, she went to see the exhibition and was horrified by the huge diagrams and cardiograms with captions carefully written out in big letters: "Irma's pulse after a run of 200 metres," "Teresa's heart," and so on. In the next room her pupils were demonstrating the beauty of man's natural movements and various other exercises.

While recognizing the legitimacy and necessity of such investigations, Isadora could not forget the terrible shock she had received when the whole "poetry of feelings" she had tried to instil in the dances she was creating was anatomically assessed by cardiograms and X-rays. Duncan immediately took her pupils away. The fact is she could not overcome her inner conflict between the artist and the pedagogue and disguised it by the formula: "I do not teach children. I give them joy."

A. I. Vyshinsky, the head of the Department of Professional Education, included Duncan's school in the network of his institutions. The poet Valery Bryusov, founder of the symbolist movement in Russia, whom Gorky described as "the most cultured writer in Russia," was appointed head of our section of artistic education.

Both Vyshinsky and Bryusov understood the purpose of Duncan's aims and the tasks of her school. Unfortunately, after their departure the school kept being transferred from one department to another and even to the Department of Science (where we were listed as a higher educational institute and official letters were addressed to me as "Rector of the Duncan School," though the oldest of our students was only twelve).

As the Duncan Theatre-Studio, the school later played an important creative role as part of the Department of Musical Institutions of the Arts Council.

The Education Commissariat's "commissions of investigation" did not understand the aim and purpose of the school and during their visits to Krasnoye poked about for "systems" and "methods" and completely overlooked the charm of the naturalness of the movements in Duncan's dances. Professor Molkov, in an interesting way that was anything but scientific, found that peasants did their weeding in vegetable gardens by squatting on their haunches, spreading their knees, and working quickly with their hands along the beds in that comfortable and natural position; townspeople, on the other hand, usually work standing, bending from the waist; the children of Duncan's school, who had been told about nothing, began weeding, quite naturally, in the same way as the peasants.

The "dunclings" knew nothing about these experiments. They went through their physical training in the morning in the park playground, had their swimming lesson in the river Nara, went gathering wild berries and mushrooms, danced on the lawns, had their English lesson, and accompanied me when I cycled to Nara on the pretext of "seeing me off as far as the road." They then begged me not to send them back and walked the five miles to the town, where they were interested in everything. They invaded the local "tea-room," ate ring-shaped rolls, and drank tea served in huge teapots decorated with flowers.

The summer drew to a close, and we began making preparations for an American tour. We were to travel via Petrograd and Riga, where we were to give a number of performances. The steamship tickets had already been paid for by Duncan's manager in New York, and the Moscow office of the White Star Line was showering us with brochures.

We left for Petrograd with a large complement of young dancers, of whom only twenty were to sail to New York. The rest had to return to Moscow. In Petrograd we were to perform in the old Mikhailovsky Theatre where a company whose producer was N. F.

Monakhov, was playing. The poet, Alexander Blok, had been the literary adviser but he had died shortly before our arrival.

After our first performance the Petrograd *Pravda* published a number of comments headed "A Breath of Fresh Air" and "Great Joy"...

Monakhov, one of our most popular and talented musical comedy actors, who had only recently gone to the legitimate theatre and earned new fame as producer and actor, invited us one day to meet his company. He spoke at some length about our performance, emphasizing the inter-relation of Stanislavsky and Duncan and speaking very highly of the art of the "dunclings," of their con-scientiousness and their remarkable discipline. He held them up as an example to his own company.

We lived on Stone Island, a former resort of Petersburg aristo-crats, where we slept between fine linen sheets with the Romanov monogram and crest, taken from the Winter Palace. We drove to the theatre in antediluvian court brakes drawn by two horses.

We did not have a chance of going to Riga, let alone America, for the American consul in Riga refused to give us visas—the result of the Duncan-Esenin American visit.

But we were not downhearted. Inspired by the success of our first tour, we returned to Moscow in high spirits and announced a Sunday matinée in the Comedy (former Korsh) Theatre. The suc-cess of our performances exceeded all expectations. After the per-formance the students, who filled the theatre, carried the "dunclings" to the bus.

This is what *Izvestia* wrote about the performance of Duncan's school in the Comedy Theatre on April 15, 1923:

"In 1921 Isadora Duncan founded a school for children in Moscow. In it the children were not only taught the art of dancing, but also brought up according to the method of Duncan, who aims at creating a new harmoniously developed human being by fostering from an early age the feelings for beauty combined, above all, with naturalness in the movements of the body. The work of the school, demonstrated in April at the Comedy Theatre, shows great progress. Their dances really seem to flow out of life itself, showing patterns of children's games or simple runs and jumps; they perform it all with such natural ease and rhythmic grace and, at the same time, with such evident pleasure that, looking at them, one involuntarily remembers H. G. Wells's novel *Men Like Gods*: the people of that happy utopia must have been like that! The performance evoked the warm sympathy of the audience, half of whom were also children, and was concluded with the singing of the Internationale."

The Duncan studio went on its first tour in 1925. Isadora was in Paris at the time. We sailed down the Volga from Nizhny-Novgorod to Astrakhan. On the steamer we had a surprise meeting with Stanislavsky. During Duncan's stay in Moscow, her pupils often met Stanislavsky. He also visited the dancing lessons at Duncan's school. When the Duncan pupils, in their red velvet tunics, went at Stanislavsky's invitation to a performance of the Moscow Art Theatre, he let them have a box and invited them to his dressing room during the intervals, talking and treating them to chocolates and sweets.

Our unexpected meeting with Stanislavsky took place after we had changed steamers at Saratov for Astrakhan: Stanislavsky was taking the air on deck and enjoying the beautiful countryside along the banks of the Volga. It seems he was having a rest by sailing from Nizhny to Astrakhan and back on the same boat.

We approached Astrakhan one hot morning.

Stanislavsky had no special plans that night and, learning that the studio of Isadora Duncan was to give its first performance, he asked if he could come. We were all pleased and excited.

"May I announce your presence in the theatre?" I asked. But he begged me not to, but before we left the boat his secretary came up to me and told me that in spite of his shyness he would really be pleased "to meet the Astrakhan public."

We decided to proceed with my plan. After the third bell, when the lights in the auditorium went down, I went out in front to make my usual short introductory speech. But before I began I told the audience Stanislavsky was in the house. After a moment's silence the theatre blew up. The audience jumped to their feet and applauded lustily for a very long time. Stanislavsky stood in his box, looking very pale, and bowed to the audience, tears streaming down his cheeks. After the performance, in which Irma and the studio had scored a big success, a huge crowd waited for Stanislavsky outside the theatre and escorted him to the landing stage.

We also gave performances in Moscow, and this helped our

finances. In those years (after the Volga famine) Duncan's school, like others, was supplied by the People's Commissariat of Food with the basic rations, by the Association of the Workers in the Arts with lunches, and by the Catholic Mission from Rome (there *was* such an organization in those days) with "a second lunch." These lunches and rations would have been hardly sufficient to keep the school going had not Isadora and her friends sent us parcels from abroad. These contained white flour and occasionally rice and sugar, tins of lard, cocoa, and condensed milk. The staff of the school (I reduced it from sixty to twenty) were also glad of the school rations, for then wages were incredibly small.

This state of comparative prosperity came suddenly to an end. On the 11th of November (I have never forgotten that day) Lunacharsky asked me to attend a meeting of the Board of the Commissariat of Education, which was to discuss the question of the position of Duncan's school. When I arrived Lunacharsky's secretary told me that the school had been placed at the end of the agenda. "There is going to be a break now," she said. Soon the door of Lunacharsky's office was opened and the members of the Board filed out, smoking cigarettes. Lunacharsky, too, came out. He looked rather embarrassed, I thought.

"We've just been discussing your problem," he said, as he sat down beside me.

I was very surprised, for I had been specially invited to take part in the discussion.

"We discussed your particular problems before the break," Lunacharsky said. "You see, I did not know you were here." Then he added: "We have decided that your school will no longer be financed by the State."

I must have looked like a question mark, for our removal from the State budget meant that our school would be the only one in the country to depend on its own resources.

"How are we to raise the necessary funds?" I asked the Commissar of Education.

"Try to organize performances. I'm sorry but I'm afraid I could do nothing," he replied and once more I realized the difficulties Lunacharsky had to overcome in his own Commissariat.

A short time later he explained these difficulties in a letter to the Commissariat of Food: "All my efforts to guarantee the existence of the Duncan school are frustrated by the narrow-minded

141

opposition of people who are of the opinion that the school is a luxury."

Moscow was going through difficult times, and it fell to me to find a solution of the problem of securing the existence of a large family of forty children, twenty employees, and two houses.

The following summer we were given the picturesque estate of Litvinovo for the children. But we remained in Moscow for a long time, and for an important reason: together with Podvoysky we decided to organize a mass gymnastic display in the sports arena of the Red Stadium, opposite the site of the present Central Park of Culture and Rest. Posters appeared in Moscow with the legend "Duncan's School for Workers' Children" inviting Moscow children to join the school in the gymnastic display it was organizing, and six hundred children living in the Zamoskvoretsky and Khamovnichesky districts enrolled. To the accompaniment of a military band they marched gaily in their red tunics along the roads from Prechistenka to the old Crimea Bridge. Six red squares of a hundred children each were drawn up on the green grass. Each company was under the supervision of two instructors, and two more "dunclings" assisted. Irma Duncan and I with a megaphone took up a position in the centre.

Pravda wrote: "The children of Duncan's school, who gave up their holidays for the sake of the six hundred children of the Zamoskvoretsky and Khamovnichesky districts, supervised their physical exercises daily in the sports arena of the Red Stadium. These exercises yielded excellent results: the children, who at the beginning were sickly, weak, and shy, soon began to grow strong, confident, and were literally transformed...."

The children (both instructors and pupils) were enthusiastic about the exercises. Sometimes not even the rain interrupted the daily routine. It was only a storm that made everybody run for shelter, but the storm over, all the children, soaked to the skin but cheerful, marched gaily together with the pupils of Duncan's school and the military band through the puddles that reflected the brilliant sunshine, and they saw their instructors back to the very door of the school.

The work with the children brought to an end the unceasing attacks on the school by the "official commissions," though from time to time they renewed their criticisms.

"What kind of aesthetic education is this?" exclaimed a lady, whose face was plastered with powder, a member of one of these commissions, as she watched the children, wearing simple, clean white dresses, sitting down at a table decorated with bunches of wild flowers and drinking tea out of soup plates with tablespoons.

I don't mind admitting that the school's crockery still left much to be desired, but the tea was all right.

Two members of one of the commissions of the Commissariat of Education, who examined the results of the physical education according to Duncan's system, frightened the children: one of them was a hunchback and another a cripple. That did not, of course, reflect on their competence or on their erudition, but those who appointed the commission (actually, "on the beauty of the human body") should have given thought to its composition. One member of this particular commission asked me why we did not have any "proletarian children" at the school.

"Ninety per cent of them are children of workers," I replied, but seeing a look not only of incredulity but undisguised indignation on the faces of the members of the commission, I lost my temper. "You are misled by the appearance of these children," I said. "You are mistaken. What you take to be 'breeding' is merely the result of the atmosphere in which the children live and of the method of their artistic and physical education."

To convince the commission, who suspected the presence of "blue blood" in the children of factory and railway workers, I showed them their documents and admission forms.

There could be no question of defraying the expenses of the school by the few performances we could give. The forty children of the school had to be fed, dressed, washed, given medical care and general education. To make our school self-supporting we had to announce the admission of a so-called parallel group of scholars, whose curriculum did not include any professional training. Their twice weekly dancing lessons were more in the nature of physical exercises.

The school was often visited by different delegations and sometimes by artists and sculptors. The sculptors, in particular, were very keen on being admitted to the lessons. They argued that ancient sculptures and paintings on vases conveyed only the fixed beauty of man's natural movements, whereas at the school they could see for themselves the dynamic continuation of these movements in their infinite variety.

Among the Visitors were Gustave Inare, the only surviving participant of the Paris Commune, Pyatnitsky, the founder of the famous choir, and Kolontay, the Soviet woman diplomat.

One day a delegation from the Japanese embassy came to visit us. They happened to come at a time when the "parallel" group was having its dancing lessons. At that lesson several pupils of the "original" group came to Irma's assistance and demonstrated the movements to the new pupils. This resulted in an unfortunate misunderstanding: I noticed the Japanese whispering to each other, shrugging their shoulders and quite clearly expressing their dissatisfaction. The striking difference between the light and free movements of the Duncan pupils and the clumsy and constrained movements of the pupils of the "parallel" group led the Japanese to believe that they were being intentionally shown "some kind of monkeys" as "a contrast." They refused to believe us when we told them that the young instructors had not so long ago been like the new pupils.

Many years later the Isadora Duncan studio was invited to give a performance at a reception at the Japanese embassy, and their dances were a great success. *The Volga Boatmen,* produced by Duncan on the theme of Repin's famous picture, made a particularly strong impression.

The work with the children in the sports arena of the Red Stadium would have assumed a much more interesting and fascinating form if Isadora Duncan had taken part in it, for those displays were the beginning of the realization of her greatest and most passionate dream.

I therefore sent a telegram to Isadora in Paris, insisting on her immediate return to Moscow.

XV

Porters were scattered all along the platform. The train was approaching. Irma and I stood waiting with bunches of flowers in our hands.

At last the train, approaching menacingly at high speed with a white plume of steam over its engine, stopped. We saw them at once. Isadora and Esenin were standing at a window of the railway carriage and beaming happily at us. On coming down onto the platform, Isadora, taking Esenin gently by the wrist, drew him to herself and, inclining her face towards me, said with a serious look:

"Hier bringe ich dieses Kind in sein Vaterland, aber ich habe nichts mehr mit ihm zu tun...."[1]

But those were only words. Feeling proved stronger than decisions taken after much suffering.

The school had moved to Litvinovo for the summer. We decided to go there together. There could be no question of taking Isadora for fifty miles by suburban train and then being jolted about in a cart along a country road. She could not consider going to Litvinovo except by car.

With some difficulty I succeeded at last in getting hold of an open car and the two Duncans, Esenin, and myself left for Litvinovo. On the way we passed some cows. Catching sight of the herd, Esenin craned his neck. "Cows," he said, without taking his eyes off them. When we came to another herd crossing the road, he again said:

[1] Here I've brought this child back to his country, but I've nothing more to do with him.

"Cows...." Then, with sudden excitement and regarding each of us in turn, he said, talking very fast: "Now, what if there weren't any cows? No, no. Without cows there would be no villages, and one can't imagine Russia without villages."

Everything was perfect so long as we sped along the highway which ran alongside the railway track, but as soon as we turned off the highway the car kept stalling on the country road to Litvinovo and when towards evening we entered a forest it stopped altogether. While we tried to get it going, it grew dark. It was only about two miles to Litvinovo, and I proposed that we should walk there. We did so, but because of the darkness we found walking difficult. Suddenly we saw some reddish lights moving towards us and throwing pink reflections on the black trunks of the trees. In another instant these lights cut through the darkness of the forest with tongues of flame. We saw a circle of "dunclings" in red tunics, carrying pitch torches in their hands. Worried by the long absence of the car which was bringing Isadora to them, they had come to meet us in the forest.

Fascinated, Isadora gazed with happy, wide-open eyes at those lovely, sun-tanned children who surrounded her in the dark forest at night. It was so wonderful to go back together to Litvinovo, to enter the big house, decorated with fresh-smelling birch branches, to sit down at a table with burning candles and bunches of wild flowers picked by the children.

Isadora, entranced, watched the dances of the children and Esenin, too, could not conceal his pleasure when he saw how successful they were. He kept slapping his knees and laughing in wonder and delight.

We spent several days in Litvinovo. Esenin and Duncan told us all about their adventures abroad. Esenin enjoyed the daily dancing lessons Irma gave on the green lawn near the house. Sometimes we all went for a long walk and came back as hungry as wolves. The composer Ilsarov paid us a visit just then. Esenin sat beside him at the piano twice, reading his poems in an undertone and repeating some a few times, while Ilsarov quietly improvised on the piano. Unfortunately, I never discovered afterwards what came of it or, indeed, if anything did come of it.

It began to rain. Huge yellow puddles covered the paths, flooding everything around: our spirits fell. Sometimes it looked as though it would clear up. A golden ball would break through the clouds and kindle green sparks on the swaying trees, but all too soon the rain covered everything within sight with a slanting net: the park, the white ruins of the mansion, the grey sheds, the wet, dark roofs of the cottages. It went on raining for three depressing days. We decided to go back to Moscow and, soaked to the skin, reached the station in the carriages I had been lucky enough to get.

In the warm, dry compartment we came to life again and kept talking till we arrived in Moscow.

Next day the poet Ryurik Ivnov came to see Esenin, and all five of us went to have dinner at the Hermitage-Olivier restaurant. We were given a separate room with a small verandah looking out on to a small garden. We were all in excellent spirits. In the garden a large company was sitting round two tables which had been placed close together. I noticed Grigory Vasilyevich Chicherin, the Commissar for Foreign Affairs, among them: he seemed to be entertaining some American delegation. I told Isadora about it.

"I'd very much like to have a talk with him," she said, brightening up. "Please ask him when it could be arranged."

I went down into the garden and told Chicherin, with whom I had worked as secretary, about Isadora's wish to meet him. Chicherin said that he would be very glad to receive her at his office any day after twelve.

When I returned to our table, I noticed a change in the atmosphere; Esenin looked angry and Isadora looked unhappy.

"Ilya Ilyich," Esenin said to me, pointing a finger at Isadora, "when we were abroad she said that you and Irma were 'swine,' but now she's all over you."

"*Das ist eine Lüge* [That is a lie]!" Isadora, who understood what he had said to me, declared calmly.

"No, it isn't! You did say that!" insisted Esenin, looking very pale as he continued to perforate the air with a finger in the direction of Isadora.

"Why?" I asked him.

"She said that you and Irma were exploiting her art."

"*Das ist eine Lüge!*" Isadora repeated.

"That is strange, Isadora," I said, turning to her. "Sergei Alexandrovich could not just have invented it. Yesterday you thanked me so much for the school, but abroad you called us names. Was it because we gave performances here?"

"Er lügt [He lies] !" Isadora cried again, glancing at Esenin with smouldering eyes.

Irma, who was sitting down looking pale, hung her head. Esenin jumped up and rushed to the door. I just had time to pay the bill.

Esenin went away. Ivnov said goodbye, looking very embarrassed. We went back to Prechistenka. Isadora tried to convince us that Esenin had misunderstood her, but I was quite sure that what Esenin had told us was true.

At home Isadora calmed down and meekly agreed to Irma's demand that the three of us should at once leave for Kislovodsk. "You've had enough disgraceful scenes all over Europe and America," Irma said. "You're seriously ill and you must have medical treatment at a spa."

Irma began packing. Trunk lids came crashing down, straps were tightened: everything was readied for the journey.

Esenin had hurt Isadora's feelings. She again became obsessed with the thought of the inevitable end of their relationship. Irma insisted on an immediate break.

I told "my ladies" that I would not be able to leave for Kislovodsk for three days and that I had arranged for them to leave for Mineralnye Vody next evening by express train. As for myself, I could not get Esenin out of my head. I did not know where to find him. It may have been just sentimentality, but I literally suffered that evening when I tried to imagine Esenin's feelings when he came back in a few days and found that Isadora had gone.

I sent our porter, our doorman, and our housekeeper to Esenin's haunts and told them to bring him back at any cost. Our "ladies" knew nothing about it and went on packing. Irma told me that if Esenin turned up Isadora was not to see him. Isadora, evidently agreeing with her, said nothing. The first to return was our porter Filipp Sergeyevich (for some reason he always squatted down and propped his face on his hands when speaking to me).

"Found him," he said. "Sober as a judge, he is, sir," and, squatting down, he added. "He'll be here presently."

I went to have a look at what Isadora was doing, but the moment I entered the room, someone ran in with the news that Esenin had arrived.

Isadora rushed into Irma's room and Irma at once locked the door. But she forgot to lock the other door from the "Gobelin hall."

I met Esenin in the entrance hall. He looked agitated.

"Isadora is going away," I said.

"When?" he asked with a nervous start.

"Altogether—from you."

"Where is she going to?"

"To Kislovodsk."

"I want to see her."

"Come along."

I pressed down the bronze door handle and opened the door quietly. Isadora was sitting on the semicircular sofa with her back to us and did not hear us enter.

Esenin went up to her inaudibly from behind and, leaning on the arm of the sofa, bent over Isadora.

"I love you very much, Isadora," he whispered a little hoarsely. "I love you very much."

It was decided that Esenin would leave for Kislovodsk with me in three days. He was given strict instructions to spend the nights with me in Prechistenka. He agreed without hesitation, smiling as though nothing had happened and not taking his eyes off Isadora. "Tomorrow," he said, "I'll see you off to Kislovodsk and then I and Ilya Ilyich will join you."

I asked V. N. Afanasyev, the manager of Duncan's tours, to get tickets in a sleeper compartment. He replied that he was quite sure he would be able to get tickets on an international train. That was precisely the sort of thing Afanasyev was good at, for he was a self-confident and brilliant administrator. I gave him a white crackling note, in the corner of which was the figure 10 within a dark circle. Ten roubles was quite a big sum that year: it was certainly enough for the purchase of two seats on the international Moscow-Kislovodsk express.

We arrived at the station an hour before the departure of the train. Afanasyev appeared exactly at the appointed time: he had no tickets. That did not in the least sadden either Isadora or Esenin: their parting was postponed for one more day! They did not conceal their pleasure.

We went back to Prechistenka. I got the tickets myself and on the following day Esenin and I saw Isadora and Irma off to Kislovodsk. A day later I sent Afanasyev there: Isadora had decided to give performances at the different Caucasian spas and afterwards to go on a short tour of Transcaucasia.

On the first evening Esenin did return home early. He told me of the chaos in the Writers' Shop and cursed his publisher. He also discussed his favourite idea with me: he thought it absolutely essential that poets should publish their own journal. Then, with a sorrowful countenance, he paced the room where everything spoke of Isadora. He left early in the morning without going to bed.

Next day he came running, looking very excited. "I can't go," he said. "I'm staying in Moscow. Very important business! I was summoned to the Kremlin. They're giving me money for the publication of a journal!"

He rushed about madly from the drawers of the desk to the suitcase and back again.

"Such important business! I'll write to Isadora. Explain everything. And as soon as I get things going here, I'll join you there!"

That evening he did not come back. At night he arrived with a whole crowd of people who disappeared with him in the morning.

Next morning Esenin came to say goodbye. His suitcases were for some reason tied up with ropes.

"I shan't live here alone," he declared. "I'm moving back to Bogoslovsky Street," he replied to my questioning glance.

"Why the ropes? What's happened to the straps?"

"I don't know. Someone must have taken them."

And he went away. Almost for good.

In the evening I left for Kislovodsk. Soedich, our business manager, left with me.

XVI

The first thing that caught my eye on entering Duncan's room in the Kislovodsk Grand Hotel was a narrow sheet of white paper pinned to the head of her bed: it was the doctor's prescribed diet and regimen for the day. Both Isadora and Irma had long faces; they conversed in soft voices, moved about slowly and importantly, fully conscious of their illnesses. I did my best to look as grave as the occasion demanded and proposed that we all go to the Casino. Duncan already knew from my telegram that Esenin was not coming.

Two bottles of the local waters, "Narzan," were standing chastely on the table. Then a glass of milk was put at Isadora's place, while the rest of us observed a melancholy silence. I was informed that from the very moment of their arrival in Kislovodsk and the start of their cure not a drop of wine had passed the lips of the two Duncans. Having offered the expected apology, I ordered a bottle of white wine. The iced and nicely wiped bottle of sunny Tsinandali brought life to the table, but it only evoked martyred looks from the two ladies. I poured some wine into my glass. Isadora turned away, Irma cleared her throat. Then the ladies exchanged a long look in silence. I raised my glass, drank their health, and refilled it. Isadora heaved a sigh, Irma uttered a short laugh.

"If you agree that milk does not quench the thirst and admit how many of these bottles you have drunk before today, I'll order another bottle and two glasses," I said, draining my glass again.

The admission came at once, the decorative glass of milk was taken away, and the diet list, which had also appeared in honour of my arrival, disappeared from the wall.

A performance by Duncan was announced to take place at the Casino. The performance included the *Sixth Symphony,* the *Slavonic March,* and the *Internationale.*

On the morning of the performance Isadora suddenly took it into her head to visit the castle of "Love and Perfidy."

"You always maintain that no experiments should be made on the day of an important performance," I said, but she refused to listen to me.

"You won't see anything of interest there," I said in a vain attempt to break down her resistance. "The whole romance is in the name. All you'll find there is a not very high cliff with a few ruins and inscriptions of visitors left by those who wished to immortalize their names. Even the Causasian restaurant which used to be there has probably gone out of business."

Isadora told me that on visiting the dungeons of the Castle of Chillon she found among the thousands of names Byron's signature (a forgery, by the way). However, when Duncan got stubborn about anything it was difficult to get the better of her. I tried a last argument.

"It's all very well for you and Irma. You sit comfortably on the soft seats of the carriage, while I have to make do on the collapsible seat and feel the driver brushing against my bald head. I shouldn't mind going on horseback, but I haven't brought any leggings."

"Take Afanasyev's topboots," Isadora said, glad to have got the better of the argument.

I hired a carriage, put my two ladies into it, and made up my mind to get a saddle-horse.

"Why go galloping for ten miles in the heat?" I thought to myself. "I'll get a horse with a cossack saddle in which I can sit as in a chair."

"Give me that chestnut mare," I said.

The guide brought out a fine stallion and held out a riding crop to me.

I refused to take it, but he kept insisting.

"I expect it must be a restive horse," I said to myself and, prompting it with my heels, gave it a tap with the crop. It jogged obediently along Topolev Avenue, but for some reason kept turning its head round as though to look for something. I decided to overtake the carriage and (against all the rules on a stony road) changed to a full gallop. My horse moved off willingly enough, but even at a

152

The playbill of Isadora's last performance, in Paris, 1927　▶

Vendredi 8 Juillet 1927, à 15 heures
UNIQUE RÉCITAL

ISADORA DUNCAN

Avec le concours de

l'Orchestre des CONCERTS PASDELOUP

sous la direction de M.

Albert WOLFF

AU PROGRAMME

Symphonie inachevée	*Schubert*
Ave Maria ..	—
Marche de l'Or du Rhin	*Richard Wagner*
Marche de Siegfried	—
Prélude et Mort d'Yseult	—

PRIX DES PLACES (*Location et timbres en sus*)

VENTE DES BILLETS AU THÉATRE MOGADOR

Isadora—drawing by Leon Bakst

Three sketches by Leon Bakst of Isadora dancing *La Marseillaise*

Isadora: by Bakst

by Olaf Gulbransson
in *Simplizissimus*

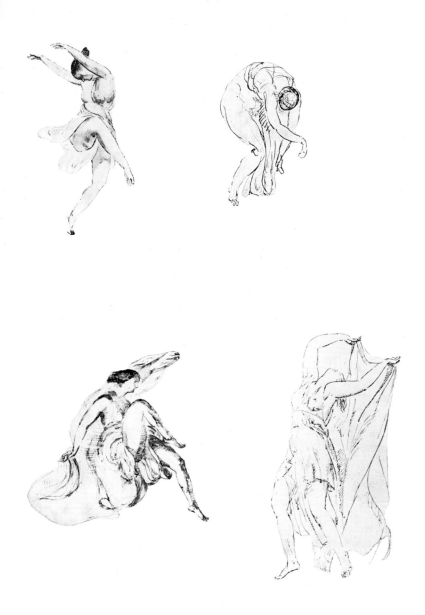

Four impressions of Isadora by the artist José Clara

Esenin and his mother Tatiana, Moscow, 1925

Room No. 5 in the Hotel Angleterre, Petrograd, photographed shortly after Esenin committed suicide there on December 28, 1925

◀ Sergei Esenin in 1924

gallop it kept turning its head and, at the crossroads, paved with large flagstones, it suddenly turned right. As I learned later, it was used to taking excursionists on a trip accompanied by a whole herd of horses and, feeling lonely, it was now looking round for its friends; not finding them, it went back at a gallop. But it slipped on the flagstones and fell, pinning down my right leg. I regained consciousness in the doctor's consulting room. The doctor diagnosed internal bleeding and a cracked bone in my foot.

My foot swelled up, it was extremely painful, and there could be no question of any work. And yet the stage had to be prepared, the lighting had to be organized for the performance, and, during the whole of this complicated business, careful instructions had to be given for the raising and lowering of the curtain. Even more important, I was supposed to make the introductory address.

I sent Soedich to see what he could do about getting the stage ready and, having done all he could, he came back with the news that there was something wrong with the lighting. Isadora kept cursing both "love" and "perfidy." The doctor applied a compress to my foot. Soedich got a wheel chair from somewhere, Isadora placed her velvet cushion under my foot, and I was carried in the chair straight onto the stage. Everything was done there and then, but I had to give up the idea of making my introductory speech.

Duncan was ready, the auditorium was packed. I was wheeling myself round the stage, giving the final instructions, when a little man in a black leather jacket and carrying a briefcase made a sudden appearance.

"Who is Duncan's manager here?" he said in a loud voice, stopping at the curtain.

I wheeled myself up to him.

"The *Slavonic March* is not to be performed today," he said. To my perplexed question, he showed me the warrant of the Secret Political Police (Cheka). "You collected half of Kislovodsk this morning to listen to your orchestra in the Lower Park. They played 'God Save the Tsar' at their rehearsal."

He demanded that the *Slavonic March* be removed from the programme. When told that Duncan had danced the march at a performance at the Moscow Bolshoi Theatre in the presence of the government on November 7th, it made no impression on him. I showed him a brochure issued in Moscow in which it was stated

◄ Esenin's tomb in the Vagankovsky cemetery, Moscow

that, however paradoxical it might sound, the old Tsarist anthem in the *Slavonic March* sounded revolutionary.

"Moscow's one thing, here's another," he said. "Cut it out!"

"I'm not Tchaikovsky," I replied. "No conductor would agree to make such cuts in the score of a symphonic orchestra ten minutes before the beginning of the performance."

"I will not permit the Tsarist anthem to be played here!" he repeated again.

I proposed that he should invite Duncan and the conductor to come out on the stage and inform the audience that they would try to make cuts in the *Slavonic March* if that were possible.

"If you make such an announcement, I shall arrest you on the spot," the commissar declared heatedly.

At that moment Duncan came up to me.

"What's going on here?" she asked.

I told her. She pushed me away and went out in front of the curtain to the footlights.

"Comrades," she said, "who'll interpret for me? In English, German, French?"

Someone in the front rows offered to be her interpreter, but she went on in her broken Russian.

"Comrades, I've just arrived from America. I danced the *Internationale* in New York a dozen times and every time the police appeared. Now I'm here again. Soviet Russia! But on the stage again—police!"

There was a murmur of astonishment in the auditorium, people began talking, moving about. In the reserved box a man in a tunic arose.

"Comrade Duncan," he said, "don't worry. I am the president of the Piatigorsk Executive Committee and I shall find out at once what's the trouble."

He quickly walked onto the stage. The commissar saluted and explained the position.

"Stop interfering!" the president of the Executive Committee ordered. "Let's get off the stage."

Returning to his box, he addressed Duncan, who was still standing in front of the curtain.

"Comrade Duncan," he said, "please, carry on with your performance."

Duncan disappeared in the folds of the curtain and the lights in

the auditorium went out at once. The bassoons rumbled, the first
movement of the *Sixth Symphony* began. Duncan danced in an
atmosphere of the greatest enthusiasm. After the *Slavonic March*
the audience gave her such an ovation that we could not proceed
with the programme for a long time.

Fortunately, there was no performance on the following day.
Isadora and Irma went for a walk in the Upper Park.

Under my pillow lay a huge heap of money: the takings of last
night's performance. For that reason I asked the porter to lock my
door on the outside and take the key with him. An hour later there
was a loud knock on the door.

"Who's there?" I asked.

"Open up!"

"I can't get out of my bed and I haven't the key. Who is it?"

"It's someone from the police department," said the hotel
manager, whose voice I recognized.

"Get the key from the porter."

A few minutes later the key was turned in the keyhole and in
came the commissar of the Transcaucasian Secret Police whom I
had already met, accompanied by two Red Army men with rifles
and the manager of the Grand Hotel.

The commissar showed me a search warrant and an order for my
arrest. On my desk lay a long telegram that I had had no time to
send addressed to: Lunacharsky, People's Commissar of Education, Chicherin, People's Commissar of Foreign Affairs, and Krasin,
People's Commissar of Foreign Trade. In the telegram I reported to
the three commissars, who were directly responsible for Duncan's
invitation to Soviet Russia and her residence and work there, last
night's incident at the Kursal.

The Cheka commissar put the telegram in his briefcase and told
me to dress.

"You can take away my telegram," I said. "I can write another.
But if you want to take me away, you'll have to get a stretcher. I
can't dress, but I can pull a blanket over myself. Will you," I
addressed the hotel manager, "go to the Upper Park, please, and
fetch Isadora Duncan. Her things are here and you must search the
room in her presence."

The manager ran out of the room and returned immediately with
Duncan and Irma, whom he had met on the stairs.

When I told her what had happened, she turned round angrily

and, saying to me: "I'll write at once!" went towards the door. The commissar signalled to the sentry, who barred her way with his rifle.

Turning to the commissar, pale with anger, she shouted at him in her broken Russian:

"*Shvolich:* [*Svoloch*—dirty swine!]" and, pushing aside the sentry, went out of the room and told the hotel manager to follow her.

"What's the matter with her? Calling me names?" the commissar asked me, taken aback.

"Why, no, it's something in English," I replied, trying to calm him, but feeling rather upset myself by Isadora's lack of control.

The commissar sat down at the table, quickly wrote something, and asked me to sign an undertaking not to leave the hotel. I signed it without altering a word, after which they all left my room.

Isadora returned late. It seemed that in spite of the late hour she had taken it into her head to pay a visit to the local authorities to protest against the action of the Secret Police.

We had only just turned in when, at five o'clock in the morning, there was again a knock at my door. A man in a leather jacket came in and introduced himself as the president of the Kislovodsk Executive Committee. He came to offer his apologies.

We did not fall asleep till six o'clock. In the morning I sent off a telegram and a report on the incident about the *Slavonic March,* which was soon published in the Moscow stage journal, the *Worker-Spectator.*

Isadora asked me whether she could give a performance where the Russian poet Lermontov was killed. I realized that Esenin must have spoken to her about Lermontov. Duncan, who had read many works of Russian classical prose writers, knew very little about Russian poetry.

At her appearances at Mineralnye Vody, Duncan performed the *Sixth Symphony,* but in Piatigorsk she changed her programme and told me that she would dance Schubert's *Unfinished Symphony.* Isadora did not give her reasons for the change, but on the day of her performance in Piatigorsk she was very sad. She told me she was sorry not to have been able to visit the place of Lermontov's duel, kept asking me about Lermontov, and also talked a lot about Esenin. She danced the *Unfinished Symphony,* which I saw then for the first time, with great feeling and was quite extraordinarily lyrical.

I told her about Lermontov's poem of the novice—*Mtsyri*—and promised her that when we were in Tiflis I would take her to ancient *Mtskhet*, at the confluence of the rivers Kura and Aragva, at the foot of the mountain on top of which can be seen the ancient "monastery of Mtsyri."

The next stopping place on our itinerary was Baku but before describing our journey there I should like to make a small digression.

In his reminiscences about Sergei Esenin, published in 1928, Vasily Kachalov, the famous Moscow Art Theatre actor, writes that during his first meetings with the poet in Moscow in the spring of 1925, Esenin told him about "his journey to Teheran." In the summer of the same year Kachalov met Esenin in Baku and was told that he (Esenin) was "about to fly to Teheran." Finally, meeting the poet again in Moscow later that summer, Kachalov was told that "he had flown" to Teheran and "returned to Moscow." The words "he had flown" Kachalov put in quotation marks. Why? Because he obviously had some doubts about it.

Esenin had never been to Persia. In Baku, it is true, he did all he could to obtain permission to fly there, but Sergei Kirov, who was at the head of the Azerbaijan's Central Committee, dissuaded him. It is said that Kirov told him that in Europe he had had an intimate friend with him while in Persia he had no one, and in that connection he mentioned Griboyedov's tragic death in Persia.[1]

And yet Esenin had quite a good idea of Persia not only from what he was told by a friend who had worked at the Russian embassy in Teheran, but also from the personal impressions he had received with Isadora's participation.

Isadora liked Baku very much but, stimulated by Esenin's constant desire to go to Persia, she always wanted to see more and more exotic places. I gladly satisfied her wish by taking her in a cab to the village of Shikhov which was, of course, in no way different from the same kind of village over the border in Persian Azerbaijan. Isadora liked that village so much that she dragged me there every day.

In the heat of the day such a journey was far from pleasant. We had to trail along in a cab past the bare Tyurksk cemeteries buried

---

[1]Alexander Griboyedov, author of the famous comedy *The Misfortune of Being Clever*, and Russian ambassador to Persia, was assassinated by a mob in Teheran on January 30, 1829.

in scorching sand, but Isadora simply adored the sight of houses without windows, narrow lanes, and the unusual silence of what seemed to be a totally deserted "Persian" village.

More often than not it was just the two of us who drove there, for Irma was not particularly keen on the journey. Sometimes, on the way to the village, we went down to the sea and, buying a watermelon from an old fisherman, settled on the beach, broke the melon on a stone, and enjoyed eating it.

Back in Moscow, we told Esenin about our trips to the "Persian" village. Living later in Baku, Esenin remembered our stories and quite likely made several visits to the village of Shikhov.

The windows of the Baku wineshops and greengrocers' shops were full of bottles of brandy and the local grape vodka. I have already mentioned that Isadora never went on stage without first drinking a glass of champagne. There was no champagne in Baku, and she had a small glass of the dark and very strong Caucasian brandy instead. After the first performance of the *Sixth Symphony* we announced Duncan's appearance in a Wagner programme, which began with *Isolde's Death*. Having adjusted her cloak, I gave the signal and the curtains slowly rose to the sound of Wagner's music.

Duncan lay on the rug. In another moment she would start rising slowly. The poignant music of *Isolde* filled the auditorium. Duncan was still lying on the rug. But there was nothing unusual about that: she never repeated herself. However, it went on a little too long. Too many bars of the music had been played. I was beginning to feel alarmed. I called Duncan softly. She did not stir. I glanced at the conductor: he looked puzzled and worried. After calling to Duncan again, I signalled for the curtain to be lowered slowly and went up to Isadora. I touched her on the shoulder and heard her breathing quietly. She was asleep. Pulling off her cloak I raised her. She opened her eyes and gazed serenely at me. Then, raising her hand to her forehead, she asked:

"What's the matter with me?"

"Are you ill or have you fallen asleep?" I asked.

"I don't know. What was I given to drink? It was like fire. I was stupefied and I don't remember how I got on to the stage...."

"Will you be able to dance or shall we cancel the performance?"

"No, no! I'm going to dance. Tell the conductor. Let him start *Isolde* again."

The performance went on.

It seems that Soedich had been in a hurry and, grabbing a large glass of spirits, had given it to Isadora without telling her what it was.

Fortunately, the audience did not notice anything, believing that all was as it should be and that the long musical interlude and the motionless Duncan was a prelude to *Isolde's Death*.

Baku had an excellent symphony orchestra, which had allowed Duncan to include a Wagner programme in her performances. This was usually impossible because most Russian orchestras did not have a sufficient number of French horns to play the *Ride of the Valkyrie*. Delighted by the playing of the Baku orchestra, Duncan insisted that all her performances should be given with its participation.

In addition to Wagner, Duncan danced the *Sixth Symphony*, the *Slavonic March,* and the *Internationale*.

Isadora gave a performance in the workers' club at the Balakhany oil wells. The working class audience gave her a terrific reception: it can be stated without fear of contradiction that it was a triumph for symphonic music, a triumph for Duncan.

The local organizations, learning from the papers and from my introductory address about the Duncan school in Moscow, raised the question of founding a branch of the school in Baku. Captivated by the sun of Transcaucasia, its people and its music, Duncan found that Baku possessed the right climate for her school: its pupils could dance out of doors. Naturally there could be no question of transferring her Moscow school to Baku, and we did not have enough instructors to open a branch. She proposed to select a number of gifted children of oil-well workers for admission to the Moscow school with a view to training them as instructors for the future Baku school. With that idea in mind, a children's matinée was announced including the "test" I described earlier as well as dances to the music of Schubert, Schuman, and Chopin.

Irma fell ill and Isadora and myself left for Balakhany accompanied by a pianist and a violinist. Duncan conducted the "test" excellently and selected twelve children. Before the second part of the matinée, she came up to me.

"What am I to do?" she asked. "You see, many of the dances should really be performed by Irma. I have not danced them for many years. They are the dances of my youth."

"Well, give me the chance to see what I have never seen," I implored her.

"All right. I'll dance everything I can before the children. But some of the dances will be for you only."

I now saw for the first time many waltzes and écossaises of Schubert, waltzes and mazurkas of Chopin, which Duncan had not danced for a long time. I was particularly impressed by one Chopin marzurka, often played by pianists at concerts and therefore well known to many people. Now I suddenly saw that mazurka in quite a new light, in so clear a form that I involuntarily repeated to myself: "Music that can be seen!" It was a kind of supernatural synchronization of musical sounds, thought, and movement.

A kind of cloud ran over Isadora's face and I had a feeling that everything around had grown dark. Why, of course, the girl had entered a dark forest. Here's the tree she nearly stumbled against. I could see the tall, spreading, silent tree with branches—hands flying upwards. The girl tried to shake off the panic that had suddenly got hold of her. She was successful and, humming a tune, she joyfully rushed towards the light and once again ran against a tree standing silently in her way, a still higher, more enigmatic, more terrible tree. It was getting darker and darker. The girl now had to retreat more often before the gloomy trees. A last effort, a last timid and feeble attempt to break through the implacable tree-trunks that barred her way on all sides... The music suddenly stopped.

The end of the mazurka? No! An anguished pause. The girl's eyes widened. The darkness grew denser. The music began again... But what eerie music! What was that? The last chord came crashing down like a clap of thunder from the dark sky... The girl fell to the ground like a blade of cut grass.

Of course, in composing that mazurka Chopin did not see that forest, not that girl. Duncan again created, as in Tchaikovsky's *Sixth Symphony*, a parallel image.

Her art of the dance, the beautiful naturalness of movements, their inconceivable lightness and expressiveness—Duncan knew how to transmit it all to her pupils as though her own blood ran in the veins of some of them. She came to life in the movements of her pupils, in the turns of their heads, in the forceful movements of their outstretched arms, in the characteristic way in which they threw out their knees to create a single supple line from the leg to the torso and from the forearm to the hand. Again and again we saw a resurgent Isadora before us.

But such dances as Chopin's mazurka were unrepeatable. It was beautifully danced afterwards by Irma and some of the more talented pupils of the Moscow school, but they could not rise to the heights of Duncan's expressiveness in this miniature. Only one of Isadora's pupils, the young Tamara Lobabovskaya, with her extraordinarily inspired, beautiful face, could at moments create the image of the girl conceived by Duncan.

We went to Tiflis. In the corridor of our compartment, with its soft seats, a man stopped me.

"Is it true," he asked, raising his voice to drown the noise of the train, "that Isadora Duncan is travelling in this compartment? I have a letter for her from Esenin."

"Oh?"

"Hearing by chance that I was going to the Caucasus, he wrote the letter and asked me to hand it to her, saying, 'Duncan is somewhere in the Caucasus.'"

That was just like Esenin.

In the letter, Esenin wrote everything he had told me in Moscow before my departure, and he concluded it by promising to go to the Crimea if Isadora intended to go there. Duncan examined the letter closely for some time. It was written in Esenin's peculiar handwriting.

"The Crimea?"

In the evening she again repeated the question: "The Crimea?" and added: "Why did he stay in Moscow? There won't be any journal!"

But the word "Crimea" stuck in her mind and emerged unexpectedly, introducing a sudden change in our itinerary.

She got out Esenin's letter and gazed for a long time at its lines.

"Dear Isadora,

I am very busy with publishing matters and cannot come. I often remember you with all my gratitude to you. From Prechistenka I moved first to Kolobova and now I have moved again to another apartment which Marienhof and I are buying.

My affairs are excellent.

I never expected a great deal

I am given a lot of money for my publishing business.

I wish you success and health and less drinking.
Regards to Ilya Ilyich.
Love, S. Esenin.
29.VIII. Moscow."

Unfortunately, nothing came of it all. Esenin took the collapse of his plans very much to heart. He certainly seemed to have counted on his journal. All this had a great effect on his mental condition. From that summer, spent in sweltering, deserted Moscow, Esenin somehow visibly went to pieces.

After businesslike Baku, Tiflis seemed idle, smart, exhausted by the sun, the abundance of fruits, wines, and gaudy women. Duncan was entranced. She was enchanted by Georgia. On leaving the Hotel Orient, in which rooms had been booked for us, we went down the hill past a majestic ancient church which pierced the sky with its sharp steeple. A thin veil of smoke smelling of roast mutton floated in the air. From the cool cellars of the Caucasian restaurants issued a breath of wine and the spicy smell of herbs. Huge goat-milk cheeses lay in yellow-white rounds next to the paper-light cheese-cakes; crimson tomatoes blazed and burst open from an excess of ripeness; heaps of long cucumbers showed up green next to the white hillocks of ears of corn; purple eggplants, hideously fat yellow melons, bright green arrows of gigantic onions, mountains of figs cracked with sweetness, grapes of every colour, black swelling plums, huge bunches of flowers, pyramids of bronze pears and red apples, gigantic striped watermelons and golden mouth-watering quinces... Hollow sounds of native drums, zithers, and other national instruments, the uneven hum of guttural voices, the noise of dice falling on to the street and the silent players surrounded by excited crowds of onlookers... It was the Maydan, the Tiflis street market.

Suddenly Duncan noticed transparent silk shawls, swelling like sails—amber, purple, sky-blue and pale pink. White crests of spray seemed to run over them....

Duncan moved along slowly through the crowd towards the airy silks with wide-open eyes.

"Is it possible?" she was saying, without taking her rapt eyes off the shawls. "Have I at last found what I have been constantly dreaming of? All the silks of Europe and America are nothing compared with this miracle!"

Taking a golden shawl in her hands, she waved it over her head.

"*Sie flattert! Sie flattert!* [It flutters! It flutters!] Such a material follows my every movement! It lives and breathes!"

Next day the Council of People's Commissars of Georgia, which had its quarters in Tiflis, gave a banquet in honour of Isadora Duncan. Earlier that day, Isadora, smiling enigmatically, asked Irma and me to come to her room and, arming herself with a pair of scissors, walked up to the pile of Caucasian silks.

"Would you like to see me make two evening dresses with the help of scissors and without a needle and thread?"

Choosing a golden-yellow shawl, she folded it in two, made a cut for the head, two more cuts down the side, and threw it over Irma. Pulling the two parallel ends through the side slits, she tied them in a wide knot and let the shawl fall down the back in the shape of a light cloak.

A few more minutes—and another evening dress for herself.

"We shall wear these dresses this evening at the banquet," declared Isadora.

The "evening dresses" were very effective, elegant and modest, leaving only the arms and the neck bare. I was a bit in doubt about the two side slits without any stitches, but they seemed to be tightly closed by the shawl's wide ends which crossed each other on the inside.

The dresses made a great impression. The Tiflis ladies were enraptured by the originality and beauty of the "Parisian *toilettes*."

Duncan let the fashion-hungry women have a good look at "the latest Paris models," but at the banquet she could not help making a speech.

"These dresses you admire so much," she said, "have been bought in your Maydan and I made them today with the help of only a pair of scissors. You do not value the beauty which is right in front of you, and you are all trying to keep up with the Paris fashions which would look ridiculous in this country of hot sun, beautiful fruits and flowers, and quite incredible vegetables. Have a good look round you and you will see things that till now have been hidden from your beautiful eyes. I drink to your beautiful country."

The ladies were disconcerted. They did, nevertheless, jump up from their seats and almost undress Isadora and Irma in their eagerness to inspect the new "fashion."

One day we went up to the top of Ptatsminda in the little carriage of the funicular railway. Tiflis spread out in a huge hollow at the foot of the mountain.

The steel cable drew the little carriage up the sheer mountainside past the monastery of St. David. I pointed out to Isadora the monuments which showed up white among the dense foliage.

"What's that one?" she asked.

"That's Griboyedov's tomb. . . ."

Duncan knew practically nothing about Griboyedov. She had read a great deal of Dostoevsky and Leo Tolstoy, she knew about Gogol, Pushkin, Chekhov. I told her about Griboyedov.

From the window we could not see the marble figure of a woman bending down at the foot of the cross of Griboyedov's tomb. Isadora was deeply moved when I told her of Griboyedov's young wife, Nina Chavchavadze, and the well-known inscription on Griboyedov's grave: "Your mind and your work are engraved in Russian memory. But why did my love survive you?"

"What a woman!" Duncan repeated softly a few times.

We did not stay long at the top, where no park had yet been laid out. After admiring the panorama of Tiflis, Isadora went back to the funicular and sat down at the window on the left. During the descent she kept looking at Griboyedov's grave.

The Soviet of People's Commissars organized a trip for Duncan to the ancient Georgian capital of Mtskhet, founded more than three thousand years ago.

In Mtskhet we paid a visit to the remarkable cathedral of Sveti Tskhoveli with its crypt of Georgian kings and the stone font in which, according to tradition, St. Nina was baptized. We came out chilled to the marrow by the cold stone walls and flagging. The sun blinded us with its light and scorched us with its current of hot air. We went down to the confluence of the Aragva and the Kura. From below we could see a monastery. "Mtsyri," I said, pointing to the monastery.

Without paying attention to the heat and fatigue, Isadora dragged us up the incredibly high stony and sandy hill of "the monastery of Mtsyri." She wanted to get there at all costs. We stopped at the last steps, hewn out of the sandstone, and I recited the lines from Lermontov's famous poem about the greybeard, "the half-alive custodian of the ruins" who swept the dust from the tombstones.

I had barely finished my recital when the heavy door of the

monastery was opened with a creaking noise and on the threshold appeared a grey, half-alive, decrepit and wizened old man—a monk. That was so unexpected in ruins which seemed to have been forgotten by God and men that Isadora, Irma, and I uttered a cry of astonishment. But the old man invited us affably to come into the cool semi-darkness of the church. We went in willingly in the hope of getting a drink of cold water.

The old man brought us some ice-cold water in a tin mug and we drank it avidly, wondering where such cold water could have come from, but we were later told that it came from a spring which flowed under the church flagstones. We were also told that the old monk, who lived in seclusion in the monastery ruins on top of the mountain, was provided with food by the inhabitants of Mtskhet.

When we got into our car in Mtskhet we noticed two tall trees with immense trunks. We were told that, according to tradition, about two thousand years ago pilgrims who had walked from Mtskhet to Jerusalem brought back with them Christ's bloodstained shirt, buried it at that spot, and planted two trees they had brought from Golgotha.

Duncan's performances were received enthusiastically by the effusive and musical Georgian audiences. Their enthusiasm could be perceived immediately in the theatre and particularly from the way the *Slavonic March* and the *Internationale* were received. The performances had to be extended. The older pupils of the Tiflis "plastic studio" were especially frantic in their applause. The director of the studio, the husband of its chief instructress, paid several visits to the Hotel Orient to invite Duncan to go to the studio, but Isadora declined on various pretexts. The "plastic" schools and studios had greatly multiplied in Russia long before the revolution. They adopted from Duncan only the "bare feet," chitons and tunics, "serious" music, carpets and curtains, but forgot the main thing—naturalness of movement, simplicity, and expressiveness, exchanging them for sugariness, affectation, and false pathos. It is natural that Duncan should have repudiated such "followers." She believed that body, gesture, and movement could express with great force the whole depth and variety of human emotions and experiences. Her light costume and bare feet had their profound reason. She used to say: "To hide your body, which is the primary material of the dance, just as paints are in painting and marble in sculpture, is the same as destroying all the expressive possibilities of paints and marble. . . ."

Someone wrote about her: "Like a girl of ancient Greece, she threw something over herself because of the coolness of the morning but later, after the sun had risen and it got warmer, she forgot about her cloak and danced as though it did not exist. . . ."

But what was only a means to an end for Duncan became the end in itself, not only to the Russian "plastic" schools and studios (which have, luckily, almost disappeared today), but also in Europe and especially in America.

The director of the Tiflis "studio of plastic dance" kept worrying me so much with his requests to pay them a visit that in the end I persuaded Isadora to go. We were met by the instructress, invited guests, and the girl pupils in the vestibule. The pupils presented Isadora with a huge bouquet of white roses, not forgetting to curtsey first. We were given seats in the front row. The very tall and almost naked pupils came out on the platform and arranged themselves in chessboard-order. The show began with Sibelius's *Valse Triste*. After the first movements, which had no inner connection with Sibelius's sad music, Isadora nudged me with her elbow:

"Warum? [Why?]"

A little later she nudged me again, more strongly this time, and repeated the question more loudly:

"Warum?"

I began to say something quietly to her in an attempt to avoid a scene, for by now I knew Isadora very well. But immediately the same question was repeated, this time in a loud voice that could be heard all over the hall:

"Warum?"

She rose from her seat and, repeating her question once more, turned to the instructress and the public:

"Why are you torturing these poor girls?" she said angrily and sadly. "What are you teaching them? What do these mechanical and impassive movements say to you? They fail to express not only the music, but anything at all. What I have just seen makes me feel extremely sad."

She went up to the stage and placed her bouquet of white roses at the feet of one of the pupils.

"I place these flowers on the grave of my hopes," said Isadora, and went to the exit.

A storm arose. The spectators jumped up from their seats. Isadora and Irma went out into the vestibule. They were followed by loud booing. I could hardly stop the crowd from rushing out after them.

"You've just greeted Isadora Duncan with such loud applause and now you are seeing her off with boos because she has remained true to her principles and convictions for which you extended your greetings to her."

This somewhat cooled their ardour. Isadora and Irma had time to get into the car that had been waiting for them. The director of the school joined them. After we had said goodbye to him and apologized for the unpleasant scene (I can imagine the sort of "dynamic" scene he had later with his "plastic" wife), Irma said:

"I knew it would end like that."

"Then why didn't you tell me earlier?" I asked indignantly.

"But you all insisted so much . . ." she said with a smile.

Isadora was silent, deep in thought and looking extremely sad.

XVII

From Tiflis we left for Batum, with its deep-blue sea and dense foliage of majestic palms. At the station cars were waiting for us.

"Where would you prefer to stay—in town or at the villa 'Green Cape'?" we were asked.

Without giving it another thought Duncan chose the suburban villa. The cars drove along a narrow road overlooking the sea at the very edge of precipices and abysses.

The villa "Green Cape" stood on the edge of a high cliff. Brick and clay steps led to a small shashlyk restaurant clinging to the cliff far below. Shashlyks were roasted there in the open air and the smell of roast mutton drifted up to us. Palms, cypresses, and magnolias drooped in the unbearably hot sunshine.

"The tropics," said Isadora. "How wonderful it is here! What could we have done in this heat in a stifling city?"

But at night we had a tropical downpour of rain, and we were imprisoned. The rain washed away the roads and cut us off from the city. The little food we had taken with us for the journey had been left by chance and was now quickly eaten, but we were still starving. Whetting our appetite still more, gusts of wind brought the smell of roast mutton from below, but we could not possibly get there. At last I plucked up courage and decided to walk down the slippery clay steps to the little restaurant. From a window Isadora and Irma watched me with alarm as I clumsily jumped down the steep steps and risked breaking my neck. But I returned to them in triumph bearing the shashlyk, by now cold and congealed, which was immediately devoured. In the evening we were shivering with cold and hunger. Isadora gazed wistfully at the wet, bleak cypresses standing erect in front of our windows like sombre and implacable sentinels. "I hate them," she said. "They are trees of the dead." Then she smiled slyly and whispered mysteriously to me: "Don't tell anyone that, but nature—nature is terrible!"

In the morning the rain stopped. The merciless Batum sun instantly dried the ground and a car came to take us to the city. Duncan, frightened by the tropical downpour, did not want to go back with us and decided to stay in a small room in a hotel. But Irma and I made up our minds to go back to the "Green Cape" after the performance.

That day the Black Sea Squadron arrived in Batum. All the sailors were invited to Duncan's performance. Duncan, electrified by the stormy reception given by the Black Sea sailors to the *Slavonic March,* asked the audience to sing revolutionary songs. She still remembered the singing of the *Aurora* sailors at her performance in Petrograd.

The audience began to sing. After Duncan had asked them to sing *You Fell Victims,* she came up to me and whispered that she wanted me to go into the prompter's box and when the song started to translate the words to her because she wanted to dance this funeral song. I went down into the prompter's box and when the song started began to cue her. She interpreted the words of the song wonderfully, and at times I could not help being amazed at the way she expressed the text in movements.

When the funeral song came to an end, the audience literally roared its approval, everyone rose, shouting and applauding loudly. At last Isadora went off the stage.

"Some moments were quite remarkable," I said to her. "You found such exact and completely new movements for interpreting the text!"

"I did not hear a single word," Isadora replied, looking embarrassed.

After the performance we were invited to a banquet. At the table our hosts kept filling Isadora's glass. Irma and I watched this procedure with mounting apprehension. Knowing only too well how strained were Isadora's nerves after the performance and the exciting reception given her by the sailors, we expected some escapade from her. At first she confined herself to a short and venomous speech addressed to us. Then she declared that she did not intend to go anywhere. We spent a whole hour trying to persuade her to come with us and at last Irma and I went out to our waiting car. A moment later I went back to Isadora in a last attempt to persuade her to go back to her hotel. We saw her walking away towards the hotel but, as we learned afterwards, she did not want to go back to her airless room and walked about the streets of Batum all night in the company of one of the guests, who aroused the whole town by firing his revolver on the boulevard in her honour.

At last the day of our departure arrived. Before that I sent off Soedich to organize Duncan's tour through Novorossiysk, Krasnodar, and Rostov-on-Don, whence we had to return straight to Moscow. We ourselves were to travel from Batum to Novorossiysk on board the small steamer *Ignati Sergeyev*. At the harbour I was surprised by the appearance of two large baskets, filled to the top with bottles of brandy and grape vodka. The baskets were delivered at the order of Isadora, who explained that we were leaving for Russia where "prohibition" was the law and that was why we had to get a good supply of wine in the Caucasus where it was freely sold.

On embarking, Isadora was interested to find out where the boat was bound for. When I told her that it was bound for the Crimea via Odessa, she declared categorically that she would remain on board until we reached the Crimea.

"The Crimea!" she kept repeating and explained joyfully that the Crimea had always been the dream of her life and if the boat actually sailed for the Crimea it would be stupid and inexcusable not to go there. However much I tried to make it clear to her that the performances in Novorossiysk and Krasnodar had already been announced, she refused to give up her idea of going to the Crimea first.

"Besides," she said, "Esenin wrote to me that he would come if I went to the Crimea!"

This brought our talk to an end, for I realized how hopeless it was to argue with her if she was hoping to see Esenin again.

The three of us were given a separate four-berth cabin. Afanasyev got a berth for himself not far from us. When the *Ignati Sergeyev* got into the swell which was normal near those coasts, the boat began to pitch and roll. Irma and I suffered all night from sea-sickness and lay in the cabin listening to the tinkling of the bottles and the glasses in the hands of Isadora and Afanasyev, who were busy emptying their baskets and talking unceasingly, although Afanasyev did not know any foreign language and Isadora did not speak Russian.

In the distance we sighted the bluish mountains of the Crimea, the little white houses of Yalta spread along the seashore and the narrow strip of Yalta's black pier. A tiresome autumn drizzle, caught up by gusts of cold wind, rained from a grey sky.

"Who ever heard of going to the Crimea in October?" I asked Isadora in a rage, but she showed no signs of contrition, assuring me that the weather was bound to improve, that Esenin would come, and that the performances could be cancelled.

I sent a telegram to cancel the performances. I also telegraphed the school that we were detained in Yalta. I sent a similar telegram to Esenin in Isadora's name.

Next day the rain and cold continued. In the evening, after a dinner in a floating restaurant, we returned to our hotel, cold and wet. The porter handed two telegrams to me. One was addressed to Isadora Duncan. I opened it. It said: "Don't send any more letters and telegrams to Esenin. He is with me and will never go back to you. Galina Benislavskaya."

"Where are the telegrams from?" asked Isadora.

"From the school."

"Why two?"

"They were sent one after the other."

Going up the stairs she asked me about the telegrams again.

"Nothing in particular," I replied. "Why are you so interested?"

A little later she came into my room and again asked me about the contents of the telegrams. Her intuition was infallible and the telegrams aroused in her a kind of inexplicable uneasiness.

Next morning there was a change in the weather: it was warm and sunny. Irma and I decided to tell Isadora about the strange telegram signed by a Galina Benislavskaya, whom none of us had ever heard of.

Isadora was crushed by that telegram, but she pretended only to be hurt by it. I told her that I had already telegraphed my deputy in Moscow and asked him whether Esenin knew of the contents of the telegram.

In the afternoon, Isadora and I went for a walk on the sea front. Of all the towns I had happened to visit Yalta was, next to my beloved Moscow, the place I liked most. I knew every corner of every house, every balcony, and every tree on its front. There was a florist's shop which had stood almost across the beach for the last ten years with a softly murmuring little fountain in its shady, cool interior. There was a delicate odour of cut roses. Isadora and I went into the shop and bought the last roses in their glass vases. On leaving the shop, we stopped under a large Japanese mimosa. We talked of royalty. Not too long ago the widow of Alexander III and her daughter, the sister of Nicholas II, lived quite near the place where we were standing. I told Isadora about the widow of Alexander III, about her relationship to the English and German royal houses. She was known as "the evil genius of Russia."

"Your old empress," said Duncan, "occupied such a central position thanks to her origin and blood relationship. But there was a woman who was not of royal birth who reigned for many years by virtue of her personal charm. I mean Hortense Beauharnais, the daughter of Josephine and the stepdaughter of Napoleon I and the wife of his brother Louis Bonaparte, King of Holland. She was the 'lady love' of the Russian Emperor Alexander I and the French King Louis XVIII and, finally, the mother of Prince Louis Napoleon, the future Napoleon III." She was silent for a moment, then said: "On the grave of Hortense, who was buried next to Josephine, her son, who had become emperor by that time, put up a memorial with the inscription: 'To Queen Hortense, her son Napoleon III.'"

It was always interesting to talk to Isadora. This time she talked about all sorts of things, but carefully avoided mentioning Esenin.

After a moment's reflection, Duncan suddenly asked:

"Did Russia ever have Russian queens?"

"Before Peter the Great," I replied, "nearly every queen was Russian, but the later Romanovs married only foreign women."

Isadora went on talking about it. I felt that she was trying hard not to mention the cruel telegram that had given her so much pain.

We walked back to the hotel.

"What do you think?" she asked. "Would there be a reply to your telegram by now?"

"We ought to get one in the evening," I said.

"I read somewhere that a Russian princess became a French queen by marrying Henri I and that since then all French queens took their oath of allegiance in Rheims cathedral by placing a hand on the Bible she had brought from Russia."

"That was Anne, the daughter of the Kiev Prince Yaroslav."

"Are you sure?" asked Isadora and, seeing my puzzled face, added, looking embarrassed: "I'm speaking of the reply to your telegram. Do you think it will arrive this evening?"

The telegram was already waiting for us. It said: "Sergei knows contents of telegram."

Isadora went slowly upstairs. Seeing Irma, she whispered something to her and both leaned over a sheet of paper like a couple of conspirators. Presently Isadora, looking questioningly at me, handed me the telegram they had both composed: "Moscow Esenin Petrovka Bogoslovsky Bakhrushin's house. Received telegram probably from your maidservant Benislavskaya writes not to send any more letters to Bogoslovsky have you changed address please explain by telegram love you very much Isadora."

We received no reply. Indeed we could hardly have received one, for we left for Moscow next day, October 12th.

Many years later, when neither Esenin nor Isadora nor Galina Benislavskaya was alive, I discovered that Esenin did reply to Isadora's telegram. On a sheet of paper he had started to draft his reply in pencil: "I told you in Paris that in Russia I should leave you. You hurt me. I love you but will not live with you. Now I am married and happy. I wish you the same. Esenin." In her diary Benislavskaya wrote that Esenin had given her the telegram to read. He said: "If I am to end it I'd better not mention love, etc." Esenin turned over the page and wrote in a blue pencil: "I love another. I'm married and happy" and signed in large block letters: "Esenin."

He was neither happy nor married. I thought that Isadora never received that telegram because it had never been sent, but the text of the telegram typed out by Esenin had a post office receipt attached to it showing that the telegram had been sent to Yalta on October 13th, and it gave its cost as 439 roubles 50 kopecks.

Who was Galina Benislavskaya? I came across that name a second time long after Duncan, Esenin, and Galina were dead. One winter day I was asked to help in the arrangement of a funeral. I arrived at the Vagankovsky cemetery. In the chapel there was a joint funeral service for over thirty dead. It was stifling inside the chapel and I decided to wait till the end of the service and walked along the paths between the graves. Suddenly I saw an inscription on a white plaque attached to a tall, massive iron cross (the grave was surrounded by the same sort of sombre iron railings): "Sergei Esenin."

I could never force myself to go to that grave, shocked as I was by Esenin's suicide. On the day of his funeral I was in Minsk, where the studio was giving performances, and I could not be present. Now, struck by this coincidence, I rushed up to the grave, fell through a snow drift, and caught hold of the iron railing of the adjacent grave. I could not help noticing that it repeated in a somewhat smaller shape the sombre design of Esenin's grave. On a white plaque I read in block letters the inscription: "Galina Benislavskaya." That girl had loved him devotedly and selflessly. Esenin had met her before he had met Duncan, but never spoke of her. Although on intimate terms with him, she never uttered a word of protest against his marriage or his departure abroad with Duncan. But when Duncan had left for the Caucasus, Esenin went to live in her rooms in Bryusov Lane and even took with him his sisters Katya and Shura. It was then that Galina wrote with his consent her dramatic telegram to Isadora (he told me about it himself afterwards).

During the last year of Esenin's life Galina, who had been working as secretary of the paper *The Poor,* devoted herself entirely to looking after his publications. Esenin never concealed his true feelings for her. While considering Galina one of his best friends, he wrote to her in March 1925: "Dear Galya, you are near to me as a friend, but I never loved you as a woman." Nevertheless, Galina remained with him and continued to take care of him. She left Esenin only after his marriage to S. A. Tolstoy, Leo Tolstoy's granddaughter. Esenin was upset by her departure. He knew that no one would be able to prevent his suicide now. About a year after the poet's death, on December 3, 1926, Galina committed suicide on Esenin's grave, leaving instructions for her burial next to him. She left two notes. One on a postcard: "December 3, 1926. I took my own life here, though I know that after this they will heap even more abuse on Esenin. But that won't make any difference to him or to me any more. In this grave is buried everything I hold dear." Galina must have gone to Esenin's grave during the day. She had a revolver, a Finnish dagger, and a packet of cigarettes. She smoked all the cigarettes and when it grew dark broke off the top of the

packet and wrote on it: "If the dagger is stuck into the grave after
the shot, it means that even then I did not regret it. If I regret what
I am doing, I shall throw it far away." In the darkness she wrote
another line on top of the previous one: "Missed." She fired several
times and only the sixth time did she shoot herself through the
heart.

Isadora's love for Esenin brought much unhappiness into her life.
Her love for him was the symbol of her great, all-embracing love for
Russia. Shortly before her death this love for Russia drew her
passionately to the country where she had hoped to remain to the
end of her life. Perhaps it was because of this that in Paris Isadora
had taken the decision she had told me about on the platform of the
Byelorussky Station in Moscow. Perhaps that was why she had so
unselfiishly agreed to leave for Kislovodsk. And if the arrival of
Esenin that evening at Prechistenka made her hesitate, the cruel
telegram merely aroused in her the feeling of a woman scorned.

Esenin's love for Isadora arose and developed quite differently.
The moment he heard of the arrival of Isadora Duncan in Moscow
he fell in love with her name. After meeting her, the poet gave
himself up entirely to his feelings. Later on a reaction set in. At
first, though, the weak shoots of that feeling imperceptibly grew into
a great, real, and sensual attachment. "Is not sensuality part of a
powerful and real love?" Esenin said to me one day. "Are we
walking on clouds and not on the earth?"

Isadora, enchanted by the natural beauties of the Crimea, went
on long walks, but she was urging me to go back to Moscow. The
telegram of the unknown Galina Benislavskaya hurt and offended
her by its peremptory interference in her relationship with Esenin.
That the telegram should have been sent with Esenin's knowledge
increased her nervousness.

We could not leave for Moscow at once, as she wished to do. We
had to wait for Soedich, who was in trouble. He had gone to arrange
Duncan's performances in Novorossiysk and Krasnodar. In
Novorossiysk he was robbed. After arranging a performance of
Isadora Duncan in Novorossiysk and borrowing some money from
the local concert organization, he left for Krasnodar, hoping for a
large sale of tickets in a city where Isadora was to appear for the
first time. But in Krasnodar he got my telegram: "Cancel
Novorossiysk and Krasnodar leave for Moscow." Having received

my telegram, he did not risk applying to the concert organization and, after figuring out his resources, left his hotel without paying his bill. On what remained of his money he bought a ticket to Novorossiysk and from there took a boat for Yalta. From the boat he sent me a telegram: "Been robbed wait for me."

While we were waiting for Soedich, Isadora kept dragging me off for walks in Yalta and its environs, trying to find some distraction from her painful thoughts by talking to me. To talk to Isadora was always interesting. Now, realizing her state of mind, I tried to distract her with all sorts of subjects. So after talking about Queen Hortense and the Russian empresses, we got to discussing Greece, Venizelos, and Catherine II.

"That's where my school should be!" said Isadora, walking along the Livadiya road. "There the children could dance all year long in the open air and not in the ballrooms of cold Moscow. The climate of Greece predetermined the clothes worn by the ancient Greeks, their drama, their sports festivals, their physical development, and the unsurpassed beauty of their bodies. I believe I told you about the failure of my last visit to Greece when Venizelos was fired by the dream of the renaissance of ancient Greek culture and invited me to be his assistant in that work. When his ministry was defeated, all his plans came to nothing. But the Crimea is a second Greece. Why, the ancient Greeks even had colonies here!"

"There was another woman," I said, "who was inspired by a desire to re-create ancient Greece in the Crimea. It is true, though, there was also a political motive there."

"Who was that?" Isadora asked, becoming suddenly interested.

"While journeying along the Dnieper and through the Crimea, Catherine II was hatching all sorts of secret plans to destroy Turkey and re-create Greece—a Greek empire, for which she already had an emperor in mind, her grandson Konstantin."

Duncan knew, of course, about Catherine II, about her correspondence with Voltaire, about Potemkin. . . .

"And where was the Temple of Diana of Tauris?" asked Isadora.

I myself was interested in that question, having read that Strabo had counted a hundred and fifty Greek stages from modern Sebastopol to the temple.

"When Pushkin rode on horseback from Gurzuf he saw the ruins of the Temple of Diana, about which there was a controversy at the time, and even wrote a poem which, I believe, began with the lines:

"Why these cold doubts,
I believe a great temple was here...."

"I'd love to be there," Isadora said wistfully.

"I'm ashamed to say that, although I have visited the Crimea so many times, I still do not know whether those ruins still exist. Catherine II saw them when she travelled in the Crimea with the Austrian Emperor Joseph II and Potemkin. She drove in her carriage as far as the present-day Baydarsky Gates. There was no road after that. There was only a bridle-path. The road we are walking along now was built by soldiers during the reign of Nicholas I. Catherine saw the Temple of Diana from the sea."

And I told Isadora that Catherine II, sailing in her yacht past the Temple of Diana with her companions, among whom was the old Prince Charles de Ligne, gave the prince the ruins of the temple as a present. The prince at once dived from the yacht into the sea in his silk coat and plumed tricorn. Scrambling out on to the shore, de Ligne went down on one knee and, taking off his hat, greeted the empress as the new owner of the ruins. He was soaked to the skin and the frightened empress sent him her own warm dressing gown, in which the chattering Prince was brought back on board the yacht.

Isadora burst out laughing. Then for some reason she remembered that she had frightened a Greek priest in Greece.

"I always wanted to find out," she said, "how the ancient Greeks managed to dance the ten kilometres during the great festival of the Eleusian Mysteries. One day I got up at five o'clock in the morning after making up my mind to dance that distance myself in a light tunic. I was dancing along the highway when I noticed that I was approaching a Greek priest who was breakfasting at the side of the road. Seeing the dancing and apparently resurrected maenad, the priest looked at me with wide-open, frightened eyes and, flinging his staff on to the grass, hitched up the skirts of his cassock and ran away from me at such a speed that even a maenad could not have overtaken him. He ruined my test, for I could not help stopping and laughing my head off. But that merely quickened his run."

She laughed. I was glad. These conversations took her mind off Galina Benislavskaya's telegram, even though only for a short time.

We left for Simferopol in an open motor car, followed by a small lorry with our luggage and Soedich. Passing Nikitsky Park, Gurzuf, and Alushta, we drove through the pass and, chilled to the marrow, were approaching Simferopol. It was getting dark. We were all silent. We were all in rather low spirits. Suddenly a man jumped out of a vineyard and, raising his hand, stopped our car. He went up to the driver and talked to him for a long time in whispers, glancing at us from time to time. Afanasyev became worried.

"What's the matter?" he shouted, casting a look down the road where our lorry could no longer be seen.

He got no reply. The suspicious individual sat down next to the driver, putting something under his feet. The driver opened the throttle.

Afanasyev tried to explain something to Isadora in whispers and by gestures.

"A bandit?" she asked me, motioning towards our new passenger with her head.

I shrugged my shoulders. Suddenly the suspicious stranger turned to me and asked:

"Tell me, is it true that Isadora Duncan is travelling in this car?"

When I told him that it was, he asked the driver to stop and, producing the suspicious parcel from under his feet, turned to us with a beaming face. It was a bottle of wine and a bunch of pink grapes. He asked us to "celebrate the auspicious meeting." It turned out that he was a student who spent his holidays at his father's house in Simferopol. He was an admirer of the arts and, of course, of Isadora Duncan. The meeting was particularly propitious to us, for we had to leave the only free room at the hotel because of bedbugs, which crawled on the walls and provided a living tapestry to the floral design of the wallpaper. The student proposed that we should spend the night at his father's little house.

At last we left for Moscow, although the Crimean Soviet of People's Commissars, learning of the arrival of Isadora Duncan, wanted to arrange a performance in Simferopol. But Isadora was anxious to get to Moscow as soon as possible.

At one of the railway stations I bought a number of the *Red Niva*, in which a new poem by Esenin was published. When I translated it to Isadora, she cried: "He wrote it for me!"

However much we tried to convince her that the first two lines of the poem:

> "*You are just as ordinary as all of us,*
> *The hundred thousand others in Russia . . .*"

178

showed clearly that it could not possibly refer to her, she insisted obstinately that it did.

That poem, as we soon learned, was dedicated to Miklash-evskaya, an actress of the Kamerny Theatre, a very beautiful woman with whom, it was rumoured, Esenin had fallen in love. Poor Galina Benislavskaya! I was told that Miklashevskaya's name was mentioned in the dedication and that the first fifteen thousand copies of the *Red Niva* had been published with that dedication which for some reason was removed in the subsequent copies of the journal.

XVIII

In Moscow an unexpected and inexplicable change took place in Isadora. In Yalta and on the way to Moscow she had taken her rupture with Esenin very much to heart. In Moscow she shut herself up in her shell, never mentioned Esenin's name, did not attempt to arrange any meeting with him, and outwardly seemed absolutely calm. She devoted herself entirely to her work with the children and seemed to be interested only in the problems of the future of her school. She was making all the necessary preparations for her two performances which were to take place at the Bolshoi Theatre.

Among the new dances Isadora was teaching the children was an Irish jig, a gay dance to the music of Schubert. Duncan herself designed the costumes for the jig. The short tunics were to be bright green and the heads of the little dancers covered with shamrocks.

"In Ireland," Isadora said, "the revolutionary colour is green and not red because the Irish revolutionaries were hanged on trees. The legendary Robin Hood wore a green feather in his hat."

Isadora also introduced the French revolutionary dance—the Carmagnole. Dancing it, the children sang the Carmagnole in French and threw red flowers to the audience. They wore no Phrygian caps (Duncan was against any accessories or decorations), but a light red-blue-and-white scarf was thrown over their shoulders. In addition, she had the idea of creating a cycle of dances on the theme of the Russian revolution which were not, in fact, performed until a year later. Supplemented later with dances from the Irish, French and Chinese revolutions, they were immensely successful in the Soviet Union as well as in France, China, America, and Canada, everywhere, in fact, where the Duncan Moscow studio gave performances.

But the financial situation of the school was, as before, very difficult, and Duncan wrote a letter to Lunacharsky. He asked us to go and see him. We arrived before the appointed time. Lunacharsky was in conference. Suddenly the doors of his office opened and a very stately and rather plump woman came out. She walked proudly and importantly through the reception room to the exit.

"Who's that?" asked Duncan.

"Deputy of the People's Commissar Yakovleva, a 'left communist.' She is in charge of all the financial affairs of the People's Commissariat of Education."

Isadora got up from her chair impetuously. "Come on," she said. "We are wasting our time here. That woman wears a corset. You don't imagine she'd ever agree to finance Isadora Duncan, who abolished corsets all over the world, do you?"

And she forced me to leave.

I had to tell Lunacharsky later the reason why his meeting with Duncan did not take place.

At first he looked a little embarrassed, but then he laughed with amusement.

The theatrical season began. Duncan's first performance was set to the music of Tchaikovsky, and the programme of the second one to the music of Wagner. I ordered, as is the usual custom, a basket of flowers for her. It was the so-called "theatrical" basket, in imitation of a vase with natural flowers and a tall handle. Entering the make-up room before the start of the performance, I saw, next to the official huge basket, a small little flowerpot with one flower sticking out of it. A note was pinned to it. Bending down, I recognized a familiar handwriting: the letters were not close together but were scattered like grains: "From Sergei Esenin."

To offer a small flowerpot on the huge stage of the theatre was quite impossible. Indeed, that is why "theatrical" flower baskets are so imposing. I simply pinned the note from the flowerpot on to the basket.

After the *Sixth Symphony* and the interval, during the performance of the *Slavonic March* I suddenly heard a noise near the stage and, walking up to the door, I saw through the square "peep-hole" two militia men trying to keep out Esenin, who, smiting his chest, explained: "I am Duncan."

Going out at once, I took Esenin by the arm and drew him towards the door.

"Has he come to see you?" asked the militia man.

I nodded and Esenin again smote his chest in a touchingly childish way, looking offended: "I'm Duncan!" And immediately he told me joyfully and with an important air: "Ilya Ilyich, I sent flowers to Isadora."

"I know, I know. But be quiet, please. She's dancing the *Slavonic March*!"

"I want to have a look at Isadora," he said hurriedly.

"Come along, but you must promise me first not to make any signals to Isadora. You know her, don't you? She could do anything! She'll see you on the stage and rush up to you."

"No, no. I'll just look. I sent her flowers, you know."

We stopped at the first wing: he, in front of me, pressed his back against me. I was very fond of him, and at such moments I was glad that he had returned.

Esenin stood still without stirring. Suddenly I heard a loud hissing whisper: "Isado-o-o-ra! Isado-o-o-ra!"

Glancing at his face I saw a pair of shining eyes and pouting lips.

"Isado-o-o ..."

"Sergei Alexandrovich, you promised!"

"I won't, I won't..."

The *Slavonic March* was drawing to an end. Isadora bent down and froze in that position in preparation for the fight to the death. Her head was tossed back, her eyes fixed on the sky where the ominous two-headed bird hovered. The dying sound of the trumpet. The curtain descended, went up again, and descended once more. The audience was roaring. Tears streamed down Isadora's happy face. . . . Suddenly she saw Esenin.

"Oh, darling!" I heard her cry.

Her bare arms embraced his head and he kissed and kissed those arms.

I gave no more signals for the raising of the curtain.

We decided to go and have dinner at Prechistenka.

"But let Katya come with us," Esenin begged.

Seeing Isadora look up suspiciously, he quickly tried to explain in the dialect without any verbs that only the two of them understood: "Sistra! Sistra! Isadora!" and, pressing her wrists, he went on rapturously: "You know? Katya—genius. Same artist as you, as Chaliapin, as Duse!"

"Katya?" I asked in surprise.

"She sings. Ryazan songs! She sings them beautifully. It's a miracle! Isadora, you must hear how Katya sings!"

We left for Prechistenka in a large company: Esenin was excited, happy, but, unfortunately, he drank a lot.

"Sing, Katya!" he demanded.

Katya sang. She had a pleasant, tiny voice. She sang one Russian song, the refrain of which ended with a little shriek.

All applauded. Katya refused to sing any more. Esenin fell silent, brooding and covering his eyes with a hand. Then he filled his glass with wine. Isadora touched his arm and begged him not to drink any more. He jumped up, banged the table with a fist, and walked away. Then his glance fell on the glass cabinet. His bust, carved by Konenkov, stood on top of it. Esenin moved a chair towards the cabinet, climbed on it rather unsteadily, and stretched out his hand for the bust. The chair had a soft seat. Esenin swayed, balanced himself, but pulled at the heavy bust. Pulling it off the cabinet at last, he sank to the floor. Everyone was silent. Esenin looked at each one of us with heavy, darkened eyes. So does the sea darken before a storm. The storm broke and ended with the loud slamming of the door. Esenin disappeared with Konenkov's wonderful bust under his arm.

We were all stunned. I rushed out after him. The corridor was empty. I went down to the cold entrance hall. There was no one there. The front door was locked.

Walking along the ground floor corridor, I looked into the children's dining room. One window was open. So Esenin must have stepped out of it straight on to the Prechistenka sidewalk. Some time later I asked him what he had done with his bust. He replied that he must have lost it, but he could not remember where.

Twenty-five years later, during a chance conversation with the actor Dalsky, I discovered that he had Esenin's bust. That night Esenin dropped in at some party and gave him his "head" as a present. Now the bust is in the offices of the Union of Writers.

Esenin came to see us again in Prechistenka, but we did not know where he lived. The intervals between his visits grew longer and longer.

I am trying now to understand what was happening to Esenin at that time. I study his poems, try to relate them to the events of those days, try to recall scraps of conversations, intonations.

Months had passed since Esenin had left Isadora at the railway station. Months ... What could be hidden behind the veil of those many days? What feelings warmed his "heart touched by a chill" all that time?

But did not his love revive at his meeting with Isadora?

At the same time I tried to understand what was going on in Isadora's mind. She was suffering. She was holding on to her former "cold decisions" and was running away from herself by concentrating on her work. She was, all the same, waiting for Esenin to come back to her.

Somehow, imperceptibly and quite simply, the complete rupture came about.

> *"Ludicrous life, ludicrous discord!*
> *So it was and so it ever will be.*
> *Like a cemetery, the garden is strewn*
> *With gnawed bones mid the birch trees.*
> *We, too, like the visitors to the garden, shall*
> *shed our blossoms...*
> *If there are no flowers in winter,*
> *There's no need to mourn for them ..."*

He had only about two more years to live.

> *"Now I've grown more sparing in my desires,*
> *My life, were you, too, only a dream?*
> *Just as though on a resonant spring morning*
> *I had galloped away on a pink horse ..."*

Esenin never came to Prechistenka again.

Did Esenin love Isadora? "To judge by my own impressions," the well-known Russian poet Sergei Gorodetsky, who had introduced Esenin to literature in 1915, writes, "it was a deep mutual love. Only love, only unceasing amazement at the rich imagination of his companion could have kept Esenin so long near Duncan in the languishment of loneliness in a foreign land."

Nikolai Nikitin, the Soviet writer who was a close friend of Esenin's, gives the following answer to the question whether Esenin was really in love with Isadora: "I think he was. She was a great

artist and, it would seem, also a great person. This is proved by the
last pages of her life. For many years and right up to her death
Stanislavsky was highly enthusiastic about her. Would not Esenin
also have felt the charm of her personality? He spoke to me again
and again about her dancing. Their brief life together proved to be
bitter. But I do not know what wormwood had poisoned it."

Vsevolod Rozhdestvensky wrote in his memoirs: "They were
obviously bound by a strong and genuine feeling, whatever the
Esenin ill-wishers may say. There was in Esenin's passion for the
famous dancer something of his habitual vanity and his urge 'to
surprise by something quite unexpected' and at the same time also a
great deal of genuine feeling. A person of great sincerity, Esenin
could never have lied to himself."

It is necessary to dispel one fiction about the rupture in the
relations between Esenin and Duncan which has found its way in
the reminiscences of N. Verzhbitsky, first published in the monthly
Zvezda and then in book form in Tiflis.

Verzhbitsky claims that Esenin told him, apropos of his rupture
with Isadora, that "his whole protest against the middle class environment in Duncan's apartment expressed itself at last in his
being unable to look without hatred at the chairs with their thin,
spindly legs in the drawing room which were so fragile that it was
dangerous to sit down on them. Esenin broke off the legs of a few
chairs, took them to Duncan's room, and flung them silently at the
feet of the astonished dancer, then picked up his trunk and walked
out of the house."

In Duncan's room there were no chairs with "spindly legs," and
anyway the rupture came by telegraph.

Where did Verzhbitsky get this episode of the "middle class
environment in Duncan's apartment"? It is difficult to say, but, at
all events, he did not get it from Esenin, who knew Duncan's deep
hostility to any middle class manifestations in everyday life.

It is only fair to say that Verzhbitsky omitted this passage from
his published reminiscences about Esenin.

It was a blustery day in late autumn. Isadora wanted to go for a
walk. At that time, thank goodness, many of the monstrous plaster-
cast statues had vanished from the streets and squares of Moscow.
But in the Staro-Konyushenny Lane, along which Duncan often
walked on the way to the Pink House where the contributors to an

arts journal worked, there still stood a huge bust of Karl Marx in front of a school building. It had an enormous head and an immense beard stuck to the wide pedestal. Every time Isadora passed that *chef d'oeuvre* she could not help laughing.

"If he had known that seventy-five years after his death the communists would put up such statues to him," she used to say, "Marx would have shaved off his beard."

The same autumn our school, that is to say Duncan, Irma, and the "dunclings," had to give a performance at Zimin's former opera house (now the Light Opera House) after a meeting of the Government in the same building. Before the beginning of the performance someone came onto the stage and said that Klara Zetkin, who had been at the meeting, had been taken ill.

Isadora got upset and asked for the beginning of the performance to be delayed. Then she filled a glass with champagne and persuaded me to take it to Klara Zetkin and ask her, in her name, to drink it.

I went into Klara Zetkin's box with the champagne in my hand. Apologizing for my intrusion, I told her of Isadora's request that she should drink it and also her assurance that it would do her a lot of good.

Zetkin smile affably. She had a sip of the wine and asked me to thank Isadora.

"She's wondering," I said, "whether you'll be staying to see her school."

"I shall most certainly stay," replied Klara Zetkin.

In the empty lobby and corridors the bells were ringing. I hurried to get to the stage, though this time it was Lunacharsky who made the introductory speech and I had only to stage-manage the show.

Isadora was electrified by the reception she and her school received from the audience. What the audience liked, of course, was not only the dancing skill of the children, but also herself and Irma—so supple, so strong, so passionately absorbed by their dances.

Having seen Duncan in this excited state before I realized she would almost certainly make an extraordinary speech. But for the time being she was content to take Lunacharsky and myself before the curtain in response to the stormy ovation. Shouting some words of greeting to the audience, Isadora whipped off her fiery silk scarf and, throwing it over Lunacharsky's shoulders, skilfully enveloped him in it. Then, holding the two of us firmly by the hands, she began her speech. Lunacharsky quietly disengaged himself from the scarf and, whispering to me: "Carry on, please," disappeared behind the stage. After translating a few sentences, I said quietly to Isadora that she should go and leave me to announce the next dance. She obeyed, but the worst was to come.

I must explain that Isadora was prejudiced against Litkens, Lunacharsky's deputy, who she believed had taken "a hostile attitude towards" her Moscow school. She was, of course, quite wrong, but somehow it always happened that all the projects for the improvement of the school's situation invariably came to an end on Litkens's desk.

"He's the enemy of my school," Duncan kept declaring, ignoring my explanations.

Now the children of the school had proved at this memorable concert that they really had made remarkable progress, and they created a great impression by their art. The audience had given the children a tremendous reception.

At the very end of the concert, when I stepped out on to the proscenium, Isadora suddenly appeared next to me. Clapping me on the shoulder and taking me by the arm, she said in her broken Russian: "Translate!" and then asked the audience: "Did you like the children?"

Her question was answered by the loud applause of the audience.

"It's much better than the *tutti* and the 'diamonds' of the ballerinas, isn't it?"

Applause and loud laughter.

"In that case, I should like you to wait a little. Let us all go to the Chistye Prudy [Clean Ponds] to see the Deputy People's Commissar Litkens. Let him come out on the balcony and you tell him that. If he refuses to come out, I shall, as a sign of my protest before the entire world, throw myself from the Kremlin wall tomorrow!"

I remember I tried in my translation to "edit" Duncan's speech, but someone shouted to me from the dark auditorium: "You're translating something different!" But by that time I had succeeded in dragging Duncan to the other side of the curtain.

"What on earth are you doing?" I asked her. "An appeal to the masses? Is that it? Besides, Litkens doesn't live at the Chistye Prudy," I went on excitedly. "Anyway, you're quite wrong about him. What do you want him to do?"

187

"People who have tried to injure me have always ended up badly," said Isadora, frowning, and went off to the dressing-room.

"Leave him alone. You don't know him. He isn't a bad man at all. Besides, he is a sick man and is going off to the Crimea for a cure."

A few days later I went into her room.

"Litkens," I said, "has been killed by the 'green shirts' on the Simferopol road."

She gave a start and turned pale.

"This is terrible," she whispered. "I did not want to hurt him. But why does it always happen in my life that . . ." and she fell silent.

After the rupture with Esenin, Isadora suffered from fits of depression. She had to have a change of scene, and we organized for her a special tour of the Ukraine and the cities of Central Asia. Irma and I were going on a trip to Berlin and Paris, and we certainly did not want to leave Isadora by herself in Moscow in her present state. She was making preparations for her tour and we left for Berlin, where in the cellars of our embassy were Isadora's blue curtains and carpets, which she needed for her performances, and chests with a great many orchestrations from which we had to select those she wanted for her tour. In Paris I had to get her affairs in order and arrange for a tour of her Moscow school. She had been given permission by the Soviet government, and she was very keen on that idea. Besides, we had to get her house on Rue de la Pompe ready for the proposed arrival of the school in Paris.

Irma wanted to give performances in both Berlin and Paris. In addition, we had to place articles on the Moscow school in the European press, for the papers had already published all sorts of fanciful stories about Duncan's work in Moscow.

XIX

Our train left the platform of the Moscow station on the evening of January 21, 1924, at 6.50 p.m. At that very moment Lenin died, a fact which was confirmed on our arrival in Berlin. I had a letter from Moscow with a mourning stamp on the envelope. The children of the school wrote that they had insisted on their right to take leave of Lenin in the Hall of the Columns in the Kremlin and to march in Red Square. The members of the Russian legation looked for a long time at my envelope with its stamp in a black frame.

"All the people in the Police Headquarters," one of them said, "are not only terrible bribe-takers but also passionate philatelists. They will do anything you ask them for such a stamp."

The French consul in Berlin refused to issue a visa to Irma because her German passport had Soviet entry and exit visas. But for the rare Soviet stamp the official of the Police Headquarters did, in fact, do something that seemed almost impossible: he received from Hamburg in one day the birth certificate of Irma Duncan and issued her a new passport untouched by visas. The first one with the Moscow visas he kept with him and promised to return it to her after her visit to Paris for re-entry to Moscow.

After Irma's performance at the Bluethnersaal, where she had had an excellent reception, we left for Paris. But before that we paid a visit to the former palace of Wilhelm II in Potsdam, the left wing of which had been set aside for the Elizabeth Duncan school I mentioned earlier. Elizabeth was Isadora's elder sister, and she worked as matron in Isadora's first Berlin school in Grünewald. But she had, of course, a thorough knowledge of Isadora's system

189

though she herself did not dance, owing to a physical defect. The Germans did not like Isadora because of the pacifist speeches which she had made during the First World War, when, as a citizen of the United States, she had left Germany.

But her system of artistic and physical education had produced such excellent results that the Germans could not possibly refuse to recognize it (in the sphere of art all the dancers who became famous afterwards, including Mary Wigman, Rudolph von Laban, and other German followers of Duncan, always openly acknowledged her as their precursor). A Duncan school was founded, and Elizabeth Duncan was appointed the head of it. The school took Duncan's method as its basis, but it eliminated what was the most important thing in it—the harmonious development of body and soul.

We had been invited to Potsdam as honoured guests. It was pleasant to be greeted so joyfully by such charming, attractive, and well-brought-up children. It was pleasant to listen to the music to which our children in Moscow were dancing and to see the same exercises. But how remote it all was from Isadora's dream. The affectation, the overemphasized prettiness, and the mannerisms in the dances of those children certainly did not accord with Isadora's requirement: "A free spirit can only exist in a free body!"

Isadora once told me that she had been invited to a children's matinée by a school in New York, founded without her knowledge but bearing her name. The majority of the audience consisted of the fathers and mothers of the performing children. They danced the same dances as those in Isadora Duncan's real school. Everything seemed to be the same. But the audience was lethargic. The children of the New York school did not arouse the enthusiastic response which always followed the performance of Isadora Duncan's schools in Moscow, Berlin, and Paris.

"Between the stage and the auditorium," she told me, "there rose from the orchestra pit an insurmountable icy cold wall, which these pretty New York children could not thaw or break through. Their dances lacked gladness and spontaneity. Everything was artificial, even the smile. It is here," Isadora put her clenched fist to her chest, "that it must burn and knock. The motor's here!"

It was in Elizabeth's school that I remembered and understood Isadora's words.

As soon as we arrived in Cologne, at six o'clock in the morning, we ran off to visit the Cathedral. It was inexpressibly beautiful, and so high that it was lost to sight in the dark core of its sharp towers, with its reverent silent air, cut across with spectral shafts of sunlight from its stained-glass windows, and filled with the cool breath of its majestic walls and the silent flagstones of its worn floor.

Cologne itself was gay and full of life. The streets were crowded with throngs of noisy people. We went into a cinema. It was showing a film set in Russia. "Bolsheviks," covered with beards and wearing leather jackets and with butchers' knives stuck in their belts, gnashed their teeth fiercely, becoming more and more fierce with every reel. The "commissar," more hirsute than the rest, sent off a messenger to his Komsomol fiancée, who was sitting in her *kokoshnik*, the traditional woman's head-dress, at the latticed window of her tower-chamber. The "messenger," going down on one knee, held out a "casket" to her with a present from her commissar betrothed, and so on.

Irma, who was sitting next to the aisle, fell off her seat with laughter. We rushed out of the cinema before the end of the film.

We entered Belgium without being aware of it. The impression I had was of the train rushing through an endless city.

Liége! The name conjured up the heroic defence of Liége and Namur. Our train stopped there for a whole hour. I dragged Irma off to see the famous fortress and its other historic fortifications. But all we saw was a very clean, quiet, and sleek little town, which reminded me of our Dorpat.

Our train arrived in Paris at midnight exactly. We had telegraphed Isadora's brother, Raymond Duncan, about our arrival and were confident that he would be at the station to meet us.

"We must look for a crowd of people—Raymond will be there," said Irma.

"Why?"

"You'll see why in a moment."

And, to be sure, Raymond was in the middle of a crowd of people, who stared at him as at some oddity. Of medium height, spare, looking in profile like Caesar, wearing a white woollen cloak thrown over a Greek tunic and sandals on bare feet and no hat (his grey hair combed back smoothly and curling over his ears), Raymond looked quite imperturbable, calmly let the crowd examine him. A thin plaited band surrounded his high forehead, holding his hair in place.

Next to him stood his wife, dressed like any other Parisian

woman. Seeing us, Raymond threw off his assumed calm. It looked as though a hidden hundred-horsepower engine suddenly started working in him, and from that moment to the end of our visit I saw him constantly in a state of furious energy.

In another moment we found ourselves outside the station. A small taxi drove up with a screech of brakes. In less than a second Raymond had thrust us into the taxi. The driver, with quite inconceivable dexterity, pushed Irma's huge trunk next to his seat, threw our other things on to our knees, and, resuming his seat at the steering wheel, tore along the Paris streets. Raymond signalled the driver to stop outside some small shop in a little street. Large soft parcels flew through the open window of the taxi, Raymond storming in after them, and we drove off again at a terrific speed through the streets and boulevards, lit by tremulous violet, red, and blue neon lights.

"Rue de Colisée!" growled the driver.

The taxi stopped, again with a screech of brakes, outside a big building at the back of a little square. Raymond relieved the taxi of our luggage with the same tempestuous energy, and we entered his theatre-studio. In the large entrance hall we saw a printing press and next to it type cases.

"I'm publishing a paper," Raymond explained. "I set the type myself, I print it myself, and I gather the material myself."

One wall of the entrance hall was covered entirely by a huge oil painting in a very modest frame. I went up to the bronze tablet. "Raymond Duncan. 'Childbirth.' Paris Salon."

The picture showed a woman at the moment of the birth of her child. A big cut yawned in one part of the canvas.

"They accepted my painting for exhibition at the salon," Raymond said, "but after one middle-class bourgeois, shocked by its subject, had attacked it with a knife, they returned it to me."

Four small black and yellow posters hung on the walls, each announcing "evenings of dances":

> Aei Duncan
> Raymond Duncan
> Maurice Duncan
> Robert Duncan

"Who are Maurice and Robert?" I asked.

Again Raymond was only too willing to explain. "There are too many Duncans in Paris. Three of Isadora's pupils—Anna, Lisl, and Margot—who refused to accompany her to Moscow, appear everywhere as 'Duncan.' Isadora sent a telegram forbidding them to use her name, but it made no difference to them. It was then that I decided to breed more Duncans in the hope that soon there will be as many of them as there are stray dogs. That should put an end to exploiting our name. I conferred the name of Duncan on all my male and female pupils. There are many more!"

"But what do these—er—Maurice and Robert do?"

"They dance. Without music. To words."

And he showed me a photograph on which "Maurice Duncan," a man with a thick spade-like beard, was squatting in a wild pose with bent knees and with widely spread fingers.

"W-well, it's extremely interesting," was all I could bring myself to say.

"If Irma wants to we can hang the same kind of poster here on the wall with her name," Raymond said. "I will print it myself."

Irma expressed her regret with a charming smile: she was sorry to say that she would not be able to appear in Paris at all because she had hurt her foot in Berlin.

But Raymond was already leading us through the dark stalls of the auditorium on to the stage, which we mounted by a few small wooden steps. The auditorium contained long tables covered with tablecloths. "What are those tables for?" I could not help asking.

"Today is Saturday," Raymond said, turning to me as he walked up the steps, "and on Sundays I have 'a church without God' here, and vegetarian meals. You see, I am a vegetarian myself."

Behind the scenes stood large looms that Raymond had brought from Greece.

"My girl students weave Greek woollen rugs and other fabrics. These twelve rugs that I'm carrying are what I got from our shop on the way here. We sell these things in our shop," said Raymond, showing us into a room where there was nothing except a wooden structure like a huge ottoman. He threw his Greek rugs on it, spread some of them instead of a mattress, rolled up others into long bolsters for pillows, and put five rugs on top for blankets.

"It's cold here," he said calmly.

It was then two o'clock in the morning. When we got up, our teeth chattered as we walked down the steps into the auditorium where we had been invited to a vegetarian breakfast. Dejected-looking women and bearded men, much like "Maurice Duncan," were sitting at the tables and silently chewing some green stuff. We ran out to the nearest café for our breakfast. As we went out of the hall we met Aei Duncan carrying a frying pan with a hissing omelette fried with bacon for the "vegetarian" Raymond.

That evening we moved to a small, warm, comfortable hotel.

I had learned about Raymond Duncan, a very interesting and talented but rather too unbusiness-like man, in some articles Lunacharsky sent from Paris in 1912. My readers have doubtless formed an opinion of his talent for taking advantage of his famous sister from the episode of the blue notebook and Isadora's will.

Paris! I was there for the first time and yet everything seemed to be familiar to me: the names of the streets, squares, buildings....
Les Invalides. Napoleon's tomb.

We arrived in Paris in March. Mild spring air, the trees of the Champs Elysées and the Bois de Boulogne touched with green, the bright green carpets of the Paris squares and the bunches of violets on the Tomb of the Unknown Soldier. How well I remember it all!

On the very first day I went to the Louvre, to the hall of the Venus de Milo. I remember Isadora telling me in Moscow: "In the round hall in the Louvre where the statue of the Venus de Milo stands, hundreds of thousands of people come every year to see that marble miracle, the greatest work of art that has stirred the imagination of many generations of men. Embodied in the cold stone is the wonderful beauty of the living body. Why then should we not create millions of living, beautiful human beings?"

It seems quite superfluous to describe my impressions of those days, particularly as we were forced to leave Paris in a hurry. We had received a telegram from Moscow of the sudden serious illness of Georgy Khachaturov, my deputy at the school.

We nearly missed our train: the Paris taxi drivers had gone on strike. They were demanding the abolition of the prohibition of tips, and the drivers of trams and buses came out on strike in sympathy.

I was given the address of one of the last of the diehards, an old cabby who agreed to take us to the station for a hundred and fifty francs.

In Berlin we received news of Georgy's death. It seems that while Isadora was away on tour, Khachaturov, economizing on fuel, contracted pneumonia and, as we say, was "consumed" in three days. We arrived in Moscow after his funeral. This blow plunged us into a state of painful depression and aroused in me a dull feeling of irritation against Isadora, for I found out that during the whole of that time she had done nothing to help the school with the money she received for her performances.

I sent her a sharp telegram calling her attention to her serious lack of care for the school. In reply I received a telegram in German which I remember began with a curious arrangement of words by Isadora: *"Ich verstehe Ihre Telegramm um mich zu blamieren* ... [I understand your telegram as a desire to make me appear ridiculous]," etc., in which she assured me that she had done everything she possibly could to assist the school. It proved to be partly true. A remittance she had sent to the school through a bank had been delayed.

Isadora returned to Moscow.

Blue patches appeared in the Moscow sky, the asphalt in the school yard dried up. The clatter and the bells of the trams became more resonant. People coming in from the street brought with them the smell of fresh air. Spring had come. Easter was getting near. Isadora asked me to take her to one of the churches on Easter Saturday. She had long wanted to go to a Greek Orthodox church for morning Mass. We went to the nearest church—Christ the Redeemer. She called it "the great white church" and once embarrassed Krasin by saying to him: "Give me that great white church for my school."

A Komsomol Easter had been announced in Moscow. Groups of young men were standing by the church in pools of melting snow. Some wore carnival costumes. In the cold night air choral songs sounded discordantly. In the aisles of the church, the walls of which had been painted by such well-known artists as Vrubel, Vasnetsov, and Nesterov, people were standing with their hats on their heads: young people even smoked, but the church choir was something quite out of the ordinary, the soloists were the best in Moscow.

Isadora listened for a long time. Then, touching me by the elbow, she went towards the street door. In the square outside the cathedral there were still crowds of young people, and the far from merry merrymaking went on. . . .

"What do you think?" asked Isadora, stopping in her tracks. "Whose side will the aesthetic feeling of the masses be on this night? On the side of the church or the revolution?" And, walking on rapidly, she replied herself: "Of course, on the side of the church. How badly all this has been organized! Light up this square with searchlights and coloured illuminations, put bright costumes on these girls and boys. Let trumpets blare and let beautiful new songs resound! Create a holiday of youth, strength, and beauty!"

I recalled Podvoysky's remark that Isadora had come into the world too soon. If she could have seen our present-day festivals, demonstrations, physical and cultural parades . . .

We left for Leningrad.

Isadora revelled in Leningrad, its buildings, its museums. She fled into the streets from her admirers, languorous girls and representatives of the "plastic" studio with the enigmatic name of "Hiptachor."

I had not seen Esenin since his rupture with Isadora. In April he arrived in Leningrad just when Duncan's performances were taking place there. The Kamerny Theatre was also in Leningrad at the time. One day Alexander Tairov invited us to dinner. He lived at the Hotel Angleterre. Isadora alone went to the dinner.

Tairov rang up Nikolai Nikitin and invited him to dinner, too, adding that he was expecting Duncan to be present. Esenin was then at Nikitin's, and they went to the dinner together. When they arrived at the Angleterre, a large company was already sitting at table. Esenin made a general bow and sat down among the actors of the Kamerny Theatre. Nikitin writes in his reminiscences:

"Without waiting for the end of the dinner, Esenin mysteriously disappeared. Just like a ghost. Did he come just because he wanted to breathe the same air as Isadora for at least half an hour?

"Perhaps we can find some explanation in a passage of one of his lyric poems of that time:

> *Strangers' lips carried off*
> *Your warmth and the quiver of your body,*
> *Just as though a drizzle of rain*
> *Falls from a soul, a little benumbed.*
> *Well, what of it? I do not fear it,*
> *Another joy has been revealed to me. . . .*
>
> .   .   .   .   .
>
> *So few bridges have been crossed.*
> *So many mistakes have been made. . . .*

"Perhaps that love affair was also one of his mistakes. Perhaps he came to the dinner to find out once more what was hidden under that other joy, about which he writes. At any rate, I believe that this chapter in Esenin's life is not so accidental and inconsequential as many have thought and many still think. . . ."

Isadora returned from the dinner pensive and silent. She only told me that Esenin had been there and had gone away early.

One day a "man from Pskov" came to see Isadora and invited her to give a performance there. She agreed.

Irma and I left for Moscow.

A few days later I was summoned to the telegraph office where our administrator, who had gone with Duncan, was waiting on the direct line for me. He told me that on their way back from Pskov their motor car had broken in two, but that Duncan had not been injured. She had been thrown out of the car and hit her head, but luckily she had fallen into a puddle and the water had softened the blow. They were at the moment in a village, but they hoped to get to Leningrad soon and from there would go straight to Moscow.

"Something always happens to her," I thought, "but to fall into a puddle is sometimes a piece of luck."

Isadora returned to Moscow full of animal spirits and all sorts of impressions. She told me about her visit to a peasant's cottage.

"In that cottage," Isadora said excitedly, "the walls were decorated with Japanese paper fans and artificial and dried flowers. 'What are those fans and paper flowers for?' I asked my host. 'For beauty,' he replied, and I could not help thinking how much had still to be done to give those people a true conception of beauty and to develop in them a feeling of good taste. But Rodin takes the peasant just as he is, still unconscious of the beauty of his own work or the grandeur of nature around him, and manages to create unsurpassed works of art!"

She immediately began worrying me with projects for organizing a new journey to the South with the whole school, this time "to give the children a chance to have a good rest after the Moscow winter." We decided to go to Kiev.

Before our departure I prepared a surprise for Isadora. I asked her not to leave the house, then I myself went to the stadium, where Podvoysky and I organized exercises with six hundred workers' children. A huge column of children in red tunics, headed by a

military band, marched over the old Crimea Bridge. Running ahead
of the column, I went into the house and led Isadora by the hand
out on to the balcony. In Prechistenka tramcars and motor cars had
already formed a long queue. "The red danger" had occupied the
whole road for the space of two blocks. The brass instruments of
the band flashed and thundered in the sun, the endless column of
children moved along with a red glow. They raised their hands and
greeted Isadora with enthusiasm. The first chords of the *Internationale* filled the air. The red shawl trembled in Isadora's hands,
flew upwards like a banner. The balcony was so narrow that she
could not possibly dance. But that was not necessary. Her appealing
gestures and movements were as easily understood as the words of a
fiery tribune. Holding hands, they moved on in an infinite, overflowing spiral.

We left for Kiev. Walking with me across Kreshchatika, Isadora
glanced sideways at a poster:
"I see you've deprived me of my surname, leaving only my
Christian name. . . ."
And, indeed, the local organizations issued posters on which they
announced the performance of Isadora and Irma Duncan and their
school.
But something inexplicable was happening to the performances,
something that had never happened before: the theatre was almost
empty. The reason for it very soon became clear. Kiev was going
through a heat wave and nothing could inveigle the public into the
airless building of a winter theatre.
Isadora was surprised. However, she was soon rewarded and was
fully recompensed, having convinced herself of the greater than
usual interest the inhabitants of Kiev had in her art and in her
school. In the Proletarian Park an open-air festival was announced.
The symphony orchestra was seated on a shell-like platform, while
Isadora, Irma, and the school were to perform on an enormous
square, larger than the biggest stage, in front of the orchestra
platform. Instead of a carpet, we had to stretch and fix in the sand
several long and wide curtains we used on our stage. Before the
square, only a few rows of seats were placed; the rest of the huge
audience, for whom at Isadora's insistence specially cheap tickets
had been issued, had to sit round the square and on the steps which
ran down to it in the shape of an amphitheatre.

The sale of tickets for the few reserved seats began long before the appointed hour of the festival. The long queues quickly merged into enormous crowds of people. Overwhelming the keepers stationed at the gates, the crowd rushed into the park and close to the curtains which we had stretched out on the ground.

The performance was a great success, but the organizers, who had hoped to cover their losses incurred by the performances in the winter theatre, faced complete financial failure because thousands had got in without paying for their tickets.

But Isadora was very pleased, refused to accept her fee, and said that there was no greater pleasure than to appear before an audience that did not have to pay for its seats.

On her return from Kiev, Isadora devoted every day to working with the children on the green arena of the stadium. Some of these children were later admitted to Duncan's school and, later still, travelled with the studio all over the Soviet Union and visited China, France, and America.

XX

In the autumn of 1924 Isadora said to me:

"Part of my music library is still in the cellar of the Berlin Soviet embassy. There are lots of my other things there too. I would like to fly to Berlin to fetch them, and it would be nice if you could also organize a few performances there."

I telegraphed the concert bureau in Berlin and Isadora began to make ready for her departure. But she had no passport: abroad, she was registered in Esenin's passport as his wife. Esenin had kept that passport. I rang him up. He could not find it.

It was a good thing that, before that, Isadora had applied for naturalization as a Soviet citizen. On the strength of that application she was issued with an official document confirming the receipt of her application. She left the Soviet Union by air with that document.

On the eve of her departure she asked me to find her hatbox, which she had brought with her on her arrival in Moscow.

"I'm only going away for a short time," she said, "and I won't take many things with me. But that hatbox is very light and I could put everything I want in it."

"Why," I said, "it must have been in our wardrobe room for the last three years!"

The hatbox was dusted and taken to her. A short time afterwards, I went into her room and found her sitting on the rug with a shoe in her hand. Next to her was the hatbox with its lid open. Isadora looked at me for a long time in silence with unseeing eyes.

"I opened the lid," she said at last, "and suddenly I saw a huge

Isadora

Isadora Duncan a few days before her death in Nice, 1927

Isadora, by José Clara. September 1927

Raymond and Elizabeth Duncan at Isadora's funeral in Paris ▶

Four of Isadora's Moscow pupils

Ilya Ilyich Schneider with members of the Moscow school on their first tour of the Volga, 1925

Tamara Lobanovskaya in Chopin's
Mazurka, 1931

Galina Benislavskaya

A school group in Tvar. Schneider is on the right

Duncan's Moscow studio on tour in China, 1926. In the centre: Irma Duncan

Dance with a Scarf performed by the Isadora Duncan studio in Moscow, 1946

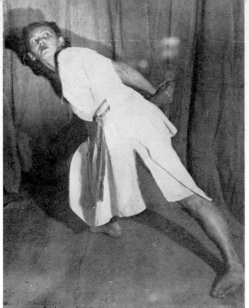

Elena Terentyerain dancing to
Tchaikovsky in Moscow, 1948

Alexandra Aksyonova, Vera Golovina and
Marie Tovopchenova in *The Three
Graces* by Schubert, a dance long in the
repertoire of the studio

Vera Golovina and Alexandra Aksyonova in *The Amazons* by
Glück, Moscow, 1940

Pupils of the Duncan school on the banks of the Dnieper near Kiev, 1946. In the centre, Ilya Ilyich Schneider

Ilya Ilyich Schneider, author of this book, as he is today

spider running up the side of the box. I got terribly frightened, and took one of my shoes and killed it. It was all over in a moment. Then I thought: That spider must have been born and lived for years in this hatbox. It was his world, black and sombre. The spider did not know the element of light. His world was limited by corners and steep sides. But it was his universe, beyond which there was Nothing or the Unknown. The spider lived in that world without realizing that it was nothing but the hatbox of a certain Isadora Duncan who had taken it into her head to fly to Berlin. Then, something he had never seen before, something he did not understand, something that blinded him came flooding suddenly into his world. And at that very moment came death! That highest, unknown power that brought him sudden death was I. The unknown power in life which men accept as God. Perhaps we, too, live in that kind of hatbox. What do you think?"

Early in the morning we left for the airport. It was the same airline "Deruluft" Moscow-Königsberg which, sixteen months before, had flown Isadora and Esenin to Europe. The German pilot was walking nervously up and down the tarmac, brandishing a Moscow cake he was taking as a present to his fiancée and muttering something under his breath. Apparently he was cursing his luck for having to fly with Isadora Duncan, who was well known "to be always involved in accidents."

That was early in the morning. That evening, in the twilight, I saw a tall dark figure walking slowly up the marble staircase of the school.

I stopped with a start.

"Isadora! Where are you coming from?"

"An emergency landing in Mozhaisk. We're flying tomorrow morning. Please, make up a parcel with twenty red tunics for me. I promised to drop them for the Mozhaisk Komsomols tomorrow. I spent several wonderful hours with them while the airplane was being repaired. I taught them dancing and free movement in the spiral arrangement of the *Internationale*. All to the music of an accordion. Don't begrudge them the tunics."

"Did the pilot curse?"

"Terribly. Can you imagine it? He thought that it was all because I was his passenger!"

Next day, as she flew over Mozhaisk, she dropped the parcel with the red tunics.

That day was the last time I saw Isadora Duncan.

Almost forty years later I met one of those Mozhaisk Komsomols in the editorial offices of *Moskva*: it was the Moscow journalist P. K. Shari, with whom I worked afterwards. Much earlier I had learned about one of the first air funerals in Moscow: the coffin with the body of the same German pilot was being sent off by air to Königsberg: he was killed in an air crash near Moscow.

From Berlin Isadora left for Paris.

It was a city she loved so much, a city in which world fame had come to her, a city in which she had undergone inhuman sufferings and had so recently spent unforgettable and anxious days with Esenin. In Paris she had fallen in love for the first time. In Paris her children had been born: her daughter Deirdre and her son Patrick. In Paris they had died. In Paris she had felt "the beginning of the end" of Esenin's love.

We are now so used to the curtains on the stages of our theatres, clubs, palaces of culture, and so on, that we forget that they were "invented" by the famous English producer, Gordon Craig. In Stanislavsky's book *My Life in Art* there is a chapter headed "Duncan and Craig." Craig and Duncan came to Moscow together. Gordon Craig was the father of Duncan's daughter, Deirdre. Patrick was her son by Paris Singer, a millionaire whose name is universally known in connection with the sewing machine his grandfather invented. To Isadora's credit be it said that her association with that millionaire was one of love. Money never interested her.

"What do I want money for?" she said to me once when discussing her life with me. "Money used to flow to me like water out of a tap. Turn it on and it flowed. If I wanted to have a contract for Spain, they sent it. If I wanted to go to Russia, there was a contract ready for me. Money flowed in. I never felt any want of it. And I do not wear diamonds."

Incidentally, during that conversation she also told me how Singer's grandfather had invented the first sewing machine. Singer had told her that his grandfather had struggled with the construction of his machine for a long time. It was ready, but one major element was still lacking. Without it, there was neither invention nor machine. When a person sews with a needle, he first pierces the cloth with it and then, letting go of the needle, catches it again with his hand from the other side of the cloth. But the machine did not have such a "hand." Singer struggled with that problem vainly until one night, exhausted by his attempts to solve the problem, he dropped off to sleep in his chair. He dreamed that a rider on a horse was rushing at him with a spear in his hand. The spear had a hole at its point, threaded with a yellow ribbon, which waved in the wind. Eureka! The problem was solved and, like all brilliant solutions, it was so simple: the hole for the thread had to be changed to the point end of the needle!

Isadora was little interested in the Singer sewing machine and the factories spread throughout the world which brought in millions to their owner. Her only wish was that Singer should help her to create her school and her theatre. One day in New York Singer walked into the room of their hotel and told Isadora to come down quickly to his car: for five million dollars he had bought her a whole city block in the style of our parks of culture and rest, containing different buildings, a theatre, a stadium, a circus, etc.

Getting out of the car, Isadora sniffed the air.

"I can't work here," she said. "It smells of horses."

Singer was furious. He tore up the contract and with it the deposit of a quarter of a million dollars he had made.

Later in Paris he bought the Bellevue Hotel for Isadora. An organization committee was appointed, the members of which included the elite of the world of art and literature, not only of France but of the whole of Western Europe. A banquet was given to celebrate the occasion.

It so happened that one evening Isadora, speaking to me about her life in Prechistenka, and coming to that afternoon hour in Paris, stopped short. Then, suddenly, she told me everything she had been through so poignantly a thousand times in her mind. . . .

Duncan sat there staring in front of her with pale moist eyes, from which two big tears rolled down her cheeks. A cold shiver went down my spine. Two big tears again gathered in her eyes and again rolled down her deathly pale cheeks.

"If you knew what I know," she said, "you wouldn't laugh so much, but cry," and she added softly: "I believe those words are ascribed to Mahomet."

I remembered other words written by Alexander Herzen: "I'd have liked to cover up a woman's face with flowers so that we should not see the tears on it."

After the speeches at the banquet had come to an end, the head waiter went up to Duncan and told her that someone was asking for her in the vestibule. She went out and was very surprised to find her children and their English nurse with them.

"What's happened?" she asked.

"Nothing. We have been for a drive and the children wanted to see you again. They begged me so much . . ."

"Go home now. I have asked my pianist to come to the studio in Neuilly. I shall work for an hour and then come home. Go now. . . ."

She went out into the street and wrapped rugs round the children's legs. The car drove off.

"I arrived at the studio," Isadora said to me. "The pianist was not there. I remember I put on my white tunic and, with a box of chocolates in my hand, walked up and down the studio, eating the chocolates and thinking: I am the happiest woman in the world. I am young, I have such wonderful children. . . . Today the dream of my life has come true. I shall have my school and my theatre! At that moment Singer rushed into the studio. He shouted: 'The children—are dead!' And collapsed on the floor. Why did I not go mad then? I could not grasp what he had said. All I could see was that he had collapsed and would probably die. I rushed up to him. . . . Perhaps that saved my reason. . . ."

She cried silently a long time.

"The car with the children drove onto the Seine embankment: a taxi cut across its path. To avoid a collision, our driver turned sharply towards the river. The motor stalled. The driver took the crank, got out of the car, and cranked up the engine. Suddenly the car lunged forward at him and drove straight for the river. At the time there was no parapet. The driver jumped aside and the car fell into the Seine. . . ."

She fell silent again, covering her eyes with a hand. Then her voice resounded hollowly again:

"The driver first beat his head on the road, then he ran off for something to my sister Elizabeth and knocked at her door—time, time passed. And they were in the river. An hour later the car was pulled out of the river by a crane. The children and the nurse were taken to the American hospital. I was later told that my little girl was still breathing. If only I could have been beside them then! I should have brought them back to life by the power of a mother's love. . . ."

What happened after the accident I learned from Irma and later from Mary Desti and from Isadora's brother Raymond, whom I saw later in Paris, and from her sister Elizabeth.

According to French law, the morgue releases the bodies of accident victims only just before the funeral. With great difficulty Isadora's friends obtained permission to take the dead children to her house. Mary Desti went to fetch the bodies from the morgue. She writes in her book: "There on a little white marble slab...were our two little angels." Not far from them lay the English girl, her face distorted and her mouth open.... When the water poured into the car, she had apparently tried to cover the heads of the children with their rugs.

For two days and nights Isadora was in a state of complete stupor. She did not even cry. She did not touch food, did not ask for water, did not utter a word. Only when they brought in the arrested driver and he threw himself at her knees did she get up and go to him: "I don't want to hurt a single hair of your head," said Isadora. "I do not believe it was a crime. Go back to your children...."

Again in a stupor, she stirred only once, when she suddenly got up and went down to the ground floor where her children were lying on a couch. Kneeling before them, she took their hands in hers. But again there were no tears. All she said was: "My poor little children..."

When they drove to the crematorium she kept repeating: "No tears... No tears... They knew no sorrow in their lives. No living."

Back home, Isadora sank into an armchair and sat there for hours, staring into the distance. Towards evening she got up and went out into the street. She was followed, but she walked without seeing anyone or anything. She walked for a long time, then came to the Seine and stood looking at its dirty-green water rolling along. She stood there a long time.

"You must let me decide what to do myself," she said to a friend who stood by her. "Nothing matters to me now, but maybe I can help others. I must be courageous, and I have decided to go on living."

After the accident Isadora left the stage for a while. Besides, she was going to be a mother once more.

"When I gave birth to a boy again, I decided to call him Patrick after my dead boy. I asked for the boy to be brought and put beside me. His little head lay on my shoulder. I bent over him and said:

Patrick! He opened a pair of large blue eyes, sighed, and died. What sort of heart could that child have had if I carried him under my heart which was wrung with suffering. . . .

"I lay in the darkness listening to them knocking together a box in which to bury Patrick in our garden. Then Mary came in and lit a lamp. I asked her to bring me some book. Shortly before the accident a stranger had sent me a book with the title: *Niobe Lamenting Her Children*. I put it on a bookshelf. Now Mary took the first book she laid her hands on and gave it to me. It was *Niobe Lamenting Her Children*. I am not a mystic, but I am not telling you about that book without good reason. But it's no use brooding on it or one would go mad. If that is true, then Ponson du Terrail with his Rocambole is but a feeble romancer. . . ."

She had a sip from her glass and took a cigarette but could not manage to strike a match. I gave her a light.

The four long plate-glass windows in her room began to brighten. It was getting light. Isadora was silent for a long time.

"Now that several years have passed," she suddenly broke the silence, speaking very softly, "I am planning to go from Paris to London and from there return to you in Moscow via Reval and Petrograd. During one of my last evenings in Paris I was invited to a reception. I was a little late but I suddenly made up my mind to go. As I was going up the staircase, I saw a friend of mine who was coming down.

" 'Going already?' I asked.

" 'It's boring there,' he replied, coming up to me and taking hold of my hands.

"I asked him about the people who had gathered upstairs, and as he named them he mentioned the name of Professor Doyen.

" 'Oh, in that case,' I said, 'I won't go up!' and I ran down a few steps."

"Isadora," I interrupted her, "why didn't you want to go up if he was there? Was he the surgeon?"

"Yes, he was. . . ."

I remembered that name well. *Operations of Professor Doyen* was the title of a short film which was shown in the Moscow cinemas after the ordinary programme. In those days the projectionists used to announce the pictures through their windows: A Drama in Six Parts, or A Highly Comic Entertainment, or a Travelogue. But for almost two years they used to show, after the

main films, the *Operations of Professor Doyen,* adding the
warning: "Nervous people, women, and children are asked to
leave." Three operations were shown, all performed by Professor
Doyen, a tall, handsome man with a well-kept beard: the trepan-
ning of the skull, the removal of cancerous tumours, and another
one...

"Yes," Isadora repeated, "the same. Doyen had a very beautiful
wife, a tall, fair-haired woman. At that time I did not know Singer,
who had had an affair with Doyen's wife without, apparently, any
objection from her husband. Singer was building surgical palaces
for him, financed his famous champagne firm *Doyen,* and, generally, promoted him regardless of cost. That film, too.... Then
Singer left Doyen's wife: he had fallen in love with me. We got
married. Apparently his own career and financial prosperity were
more important to Doyen than his wife. He never forgave me and
came to hate me. I always felt his hatred. He was a kind of
medieval enemy...."

She shuddered, shrugged her shoulders, got up, and drew a
shawl around herself. The room had been getting rather cold, and
now it was quite light. Isadora drew the curtains and returned to
her armchair.

"After the accident my chauffeur left me. He bought a villa for
fifty thousand francs. It was a great deal of money. I don't want to
think or speak of it..."

And now Isadora was again in Paris where she was to receive one
more heavy blow—the last one: my telegram about Esenin's
suicide.

XXI

I seldom saw Esenin during the last years of his life. I knew that he had gone to Leningrad again in July and to the Caucasus in September, where he lived till the end of Febraury, 1925. He returned to Moscow for one month and left again for Baku. During those sixteen months he had written a great deal. In the Caucasus he wrote *Lenin, The Song of the Great Campaign, The Ballad of the Twenty-Six, The Poem on 36, Anna Snegina, The Captain of the Earth, Stanzas, The Golden Copse, Disappearing Russia, A Letter to a Woman, A Letter from Mother, Reply,* and, finally, *Persian Motifs* and *Flowers.* "This is perhaps the best I have ever written," he wrote to Galina Benislavskaya in December, 1924.

In June he was again in Moscow. It was there that I met him. I was walking towards Petrovka when near the window of Paulo the photographer's, in which a large portrait of Esenin was displayed, someone stopped me, seizing me by the elbow.

"Ilya Ilyich, don't you want to see me at all?"

I saw before me Esenin's dearly familiar, happily smiling face and his lustrous blue smiling eyes. He was standing on one foot; the other was on the box of a shoeshine man.

"I want to very much!" I was glad to reply.

And, holding me by the elbow, he showered questions upon me. I replied hurriedly and, for my part, asked him about everything. He told me about something that pleased him very much: the State publishing house was about to issue a collected edition of his works.

The last time I saw Esenin was about a month and a half before his death: I was returning home by tram with the elder "dunclings" after a visit to the Art, a cinema. A few passengers boarded the tram at the Prechistenka Gates. One of them, wearing a grey overcoat and a light cap, walked quickly down the tram to get off. At that moment the tram started with a jerk and the passenger fell straight into the lap of one of the girls. He jumped to his feet, looking embarrassed, and we both at one and the same time seized each other by the hands, and cried:

"Sergei Alexandrovich!"

"Ilya Ilyich!"

All my love for him was stirred up inside me and a feeling of deep anxiety overwhelmed me. He had changed greatly, got thinner, turned grey, and his eyes had lost their lustre. But the smile was the same, winsome and pure as a child's.

"Good Lord, it can't be them!" he cried joyfully, looking at the "dunclings." "Haven't they grown! And where's Kapelka?" [This is what he called his favourite, Shura Aksenova.]

"Why, you've been sitting on her knee!"

"They've certainly changed!" Then suddenly turning to me, he said: "Did you know? I've got married!"

"I know."

"Don't you think it's all right? Sergei Esenin married to the grand-daughter of Leo Tolstoy."

"Yes, I do," I replied, looking sadly at his sickly face.

The tram stopped at the school. The girls said goodbye and filed into the door of the entrance hall. I, too, said goodbye. This time, for ever.

It would seem that during the last years of his life Esenin felt particularly "lucid" and yet, beginning in 1924, the theme of death is clearly detectable throughout his poems. He was anxious to get medical treatment, and soon after that last meeting he voluntarily began a two-month course of treatment at a clinic. After twenty-six days, however, he discharged himself and a day later on December 22nd, left for Leningrad.

He took all his notes, manuscripts, and books with him. "Esenin went to Leningrad to work and not to die," Ustinov writes in his reminiscences.

I received the telegram informing me of Esenin's suicide in Minsk, where the studio was appearing at the time. Isadora was in Paris. I telegraphed her. She sent back a long telegram in which, I remember, she said: "I wept so much that I don't think I have any more tears left."

We learnt from the papers that Esenin committed suicide at the Hotel Angleterre, and I remembered the room, No. 5. When we left for Moscow, someone brought into our compartment the latest number of *Ogonyok*, with the photograph of the room in which Esenin had killed himself. Under it I read the caption: "Room No. 5 in the Hotel Angleterre where Sergei Esenin hanged himself."

Sergei Esenin committed suicide in the night of the 27th to 28th of December, 1925. The door of his room was opened at half-past ten in the morning. At 11 : 15 p.m., after a civil funeral service in the Union of Leningrad Writers, the coffin with his body was sent by train to Moscow. It was placed in the Moscow Press Club. Across the street, a banner was stretched with the inscription: "Here lies the body of the great Russian poet Sergei Esenin." His funeral took place at half-past ten in the morning.

After Esenin's death Isadora sent the following telegram to the Paris newspapers: "The tragic death of Esenin caused me great pain. He had youth, beauty, genius. Dissatisfied with these gifts, his gallant spirit sought the impossible. He destroyed his young and beautiful body but his spirit will live for ever in the hearts of the Russian people and in the hearts of all who love poetry. I protest against the frivolous statements published by the American press in Paris. There were never any quarrels between me and Esenin and we have never been divorced. I mourn his death with pain and despair."

In January I received a letter from Isadora from Paris. She wrote: "Esenin's death was a terrible blow to me, but I cried so much that I cannot suffer any more and I am so unhappy myself now that I often think of following his example, but in a different way. I'd prefer the sea. . . ."

The love of Sergei Esenin and Isadora Duncan was a collision of two eras, two outlooks on life, two worlds. That explains the tragic character of their love. They were brought together by their identical views of artistic principles, their breadth of feeling, their high emotion, their inspiration, and their rebelliousness, and they gave a great deal to one another. Esenin was the last blinding flash in Duncan's life, which consumed her entirely. But Sergei Esenin's love for Isadora Duncan will live in the hearts of posterity.

It can be argued that Duncan contributed little to Esenin as a poet (though love lyrics began to appear in his work only after Duncan). It was, after all, only in 1921, in the year of his meeting with her, that he said to the writer I. N. Rozanov: "Note that there are practically no love themes in my work. My lyrics are animated only with my great love for my country." Perhaps, as Gorky writes, Duncan was for Esenin "the most perfect personification of everything he did not need." But when they went abroad she dreamed that, "like Virgil, she would lead Esenin into the world to show him all the treasures of art." That journey was of tremendous importance to the inner growth of the poet. Under its influence, his former idea of Russia underwent a change. He realized that everything he loved was old and had had its day.

Days and months passed. Isadora was still in Paris while we and the studio had gone on a long journey to the Urals, Siberia, the Far East, Manchuria, and China. According to Mary Desti, the large sale of Esenin's works after his death brought in a great deal of money and, since Isadora had never been legally divorced from Esenin, the Russian courts decreed that the money belonged to her, and so Isadora received three hundred thousand francs from Russia. But, Desti further states, although Isadora did not have even the price of her hotel bill. she refused to accept that money, saying: "You will take this to his mother and his little sisters. They need it more than I."

All this is sheer fantasy except for the fact that Isadora and Esenin had never really been divorced. In one of her letters to me from France she did write that she would never have claimed, as Esenin's wife, any hereditary rights and that everything he left behind must belong to his mother and sisters, of whom he had taken so much care when alive.

Among Esenin's heirs was also Sofia Andreyevna Tolstoy, who had no legal rights to any inheritance, which belonged to the poet's children, mother, and sisters. Esenin was never divorced from Isadora and his marriage to Sofia was therefore not legally valid. Esenin was not in love with Sofia, and he had left her before he entered the university clinic. (Esenin "married" Sofia Tolstoy on September 18th, entered the clinic on November 6th, discharged himself on December 22nd, soon left for Leningrad, and committed suicide a few days later.)

This is what the poet's sister Alexandra tells about Esenin's marriage to Sofia: "After Esenin had moved to Sofia's apartment, there was an abrupt change in his surroundings. After his apartment in Bryusov Lane, where we all had the same interests, he found his new quarters uncomfortable and gloomy. He found it difficult to live there. Having moved to Sofia's apartment and finding himself alone with her, he immediately realized that they were two quite different people, with different interests and different views of life. At the end of July, Sergei and Sofia left for the Caucasus and returned at the beginning of September. But he was quite a different person from the Esenin who had returned from the Caucasus in the spring. Then he had arrived looking cheerful, rested, and much younger in spite of the fact that he had done a lot of work there. Now he returned just the same as he had left, tired, nervous, and highly irritable. In our apartment a kind of watchful silence reigned. We spent the evenings by ourselves, without any callers, in the family circle. Even on September 18th, on the day of the registration of Sergei's and Sofia's marriage, we had no visitors. There was a lot I did not know. Nor did I know that there were serious disagreements between Sergei and Sofia. Whenever I went to see them, everything was calm and quiet in the house, but a little boring. I noticed that Sergei went out more often, returned home drunk, and found fault with Sofia. But I could not understand why he found fault with her, for usually, when in that state of mind, Sergei found fault and quarrelled only with people who exasperated him, and I was completely taken aback when, after long persuasion by my sister, he agreed to enter the clinic, but forbade Sofia to visit him there. . . ."

From China we returned to Moscow with a banner presented to us by the Chinese Communist Party. It bore the inscription: "To the flowers of the revolution." In the autumn of 1927, the studio went to the Crimea. From the Crimea we went to Kharkov and the Don Basin, where, after one performance, I took the members of the studio to an iron rolling mill to study the beautiful movements of the workers. We stood in silence, frozen in contemplation of the fairy-like scene, when I heard a loud voice shouting:

"Which is Comrade Schneider here?"

"Me."

"I've just heard a radio announcement from Moscow: your Duncan was killed in a car accident."

It was September 15, 1927.

At one of the stations I bought a paper and at once saw the

heading: "Death of Isadora Duncan," and Isadora's photograph, apparently taken from the portrait in my room.

The autobiography of Isadora Duncan, published in 1927, ends with the sentence: "Adieu, Old World! I would hail a New World!"

The second volume of her memoirs should have covered the period of her life in Soviet Russia.

In an interview in Nice shortly before her death, Isadora was asked: "What period of your life do you regard as the greatest and happiest?"

"Russia, Russia, only Russia!" replied Isadora. "My three years in Russia, with all their sufferings, were worth everything in my life taken together. There I achieved the greatest ambition of my life. There is nothing impossible in that great country to which I shall soon return and where I intend to spend the rest of my life."

In September, 1927, Duncan began to write her second book. A few sheets of bluish paper, the colour of an overcast sky, on which Duncan always wrote in Indian ink, were covered in her curious handwriting, with letters either horizontally or vertically lengthened, but falling on the paper in the same measured and perfect lines as those with which she filled every movement in life and on the stage.

On that September evening Isadora went down into the street where a small racing car was waiting for her. Throwing the end of the red shawl with the spread-eagled bird over her shoulders, she waved a farewell and, smiling, uttered her last words:

"Adieu, mes amis! Je vais à la gloire!"

She got into the small car not knowing that it was there that her death lay in waiting, a death both frenzied and cruel. Without knowing that she had only one more minute to live, to feel. A few dozen seconds, a few dozen turns of the wheel. A red shawl with a spread-eagled bird, strewn with blue Chinese asters, slipped from Isadora's shoulder, floated over the side of the car, quietly licked the dry turning rubber and, suddenly, wildly winding itself round the wheel, roughly jerked Isadora by the throat. The motor of the car was a very powerful one and so the blow, too, was of quite exceptional power: at the very first revolution of the wheel, after the shawl had wound itself into the spokes, her neck was broken and her jugular vein severed.

"There's nothing to be done," said the doctor who had been summoned. "She was killed instantly."

In Nice and at the funeral in Paris I learnt all the details. Very characteristic of that time was the hostile attitude of the mayor of Nice: though Isadora was not to be buried there, the mayor, learning that among Isadora's papers there was a Moscow certificate confirming that she wished to become a Soviet citizen, declared that he would not permit her to be buried in Nice.

The moment after the fatal accident, the driver who sat in front kept shouting: "I've killed Madonna! I've killed Madonna!"

To free Isadora's head, which had been drawn down against the side of the car, the shawl had to be cut. I happened to meet an émigré Russian artist who had witnessed the accident. It was he who had run for the scissors and cut the shawl. I never quite believe the "eye-witnesses" of such tragic occurrences, but as he happened to be sitting on the verandah of the Café de France opposite the spot where the accident had taken place, I asked him to draw it for me. He drew the diagram clearly on a box of matches. It was evident, therefore, that the accident did not take place on the Promenade des Anglais, as had been reported in all the papers, but on the corner of Rue de France and Boulevard Gambetta.

A few days later that car was sold at an auction in Nice. Some maniac smiled happily when after some heated bidding the car was knocked down to him for the, at the time, unheard-of sum of two hundred thousand francs. A no less savage crowd of eye-witnesses flung themselves on the torn shawl and, in a crazy race for souvenirs, tore it to shreds.

When, in the late autumn of 1927, Desti came to Moscow, she brought me a little piece of the fatal scarf with the spread-eagled bird and the scattered blue Chinese asters. On one petal was a dried drop of Isadora's blood. . . .

Two hours after the accident there was the sound of horses' hooves outside Duncan's studio in Nice. It was Isadora's body being brought home from the morgue. She was put on a sofa, covered with a scarf in which she had danced, and a purple mantle was thrown across her feet. The studio was filled with flowers and many lighted candles.

In Moscow, Isadora had declared that she wanted a certain air of Bach's to be played at her funeral. "My spirit," she used to say, "will never leave this earth until it hears the strains of Bach's great air." Her wish was fulfilled. In Nice as well as in Paris, where the coffin with the body of the artist had been taken, Bach's air was played and Schubert's *Ave Maria* was sung. (On the first anniversary of Isadora's death, at the memorial evening in the Bolshoi Theatre in Moscow, the orchestra played the same aria during the showing of the film of Isadora's last journey from Nice to Paris.)

There was a flood of telegrams and flowers, which did not cease on the following day, either.

A telegram arrived from the American publisher confirming the agreement for the publication of Isadora's memoirs and announcing the transfer of money through a Paris bank. She had been waiting for that money to leave for Moscow.

The bluish sheets of paper remained lying in an untouched pile on Isadora's table in Nice. The pages about the years she had spent in our country were never written.

In Paris a wreath of red roses from the Soviet diplomatic delegation was placed on Isadora's coffin. The ribbon bore the inscription : "From the heart of Russia, which mourns Isadora."

Thousands of people followed the urn to the Père Lachaise cemetery. A special mourning session under the chairmanship of M. Herriot took place at the Sorbonne three days after the funeral. The committee to perpetuate the memory of Isadora Duncan voted a resolution to raise a memorial to her in Paris. Emile Bourdelle was commissioned to do the work. Unfortunately, nothing came of it.

When the smoke from the cremated body of Isadora dispersed in the Paris autumn sky, the poet Fernand Divoire, who had delivered the funeral oration, said : "She is dead. The great door, opened by Beauty, is closed."

No, that door is not closed! The light left behind by Isadora has not gone out. Her Soviet pupils have carried her art to all the corners of the Soviet Union and beyond. Long since Isadora's death her art has brought joy to people.

On December 3, 1946, the twenty-fifth anniversary of the foundation of the Duncan school was celebrated in Moscow together with the twentieth anniversary of the Moscow State Theatre Studio named after her. In Tchaikovsky Hall and in the Stanislavsky-Nemirovich-Danchenko Theatre the studio performed Tchaikovsky's *Sixth Symphony* just as Duncan dreamed of it. During the years of the studio's existence it gave five thousand performances in the Soviet Union alone, and they were attended by more than four million people.

Isadora's legacy lies at the foundation of the art of choreography of many countries throughout the world. It has left its trace in the art of the famous Russian ballet and of calisthenics, in which hundreds of thousands of girls and women take part in the Soviet Union.

Index